Lecture Notes in Computer Science 8647

Commenced Publication in 1973
Founding and Former Series Editors:
Gerhard Goos, Juris Hartmanis, and Jan van Leeuwen

T0236189

Claudia Eckert   Sokratis K. Katsikas
Günther Pernul (Eds.)

Trust, Privacy, and Security in Digital Business

11th International Conference, TrustBus 2014
Munich, Germany, September 2-3, 2014
Proceedings

 Springer

Volume Editors

Claudia Eckert
Fraunhofer-Institut für Angewandte
und Integrierte Sicherheit (AISEC)
Parkring 4
85748 Garching, Germany
E-mail: claudia.eckert@aisec.fraunhofer.de

Sokratis K. Katsikas
University of Piraeus
Department of Digital Systems
150 Androutsou St.
Piraeus 185 32, Greece
E-mail: ska@unipi.gr

Günther Pernul
Universität Regensburg
LS Wirtschaftsinformatik 1 - Informationssysteme
Universitätsstr. 31
93053 Regensburg, Germany
E-mail: guenther.pernul@ur.de

ISSN 0302-9743   e-ISSN 1611-3349
ISBN 978-3-319-09769-5   e-ISBN 978-3-319-09770-1
DOI 10.1007/978-3-319-09770-1
Springer Cham Heidelberg New York Dordrecht London

Library of Congress Control Number: 2014944663

LNCS Sublibrary: SL 4 – Security and Cryptology

Typesetting: Camera-ready by author, data conversion by Scientific Publishing Services, Chennai, India

Printed on acid-free paper

Springer is part of Springer Science+Business Media (www.springer.com)

Preface

This book presents the proceedings of the 11th International Conference on Trust, Privacy, and Security in Digital Business (TrustBus 2014), held in Munich, Germany during September 2–3, 2014. The conference continues from previous events held in Zaragoza (2004), Copenhagen (2005), Krakow (2006), Regensburg (2007), Turin (2008), Linz (2009), Bilbao (2010), Toulouse (2011), Vienna (2012), Prague (2013).

The advances in information and communication technologies have raised new opportunities for the implementation of novel applications and the provision of high quality services over global networks. The aim is to utilize this 'information society era' for improving the quality of life for all of us, disseminating knowledge, strengthening social cohesion, generating earnings, and finally ensuring that organizations and public bodies remain competitive in the global electronic marketplace. Unfortunately, such a rapid technological evolution cannot be problem-free. Concerns are raised regarding the 'lack of trust' in electronic procedures and the extent to which 'information security' and 'user privacy' can be ensured.

TrustBus 2014 brought together academic researchers and industry developers who discussed the state-of-the-art in technology for establishing trust, privacy, and security in digital business. We thank the attendees for coming to Munich to participate and debate the new emerging advances in this area.

The conference program included 5 technical papers sessions that covered a broad range of topics, from trust metrics and evaluation models, security management to trust and privacy in mobile, pervasive and cloud environments. In addition to the papers selected by the Program Committee via a rigorous reviewing process (each paper was assigned to four referees for review) the conference program also featured an invited talk delivered by Sanjay Kumar Madria on secure data sharing and query processing via federation of cloud computing.

We would like to express our thanks to the various people who assisted us in organizing the event and formulating the program. We are very grateful to the Program Committee members and the external reviewers, for their timely and rigorous reviews of the papers. Thanks are also due to the DEXA Organizing Committee for supporting our event, and in particular to Mrs. Gabriela Wagner for her help with the administrative aspects.

Finally we would like to thank all of the authors that submitted papers for the event and contributed to an interesting volume of conference proceedings.

September 2014

Claudia Eckert
Sokratis K. Katsikas
Günther Pernul

Organization

General Chair

Claudia Eckert — Technical University of Munich, Fraunhofer Research Institution for Applied and Integrated Security (AISEC), Germany

Program Committee Co-chairs

Sokratis K. Katsikas — University of Piraeus, National Council of Education, Greece

Günther Pernul — University of Regensburg, Bayerischer Forschungsverbund FORSEC, Germany

Program Committee

George Aggelinos — University of Piraeus, Greece
Isaac Agudo — University of Malaga, Spain
Preneel Bart — Katholieke Universiteit Leuven, Belgium
Marco Casassa Mont — HP Labs Bristol, UK
David Chadwick — University of Kent, UK
Nathan Clarke — Plymouth University, UK
Frederic Cuppens — ENST Bretagne, France
Sabrina De Capitani di Vimercati — University of Milan, Italy
Prokopios Drogkaris — University of the Aegean, Greece
Damiani Ernesto — Università degli studi di Milano, Italy
Carmen Fernandez-Gago — University of Malaga, Spain
Simone Fischer-Huebner — Karlstad University, Sweden
Sara Foresti — Università degli studi di Milano, Italy
Juergen Fuss — University of Applied Science in Hagenberg, Austria
Dimitris Geneiatakis — European Commision, Italy
Dimitris Gritzalis — Athens University of Economics and Business, Greece
Stefanos Gritzalis — University of the Aegean, Greece

External Reviewers

Adrian Dabrowski	SBA Research, Austria
Bastian Braun	University of Passau, Germany
Christoforos Ntantogian	University of Piraeus, Greece
Daniel Schreckling	University of Passau, Germany
Eric Rothstein	University of Passau, Germany
George Stergiopoulos	Athens University of Economics and Business, Greece
Hartmut Richthammer	University of Regensburg, Germany
Johannes Sänger	University of Regensburg, Germany
Katharina Krombholz	SBA Research, Austria
Konstantina Vemou	University of Aegean, Greece
Marcel Heupel	University of Regensburg, Germany
Markus Huber	SBA Research, Austria
Martin Mulazzani	SBA Research, Austria
Michael Weber	University of Regensburg, Germany
Miltiadis Kandias	Athens University of Economics and Business, Greece
Nick Virvilis	Athens University of Economics and Business, Greece
Sebastian Schrittwieser	SBA Research, Austria
Stavros Simou	University of Aegean, Greece
Stefanos Malliaros	University of Piraeus, Greece

A Secure Data Sharing and Query Processing Framework via Federation of Cloud Computing

(Keynote)

Sanjay K. Madria

Department of Computer Science
Missouri University of Science and Technology, Rolla, MO
madrias@mst.edu

Abstract. Due to cost-efficiency and less hands-on management, big data owners are outsourcing their data to the cloud, which can provide access to the data as a service. However, by outsourcing their data to the cloud, the data owners lose control over their data, as the cloud provider becomes a third party service provider. At first, encrypting the data by the owner and then exporting it to the cloud seems to be a good approach. However, there is a potential efficiency problem with the outsourced encrypted data when the data owner revokes some of the users' access privileges. An existing solution to this problem is based on symmetric key encryption scheme but it is not secure when a revoked user rejoins the system with different access privileges to the same data record. In this talk, I will discuss an efficient and Secure Data Sharing (SDS) framework using a combination of homomorphic encryption and proxy re-encryption schemes that prevents the leakage of unauthorized data when a revoked user rejoins the system. I will also discuss the modifications to our underlying SDS framework and present a new solution based on the data distribution technique to prevent the information leakage in the case of collusion between a revoked user and the cloud service provider. A comparison of the proposed solution with existing methods will be discussed. Furthermore, I will outline how the existing work can be utilized in our proposed framework to support secure query processing for big data analytics. I will provide a detailed security as well as experimental analysis of the proposed framework on Amazon EC2 and highlight its practical use.

Biography: Sanjay Kumar Madria received his Ph.D. in Computer Science from Indian Institute of Technology, Delhi, India in 1995. He is a full professor in the Department of Computer Science at the Missouri University of Science and Technology (formerly, University of Missouri-Rolla, USA) and site director, NSF I/UCRC center on Net-Centric Software Systems. He has published over 200 Journal and conference papers in the areas of mobile data management, Sensor computing, and cyber security and trust management. He won three best papers awards including IEEE MDM 2011 and IEEE MDM 2012. He is the co-author of a book published by Springer in Nov 2003. He serves as steering committee members in IEEE SRDS and IEEE MDM among others and has served in International conferences as a general co-chair (IEEE MDM, IEEE SRDS and others), and presented tutorials/talks in the areas of mobile data management and sensor computing at various venues. His research is supported by several grants from federal sources such as NSF, DOE, AFRL, ARL, ARO, NIST and industries like Boeing, Unique*Soft, etc. He has also been awarded JSPS (Japanese Society for Promotion of Science) visiting scientist fellowship in 2006 and ASEE (American Society of Engineering Education) fellowship at AFRL from 2008 to 2012. In 2012-13, he was awarded NRC Fellowship by National Academies. He has received faculty excellence research awards in 2007, 2009, 2011 and 2013 from his university for excellence in research. He served as an IEEE Distinguished Speaker, and currently, he is an ACM Distinguished Speaker, and IEEE Senior Member and Golden Core awardee.

Table of Contents

Security Management

Security, Trust and Privacy in Mobile and Pervasive Environments

Maintaining Trustworthiness
of Socio-Technical Systems at Run-Time

Nazila Gol Mohammadi[1], Torsten Bandyszak[1], Micha Moffie[2], Xiaoyu Chen[3],
Thorsten Weyer[1], Costas Kalogiros[4], Bassem Nasser[3], and Mike Surridge[3]

[1] paluno - The Ruhr Institute for Software Technology, University of Duisburg-Essen, Germany
{nazila.golmohammadi,torsten.bandyszak,
thorsten.weyer}@paluno.uni-due.de
[2] IBM Research, Haifa, Israel
moffie@il.ibm.com
[3] IT-Innovation Center, School of Electronics and Computer Science,
University of Southampton, Southampton, United Kingdom
{wxc,bmn,ms}@it-innovation.soton.ac.uk
[4] Athens University of Economics and Business, Athens, Greece
ckalog@aueb.gr

Abstract. Trustworthiness of dynamical and distributed socio-technical systems is a key factor for the success and wide adoption of these systems in digital businesses. Different trustworthiness attributes should be identified and accounted for when such systems are built, and in order to maintain their overall trustworthiness they should be monitored during run-time. Trustworthiness monitoring is a critical task which enables providers to significantly improve the systems' overall acceptance. However, trustworthiness characteristics are poorly monitored, diagnosed and assessed by existing methods and technologies. In this paper, we address this problem and provide support for semi-automatic trustworthiness maintenance. We propose a trustworthiness maintenance framework for monitoring and managing the system's trustworthiness properties in order to preserve the overall established trust during run-time. The framework provides an ontology for run-time trustworthiness maintenance, and respective business processes for identifying threats and enacting control decisions to mitigate these threats. We also present use cases and an architecture for developing trustworthiness maintenance systems that support system providers.

Keywords: Socio-Technical Systems, Trustworthiness, Run-Time Maintenance.

1 Introduction

Humans, organizations, and their information systems are part of Socio-Technical Systems (STS) as social and technical components that interact and strongly influence each other [3]. These systems, nowadays, are distributed, connected, and communicating via the Internet in order to support and enable digital business processes, and thereby provide benefits for economy and society. For example, in the healthcare domain, STS enable patients to be medically supervised in their own home by care

C. Eckert et al. (Eds.): TrustBus 2014, LNCS 8647, pp. 1–12, 2014.

providers [18]. Trust underlies almost every social and economic relation. However, the end-users involved in online digital businesses generally have limited information about the STS supporting their transactions. Reports (e.g., [8]) indicate an increasing number of cyber-crime victims, which leads to massive deterioration of trust in current STS (e.g., w.r.t. business-critical data). Thus, in the past years, growing interest in trustworthy computing has emerged in both research and practice.

Socio-technical systems can be considered worthy of stakeholders' trust if they permit confidence in satisfying a set of relevant requirements or expectations (cf. [2]). A holistic approach towards trustworthiness assurance should consider trustworthiness throughout all phases of the system life-cycle, which involves: 1) trustworthiness-by-design, i.e., applying engineering methodologies that regard trustworthiness to be built and evaluated in the development process; and 2) run-time trustworthiness maintenance when the system is in operation. Stakeholders expect a system to stay trustworthy during its execution, which might be compromised by e.g. security attacks or system failures. Furthermore, changes in the system context may affect the trustworthiness of an STS in a way that trustworthiness requirements are violated. Therefore it is crucial to monitor and assure trustworthiness at run-time, following defined processes that build upon a sound theoretical basis.

By studying existing trustworthiness maintenance approaches, we identified a lack of generally applicable and domain-independent concepts. In addition, existing frameworks and technologies do not appropriately address all facets of trustworthiness. There is also insufficient guidance for service providers to understand and conduct maintenance processes, and to build corresponding tools. We seek to go beyond the state-of-the-art of run-time trustworthiness maintenance by establishing a better understanding of key concepts for measuring and controlling trustworthiness at run-time, and by providing process guidance to maintain STS supported by tools.

The contribution of this paper consists of three parts: First, we introduce a domain-independent ontology that describes the key concepts of our approach. Second, we propose business processes for monitoring, measuring, and managing trustworthiness, as well as mitigating trustworthiness issues at run-time. Third, we present use cases and an architecture for trustworthiness maintenance systems that are able to facilitate the processes using fundamental concepts of autonomous systems.

The remainder of this paper is structured as follows: In Section 2 we describe the fundamentals w.r.t. trustworthiness of STS and the underlying runtime maintenance approach. Section 3 presents the different parts of our approach, i.e., an ontology for run-time trustworthiness of STS, respective business processes, as well as use cases and an architecture for trustworthiness maintenance systems that support STS providers. In Section 4, we briefly discuss the related work. We conclude this paper with a summary and a brief discussion of our ongoing research activities in Section 5.

2   Fundamentals

This section presents the fundamental concepts that form the basis for our approach. First, we present our notion of trustworthiness related to STS. Then, we briefly introduce the concept of run-time maintenance in autonomic systems.

2.1 Trustworthiness of Socio-Technical Systems

The term "trustworthiness" is not consistently used in the literature, especially with respect to software. Some approaches merely focus on single trustworthiness characteristics. However, even if combined, these one-dimensional approaches are not sufficient to capture all kinds of trustworthiness concerns for a broad spectrum of different STS, since the conception of trustworthiness depends on a specific system's context and goals [1]. For example, in safety-critical domains, failure tolerance of a system might be prioritized higher than its usability. In case of STS, we additionally need to consider different types of system components, e.g. humans or software assets [3].

Trustworthiness in general can be defined as the assurance that the system will perform as expected, or meets certain requirements [2]. With a focus on software trustworthiness, we adapt the notion of trustworthiness from [1], which covers a comprehensive set of quality attributes (e.g., availability or reliability). This allows us to measure overall trustworthiness as the degrees to which relevant quality attributes (then referred to as trustworthiness attributes) are satisfied. To this end, metrics for objectively measuring these values can be defined, as shown in [19].

2.2 Run-Time Maintenance in Autonomic Computing

Our approach for maintain trustworthiness at run-time is mainly based on the vision of Autonomic Computing [6]. The goal of Autonomic Computing is to design and develop distributed and service-oriented systems that can easily adapt to changes. Considering assets of STS as managed elements of an autonomic system allows us to apply the concepts of Autonomic Computing to trustworthiness maintenance. MAPE-K (Monitor, Analyze, Plan, Execute, and Knowledge) is a reference model for control loops with the objective of supporting the concepts of self-management, specifically: self-configuration, self-optimization, self-healing, and self-protection [5, 6]. Fig. 1 shows the elements of an autonomic system: the control loop activities, sensor and effector interfaces, and the system being managed.

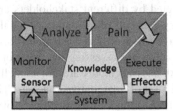

Fig. 1. Autonomic Computing and MAPE-K Loop [6]

The *Monitor* provides mechanisms to collect events from the system. It is also able to filter and aggregate the data, and report details or metrics [5]. To this end, system-specific *Sensors* provide interfaces for gathering required monitoring data, and can also raise events when the system configuration changes [5]. *Analyze* provides the means to correlate and model the reported details or measures. It is able to handle complex situations, learns the environment, and predicts future situations. *Plan* provides mechanisms to construct the set of actions required to achieve a certain goal or objective, or respond to a certain event. *Execute* offers the mechanisms to realize the actions involved in a plan, i.e., to control the system by means of *Effectors* that modify the managed element [6]. A *System* is a managed element (e.g., software) that contains resources and provides services. Here, managed elements are assets of STS. Additionally, a common *Knowledge* base acts as the central part of the control loop, and is shared by the activities to store and access collected and analyzed data.

3   A Framework for Maintaining Trustworthiness of Socio-Technical Systems at Run-Time

This section presents our approach for maintaining STS trustworthiness at run-time. We describe a framework that consists of the following parts: 1) an ontology that provides general concepts for run-time trustworthiness maintenance, 2) processes for monitoring and managing trustworthiness, 3) functional use cases of a system for supporting the execution of these processes, and 4) a reference architecture that guides the development of such maintenance systems. Based on the ontology and processes, we provide guidance for developing supporting maintenance systems (i.e., use cases and reference architecture). The reference architecture is furthermore based on MAPE-K, which in principle allows for realizing automated maintenance. However, our approach focuses on semi-automatic trustworthiness maintenance, which involves decisions taken by a human maintenance operator. In the following subsections, we elaborate on the elements of the framework in detail.

3.1   Ontology for Run-Time Trustworthiness Maintenance

This section outlines the underlying ontology on which the development of run-time trustworthiness maintenance is based. Rather than focusing on a specific domain, our approach provides a meta-model that abstracts concrete system characteristics, in such a way that it can be interpreted by different stakeholders and applied across disciplines. Fig. 2 illustrates the key concepts of the ontology and their interrelations.

The definition of qualitative trustworthiness attributes forms the basis for identifying the concepts, since they allow for assessing the trustworthiness of a great variety of STS. However, trustworthiness attributes are not modelled directly; instead they are encoded implicitly using a set of quantitative concepts. The core elements abstract common concepts that are used to model trustworthiness of STS, while the run-time concepts are particularly required for our maintenance approach.

Trustworthiness attributes of *Assets*, i.e., anything of value in an STS, are concretized by *Trustworthiness Properties* that describe the system's quality at a lower abstraction level with measurable values of a certain data type, e.g., the response time related to a specific input, or current availability of an asset. These properties are atomic in the sense that they refer to a particular system snapshot in time. The relation between trustworthiness attributes and properties is many to many; an attribute can potentially be concretized by means of multiple properties, whereas a property might be an indicator for various trustworthiness attributes. Values of trustworthiness properties can be read and processed by metrics in order to estimate the current levels of trustworthiness attributes. A *Metric* is a function that consumes a set of properties and produces a measure related to trustworthiness attributes. Based on metrics, statements about the behavior of an STS can be derived. It also allows for specifying reference threshold values captured in *Trustworthiness Service-Level Agreements* (TSLAs).

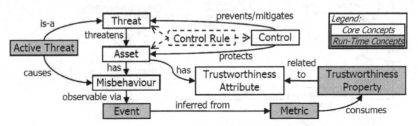

Fig. 2. Ontology for Run-Time Trustworthiness Maintenance

A system's behavior is observed by means of *Events*, i.e., induced asset behaviors perceivable from interacting with the system. Events can indicate either normal or abnormal behavior, e.g., underperformance or unaccountable accesses. *Misbehavior* observed from an event or a sequence of events may manifest in a *Threat* which undermines an asset's value and reduces the trustworthiness of the STS. This in turn leads to an output that is unacceptable for the system's stakeholders, reducing their level of trust in the system. Given these consequences, we denote a threat "active". Threats (e.g., loss of data) can be mitigated by either preventing them from becoming active, or counteracting their effects (e.g., corrupted outputs). Therefore, *Controls* (e.g., service substitution) are to be executed. *Control Rules* specify which controls can block or mitigate a given type of threat. Identifying and analyzing potential threats, their consequences, and adequate controls is a challenging task that should be started in early requirements phases.

3.2   Processes for Run-Time Trustworthiness Maintenance

In order to provide guidance for realizing trustworthiness maintenance, we define two complementary reference processes, i.e., *Trustworthiness Monitoring* and *Management*. These processes illustrate the utilization of the ontology concepts. We denote them as "reference processes" since they provide a high-level and generic view on the activities that need to be carried out in order to implement trustworthiness maintenance, without considering system-specific characteristics. Instantiating the processes will require analyzing these characteristics and defining e.g. appropriate metric thresholds to identify STS misbehavior(s). Our approach is semi-automatic, i.e., we assume a human maintenance operator to be consulted for taking critical decisions.

Trustworthiness Monitoring. Monitoring is responsible for observing the behavior of STS in order to identify and report misbehaviors to the *Management*, which will then analyze the STS state for potential threats and enact corrective actions, if necessary. In general, our monitoring approach is based on metrics which allow for quantifying the current value of relevant trustworthiness attributes. The reference process for trustworthiness monitoring is shown in the BPMN diagram depicted in Fig. 3.

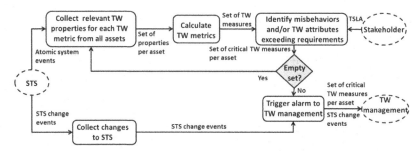

Fig. 3. Trustworthiness Monitoring Process

According to our modelling ontology, each measure is based on collected data, called atomic properties. Thus, the first step involves collecting all relevant trustworthiness properties (e.g., indicating system usage). These can be either 1) system properties that are necessary to compute the metrics for the set of relevant trustworthiness attributes, or 2) system topology changes, such as the inclusion of a new asset. Atomic system events indicate changes of properties. For each system asset, trustworthiness metrics are computed. Having enough monitoring data, statistical analysis can be used for aggregating atomic measurements into composite ones, e.g., the mean response time of an asset. These measures and further processed in order to identify violations of trustworthiness requirements that are captured in user-specific TSLAs. For each trustworthiness metrics, it is observed whether the required threshold(s) are exceeded. If so, the critical assets are consequently reported to the management, so that potentially active threats can be identified and mitigation actions can be triggered.

Each STS has its individual characteristics and requirements for trustworthiness. At run-time, system characteristics may change, e.g., due to adaptations to the environment. Consequently, another important monitoring task is to accept change notifications from the STS, and forward them to the trustworthiness management.

Trustworthiness Management. The key objective of STS trustworthiness management (see Fig. 4) is to guarantee correct system and service behavior at run-time by continuously analyzing system behavior, identifying potential threats, as well as recommending and executing possible mitigation actions. Note that we do not provide a separate mitigation process, since the actual mitigation execution is rather a technical issue that does not involve complex logic.

The reference management and mitigation process is triggered by incoming events (i.e., misbehaviors or system changes) reported by the trustworthiness monitoring. Misbehaviors identified in the form of deviations from required trustworthiness levels indicate an abnormal status of the target STS, e.g., underperformance due to insufficient resources, or malicious attacks. The management keeps tracks of the system status over time, and analyzes the causes of misbehaviors. Once threats are classified, it is necessary to analyze their effect on the asset's behavior and understand the links between them in order to analyze complex observations and sequences of threats that may be active, and identify suitable controls. Statistical reasoning is necessary for estimating threat probabilities (for each trustworthiness attribute).

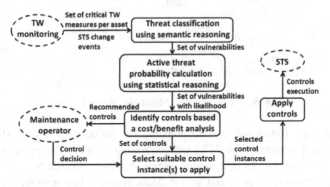

Fig. 4. Trustworthiness Management and Mitigation Process

Regarding control selection and deployment, we focus on semi-automated threat mitigation, as illustrated in Fig. 4, which requires human intervention. The maintenance operator is notified whenever new threats are identified. These threats may be active, indicating vulnerabilities due to lack of necessary controls. Each threat is given a likelihood based on the observed system behaviors. It is then the maintenance operator's responsibility to select appropriate controls that can be applied to the STS in order to realize mitigation. These controls involve, e.g., authentication or encryption. Several control instances may be available for each control (e.g., different encryption technologies), having different benefits and costs. Based on cost-effective recommendations, the operator selects control instances to be deployed. As a consequence, previously identified active threats should be classified as blocked or mitigated. The system may be dynamic, i.e., assets can be added or removed. Thus, notifications about changes of the STS topology will also trigger the management process.

3.3   Use Cases of a Run-Time Trustworthiness Maintenance System

Based on the reference processes introduced in Section 3.2, we elicited functional requirements of a tool that supports STS providers in maintaining trustworthiness. Such a system is supposed to facilitate and realize the business processes in a semi-automatic manner. We distinguish three main areas of functionality, i.e., *Monitoring*, *Management*, and *Mitigation*. The latter is included for a better separation of concerns, although we did not define a separate reference process for mitigation. We analyzed possible maintenance use cases, and actors that interact with the system. The results of this analysis are shown in the UML use case diagram in Fig. 5.

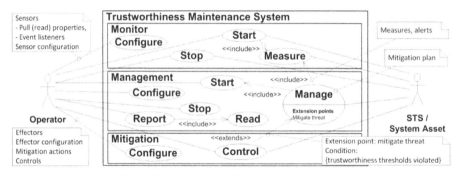

Fig. 5. Trustworthiness Maintenance Use Cases

The Monitoring functionality is responsible for collecting events and properties from the system (measuring the STS) and computing metrics. The inputs to the component are system properties and atomic events that are collected from the STS. The output, i.e., measures, is provided to the Management. The maintenance operator (e.g., the service provider) is able to start and stop the measurement, and to configure the monitor. Specifically, the operator can utilize the concept of trustworthiness requirements specified in TSLAs (cf. Section 3.1) to derive appropriate configuration.

The Management part provides the means to assess current trustworthiness attributes using the metrics provided from monitoring, choose an appropriate plan of action (if needed) and forward it to the mitigation. The operator is able to configure the Management component and provides a list of monitor(s) from which measures should be read, a list of metrics and trustworthiness attributes that are of interest, as well as management processes. Additionally, the operator is able to start/stop the management process, retrieve trustworthiness metric values, and to generate reports which contain summaries of trustworthiness evolution over time.

Lastly, the Mitigation part has one main purpose – to control the STS assets by realizing and enforcing mitigation actions, i.e., executing controls to adjust the trustworthiness level. The maintenance operator will configure the service with available mitigation actions and controls that are to be executed by means of effectors.

3.4   Architecture for Run-Time Trustworthiness Maintenance Systems

We view the trustworthiness maintenance system as an autonomic computing system (see Section 2.2). The autonomic system elements can be mapped to three maintenance components, similar to the distribution of functionality in the use case diagram in Fig. 5. The Monitor and Mitigation components are each responsible for a single functionality - monitoring and executing controls. Analyze and plan functionalities are mapped to a single management package, since they are closely related, and in order to simplify the interfaces. Fig. 6 shows the reference architecture of a maintenance system as a UML component diagram, depicting the components that are structured in three main packages, i.e., *Monitor*, *Management* and *Mitigation*.

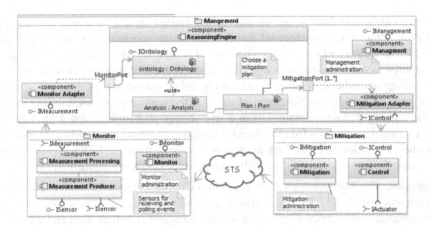

Fig. 6. Reference System Architecture for Run-Time Trustworthiness Maintenance

Trustworthiness maintenance systems are designed around one centralized management component and support distributed monitoring and mitigation. This modular architecture enables instantiating multiple monitors on different systems, each reporting to a single centralized management. Likewise, Mitigation can be distributed among multiple systems, too. This allows for greater scalability and flexibility.

Monitor. The Monitor package contains three components. The *Monitor* component provides an API to administer and configure the package, while the *Measurement Producer* is responsible for interfacing with the STS via sensors. The latter supports both passive sensors listening to events, as well as active sensors that actively measure the STS (e.g., to check if the system is available). Hence, the STS-specific event capturing implementation is decoupled from the more generic *Measurement Processing* component which gathers and processes all events. It is able to compute metrics and forward summarized information to the management. In addition, it may adjust the processes controlling the sensors (e.g., w.r.t. frequency of measurements).

One way to implement the Monitor component is using an event-based approach like Complex Event Processing (CEP) [4]. CEP handles events in a processing unit in order to perform monitor activities, and to identify unexpected and abnormal situations at run-time. This offers the ability of taking actions based on enclosed information in events about the current situation of an STS.

Management. The Management package is responsible for gathering all information from the different monitors, store it, analyze it, and find appropriate plans to execute mitigation controls. It contains *Monitor* and *Mitigation* adapters that allow multiple monitors or mitigation packages to interact with the management, and provide the reasoning engine with unified view of all input sources and a single view of all mitigation packages. It also includes the *Management* administration component that is used to configure all connected Monitor and Mitigation packages, and exposes APIs for configuration, display and report generation. The central component, the *Reasoning Engine*, encapsulates all the logic for the analysis of the measurements and planning of actions. This allows us to define an API for the engine and then replace it with different engines. Internally, an instance of the *Reasoning Engine* contains *Analysis* and *Plan* components as expected from an autonomic computing system (cf. Section 2.2), as well as an *Ontology* component. The ontology component encapsulates all required system models, which define e.g. threats and attributes. This allows for performing semantic reasoning by executing rules against the provisional system status and, estimating the likelihood of threat activeness (e.g., vulnerabilities) based on the current monitoring state. Given active threats probabilities and a knowledge base of candidate controls for each threat, the plan component can instruct the mitigation one what action(s) to perform in order to restore or maintain STS trustworthiness in a cost-effective manner, following the maintenance operator's confirmation.

Mitigation. The Mitigation package contains a *Control* component that encapsulates all interaction with the STS, and a *Mitigation* administration component. This allows us to separate and abstract STS control details, mitigation configuration and expose a generic API. The Mitigation package is responsible for executing mitigation actions by means of appropriate STS-specific effectors. These actions may be complex such as deploying another instance of the service, or as simple as presenting a warning to the maintenance operator including information for him to act on.

4   Related Work

Related work can be found in several areas, since trustworthiness of STS comprises many disciplines, especially software development. For example, methodologies for designing and developing trustworthy systems, such as [2], focus on best practices, techniques, and tools that can be applied at design-time, including the trustworthiness evaluation of development artifacts and processes. However, these trustworthiness-by-design approaches do not consider the issues related to run-time trustworthiness assessment. Metrics as a means for quantifying software quality attributes can be found in several publications, e.g. related to security and dependability [9], personalization [10], or resource consumption [11].

The problem of trustworthiness evaluation that we address has many similarities with the monitoring and adaption of web services in Service-Oriented Architectures, responding to the violation of quality criteria. Users generally favor web services that can be expected to perform as described in Service Level Agreements. To this end, reputation mechanisms can be used (e.g., [12]). However, these are not appropriate for objectively measuring trustworthiness based on system characteristics. In contrast, using online monitoring approaches, analyses and conflict resolution can be carried out based on logging the service interactions. Online monitoring can be performed by the service provider, service consumer, or trusted third parties [13, 14]. The ANIKETOS TrustWorthinessModule [15] allows for monitoring the dependability of service-oriented systems, considering system composition as well as specific component characteristics. Zhao et al. [7] also consider service composition related to availability, reliability, response time, reputation, and security. Service composition plays an important role in evaluation, as well as in management. For example, in [15] substitution of services is considered as the major means of restoring trustworthiness.

Decisions to change the system composition should not only consider system qualities [17], but also related costs and profits [15, 11]. Lenzini et al. [16] propose a Trustworthiness Management Framework in the domain of component-based embedded systems, which aims at evaluating and controlling trustworthiness, e.g., w.r.t. dependability and security characteristics, such as CPU consumption, memory usage, or presence of encryption mechanisms. Conceptually, their framework is closely related to ours, since it provides a software system that allows for monitoring multiple quality attributes based on metrics and compliance to user-specific trustworthiness profiles.

To summarize, there are no comprehensive approaches towards trustworthiness maintenance, which consider a multitude of system qualities and different types of STS. There is also a lack of a common terminology of relevant run-time trustworthiness concepts. Furthermore, appropriate tool-support for enabling monitoring and management processes is rare. There is insufficient guidance for service providers to understand and establish maintenance processes, and to develop supporting systems.

5   Conclusion and Future Work

Maintaining trustworthiness of STS at run-time is a complex task for service providers. In this paper, we have addressed this problem by proposing a framework for maintaining trustworthiness. The framework is generic in the sense that it is based on a domain-specific ontology suitable for all kinds of STS. This ontology provides key concepts for understanding and addressing run-time trustworthiness issues. Our framework defines reference processes for trustworthiness monitoring and management, which guide STS providers in realizing run-time maintenance. As the first step towards realizing trustworthiness maintenance processes in practice, we presented results of a use case analysis, in which high-level functional requirements of maintenance systems have been elicited, as well as a general architecture for such systems.

We are currently in the process of developing a prototype of a trustworthiness maintenance system that implements our general architecture. Therefore, we will define more concrete scenarios that will further detail the abstract functional requirements presented herein, and also serve as a reference for validating the system in order to show the applicability of our approach. We also aim at extending the framework and the maintenance system by providing capabilities to monitor and maintain the user's trust in the STS. The overall aim is to balance trust and trustworthiness, i.e., to prevent unjustified trust, and to foster trust in trustworthy systems. To some extent, trust monitoring and management may be based on monitoring trustworthiness as well, since some changes of the trustworthiness level are directly visible to the user. Though additional concepts and processes are needed, we designed our architecture in a way that allows for easily expanding the scope to include trust concerns.

Acknowledgements. This work was supported by the EU-funded project OPTET (grant no. 317631).

References

1. Gol Mohammadi, N., Paulus, S., Bishr, M., Metzger, A., Könnecke, H., Hartenstein, S., Pohl, K.: An Analysis of Software Quality Attributes and Their Contribution to Trustworthiness. In: 3rd Int. Conference on Cloud Computing and Service Science, pp. 542–552. SciTePress (2013)
2. Amoroso, E., Taylor, C., Watson, J., Weiss, J.: A Process-Oriented Methodology for Assessing and Improving Software Trustworthiness. In: 2nd ACM Conference on Computer and Communications Security, pp. 39–50. ACM, New York (1994)
3. Sommerville, I.: Software Engineering, 9th edn. Pearson, Boston (2011)
4. Luckham, D.: The Power of Events – An Introduction to Complex Event Processing in Distributed Enterprise Systems. Addison-Wesley, Boston (2002)
5. IBM: An Architectural Blueprint for Autonomic Computing, Autonomic Computing. White paper, IBM (2003)
6. Kephart, J.O., Chess, D.M.: The Vision of Autonomic Computing. IEEE Computer 36(1), 41–50 (2003)
7. Zhao, S., Wu, G., Li, Y., Yu, K.: A Framework for Trustworthy Web Service Management. In: 2nd Int. Symp. on Electronic Commerce and Security, pp. 479–482. IEEE (2009)
8. Computer Security Institute: 15th Annual 2010/2011 Computer Crime and Security Survey. Technical Report, Computer Security Institute (2011)
9. Arlitt, M., Krishnamurthy, D., Rolia, J.: Characterizing the Scalability of a Large Web Based Shopping System. ACM Transactions on Internet Technology 1(1), 44–69 (2001)
10. Bassin, K., Biyani, S., Santhanam, P.: Metrics to Evaluate Vendor-developed Software based on Test Case Execution Results. IBM Systems Journal 41(1), 13–30 (2002)
11. Zivkovic, M., Bosman, J.W., van den Berg, J.L., van der Mei, R.D., Meeuwissen, H.B., Nunez-Queija, R.: Dynamic Profit Optimization of Composite Web Services with SLAs. In: 2011 Global Telecommunications Conference (GLOBECOM), pp. 1–6. IEEE (2011)
12. Rana, O.F., Warnier, M., Quillinan, T.B., Brazier, F.: Monitoring and Reputation Mechanisms for Service Level Agreements. In: Altmann, J., Neumann, D., Fahringer, T. (eds.) GECON 2008. LNCS, vol. 5206, pp. 125–139. Springer, Heidelberg (2008)
13. Clark, K.P., Warnier, M.E., Quillinan, T.B., Brazier, F.M.T.: Secure Monitoring of Service Level Agreements. In: 5th Int. Conference on Availability, Reliability, and Security (ARES), pp. 454–461. IEEE (2010)
14. Quillinan, T.B., Clark, K.P., Warnier, M., Brazier, F.M.T., Rana, O.: Negotiation and Monitoring of Service Level Agreements. In: Wieder, P., Yahyapour, R., Ziegler, W. (eds.) Grids and Service-Oriented Architectures for Service Level Agreements, pp. 167–176. Springer, Heidelberg (2010)
15. Elshaafi, H., McGibney, J., Botvich, D.: Trustworthiness Monitoring and Prediction of Composite Services. In: 2012 IEEE Symp. on Computers and Communications, pp. 000580–000587. IEEE (2012)
16. Lenzini, G., Tokmakoff, A., Muskens, J.: Managing Trustworthiness in Component-Based Embedded Systems. Electronic Notes in Theoretical Computer Science 179, 143–155 (2007)
17. Yu, T., Zhang, Y., Lin, K.: Efficient Algorithms for Web Services Selection with End-to-End QoS Constraints. ACM Transactions on the Web 1(1), 1–26 (2007)
18. OPTET Consortium: D8.1 – Description of Use Cases and Application Concepts. Technical Report, OPTET Project (2013)
19. OPTET Consortium: D6.2 – Business Process Enactment for Measurement and Management. Technical Report, OPTET Project (2013)

Trust Relationships in Privacy-ABCs' Ecosystems

Ahmad Sabouri, Ioannis Krontiris, and Kai Rannenberg

Goethe University Frankfurt, Deutsche Telekom Chair of Mobile Business &
Multilateral Security,
Grueneburgplatz 1, 60323 Frankfurt, Germany
{ahmad.sabouri,ioannis.krontiris,kai.rannenberg}@m-chair.de

Abstract. — Privacy Preserving Attribute-based Credentials (Privacy-ABCs) are elegant techniques to offer strong authentication and a high level of security to the service providers, while users' privacy is preserved. Users can obtain certified attributes in the form of Privacy-ABCs, and later derive unlinkable tokens that only reveal the necessary subset of information needed by the service providers. Therefore, Privacy-ABCs open a new way towards privacy-friendly identity management systems. In this regards, considerable effort has been made to analyse Privacy-ABCs , design a generic architecture model, and verify it in pilot environments within the ABC4Trust EU project. However, before the technology adopters try to deploy such an architecture, they would need to have a clear understanding of the required trust relationships.

In this paper, we focus on identifying the trust relationships between the involved entities in Privacy-ABCs' ecosystems and provide a concrete answer to *"who needs to trust whom on what?"* In summary, nineteen trust relationships were identified, from which three of them considered to be generic trust in the correctness of the design, implementation and initialization of the crypto algorithms and the protocols. Moreover, our findings show that only six of the identified trust relationships are extra requirements compared with the case of passport documents as an example for traditional certificates.

Keywords: Privacy Preserving Attribute-based Credentials, Trust Relationships.

1   Introduction

Trust is a critical component of any identity system. Several incidents in the past have demonstrated the existence of possible harm that can arise from misuse of people's personal information. Giving credible and provable reassurances to people is required to build trust and make people feel secure to use the electronic services offered by companies or governments on-line.

Indeed, organizations that have built trust relationships to exchange digital identity information in a safe manner preserve the integrity and confidentiality of the user's personal information. However, when it comes to privacy, typical

C. Eckert et al. (Eds.): TrustBus 2014, LNCS 8647, pp. 13–23, 2014.

identity management systems fail to provide these strong reassurances. For example, in these systems, the so-called "Identity Provider" is able to trace and link all communications and transactions of the users and compile dossiers for each individual about his or her habits, behaviour, movements, preferences, characteristics, and so on. There are also many scenarios where the use of certificates unnecessarily reveals the identity of their holder, for instance scenarios where a service platform only needs to verify the age of a user but not his/her actual identity.

Strong cryptographic protocols can be used to increase trust, by not letting such privacy violations be technically possible. Over the past years, a number of technologies have been developed to build Privacy Preserving Attribute-based Credentials (Privacy-ABCs) in a way that they can be trusted, like normal cryptographic certificates, while at the same time they protect the privacy of their holder. Such Privacy-ABCs are issued just like ordinary cryptographic credentials (e.g., X.509 credentials) using a digital secret signature key. However, Privacy-ABCs allow their holder to transform them into a new token, in such a way that the privacy of the user is protected.

As prominent instantiations of such Privacy-ABC technologies one could mention Microsoft's U-Prove [2] and IBM's Idemix [3]. Both of these systems are studied in depth by the EU project ABC4Trust [1], where their differences are abstracted away to build a common architecture for Privacy-ABCs and tested in real-world, large-scale user trials. A privacy-threat analysis that we performed on the implementation of one of the pilot scenarios [4], we showed that indeed the use of Privacy-ABCs has helped mitigate many serious threats to user's privacy. However, some risks still remain, which are not addressed by Privacy-ABCs, requiring some degree of trust between the involved entities.

In this work, we focus on identifying the trust relationships between the involved entities in Privacy-ABCs' ecosystems and provide a concrete answer to "who needs to trust whom on what?". The rest of the paper is organized as follows: In Section 2, we elaborate on the definition of *Trust*, which we considered in this paper. Section 3 provides a brief overview of the related work in the area of identity management and trust relationships. Later in Section 4, we introduce the entities involved in the life-cycle of Privacy-ABCs and their interactions. Section 5 describes the required trust relationships from the perspective of each entity introduced in Section 4. Then, in Section 6, we compare the complexity of the systems based on Privacy-ABCs with the traditional systems in terms of the required trust relationships. In the end, we conclude the discussion in Section 7.

2   The Concept of Trust

A wide variety of definitions of trust exist in the bibliography [5][6]. A comprehensive study of the concept has been presented in the work by McKnight and Chervany [7], where the authors provide a classification system for different aspects of trust. In their work, they define trust intention as *"the extent to which one party is willing to depend on the other party in a given situation with a feeling of relative security, even though negative consequences are possible."* [7]

Their definition embodies (a) the prospect of negative consequences in case the trusted party does not behave as expected, (b) the dependence on the trusted party, (c) the feeling of security and the (d) situation-specific nature of trust. So, trust intention shows the willingness to trust a given party in a given context, and implies that the trusting entity has made a decision about the various risks of allowing this trust.

3   Related Work

Jøsang et al. [8] analyse some of the trust requirements in several existing identity management models. They consider the federated identity management model, as well as the isolated or the centralized identity management model and they focus on the trust requirements of the users in the service and identity service providers, but also between the identity service providers and service providers. However, this work does not cover the case of identity management based on Privacy-ABCs.

Delessy et al. [9] define the Circle of Trust pattern, which represents a federation of service providers that share trust relationships. The focus of their work however lays more on the architectural and behavioural aspects, rather than on the trust requirements which must be met to establish a relationship between two entities.

Later, Kylau et al. [10] concentrated explicitly on the federated identity management model and identify possible trust patterns and the associated trust requirements based on a risk analysis. The authors extend their scenarios by considering also scenarios with multiple federations.

To the best of our knowledge, there is no work that discusses systematically the trust relationships in identity management systems that incorporate Privacy-ABCs. However, some steps have been done in systematisation of threat analysis in such schemes, by the establishments of a quantitative threat modelling methodology that can be used to identify privacy-related risks on Privacy-ABC systems [4]. We perform our trust relationship analysis based on the risks identified by applying this methodology.

4   Privacy Preserving Attribute-based Credentials' Life-Cycle

Figure 1 shows the entities that are involved during the life-cycle of Privacy-ABCs [11]. The core entities are the User, the Issuer and the Verifier, while the Revocation Authority and the Inspector are optional entities. The User interacts with the Issuer and gets credentials, which later presents to the Verifiers in order to access their services. The User has the control of which information from which credentials she presents to which Verifier. The human User is represented by her UserAgent, a software component running either on a local device (e.g., on the User's computer or mobile phone) or remotely on a trusted cloud service.

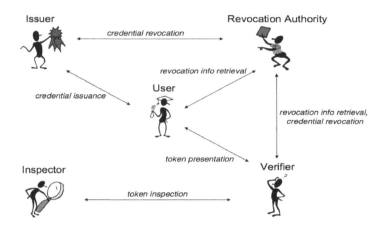

Fig. 1. Entities and relations in the Privacy-ABC's architecture [11]

In addition, the User may also possess special hardware tokens, like smart cards, to which credentials can be bound to improve security.

A Verifier is posing restrictions for the access to the resources and services that it offers. These restrictions are described in a presentation policy and specify which credentials Users must own and which attributes from these credentials they must present in order to access the service. The User generates from her credentials a presentation token, which corresponds to the Verifier's presentation policy and contains the required information and the supporting cryptographic evidence.

The Revocation Authority is responsible for revoking issued credentials. Both the User and the Verifier must obtain the most recent revocation information from the Revocation Authority to generate presentation tokens and respectively, verify them. The Inspector is an entity who can de-anonymize presentation tokens under specific circumstances. To make use of this feature, the Verifier must specify in the presentation policy the conditions, i.e., which Inspector should be able to recover which attribute(s) and under which circumstances. The User is informed about the de-anonymization options at the time that the presentation token is generated and she has to be involved actively to make this possible. In an actual deployment, some of the above roles may actually be fulfilled by the same entity or split among many. For example, an Issuer can at the same time play the role of Revocation Authority and/or Inspector, or an Issuer could later also be the Verifier of tokens derived from credentials that it issued [11].

5   Trust Relationships

In order to provide a comprehensible overview of the trust relationships, we describe the trust requirements from each entity's perspective. Therefore, whoever likes to realise one of the roles in the Privacy-ABCs' ecosystem could easily refer to that entity and learn about the necessary trust relationships that need to be established. Figure 2 depicts an overview of the identified trust relationships between the involved parties. On the bottom of Figure 2, the general trust requirements by all the parties are demonstrated.

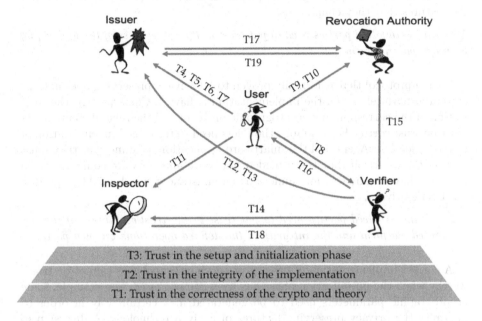

Fig. 2. Visualization of the trust relationships

5.1 Assumptions

Before delving into the trust relationships, it is important to elaborate on the assumptions that are required for Privacy-ABCs to work. Privacy-ABCs are not effective in cases where tracking and profiling methods that work based on network level identifiers such as IP addresses or the ones in the lower levels. Therefore, in order to benefit from the full set of features offered by Privacy-ABCs, the underlying infrastructure must be privacy-friendly as well. The recommendation for the users would be to employ network anonymizer tools to cope with this issue.

Another important assumption concerns the verifiers' enthusiasm for collecting data. Theoretically, greedy verifiers have the chance to demand for any kind of information they are interested in and avoid offering the service if the user is not willing to disclose this information. Therefore, the assumption is that the verifiers reduce the amount of requested information to the minimum level possible either by regulation or any other mechanism in place.

5.2 Trust by All the Parties

Independent from their roles, all the involved parties need to consider a set of fundamental trust assumptions that relates to design, implementation and setup of the underlying technologies. The most fundamental trust assumption by all the involved parties concerns the theory behind the actual technologies utilized underneath. Everybody needs to accept that in case of a proper implementation and deployment, the cryptographic protocols will offer the functionalities and the features that they claim.

T1. *All the involved parties need to put trust in the correctness of the underlying cryptographic protocols.*

Even a protocol that is formally proven to be privacy preserving does not operate appropriately when the implementation is flawed. Consequently, the realization of the corresponding cryptographic protocol and the related components must be trustworthy. For example, the Users need to trust the implementation of the so-called UserAgent and the smart card application meaning that they must rely on the assertion that the provided hardware and software components do not misbehave in any way and under any circumstances, which might jeopardise the User's privacy.

T2. *All the involved parties need to put trust in the trustworthiness of the implemented platform and the integrity of the defined operations on each party.*

A correct implementation of privacy preserving technologies cannot be trustworthy when the initialization phase has been compromised. For example, some cryptographic parameters need to be generated in a certain way in order to guaranty the privacy preserving features of a given technology. A diversion in the initialization process might introduce vulnerabilities to the future operation of the users.

T3. *All the involved parties need to put trust in the trustworthiness of the system setup and the initialization process.*

5.3   Users' Perspective

In typical scenarios, verifiers grant access to some services based on the credentials that the users hold. A malicious issuer can trouble a user and cause denial of service by not providing credible credentials in time or deliberately embedding invalid information in the credentials. For example, in case of a voting scenario, the issuer of ballots can block some specific group of users with fake technical failures of the issuance service.

T4. *The users need to put trust in the issuers delivering accurate and correct credentials in a timely manner.*

When designing a credential, the issuer must heed that the structure of the attributes and the credential will not impair the principle of minimal disclosure. For example, embracing name and birth date in another attribute such as registration ID is not an appropriate decision since presenting the latter to any verifier results in undesirable disclosure of data.

T5. *The users need to trust that the issuers design the credentials in an appropriate manner, so that the credential content does not introduce any privacy risk itself.*

Similar to any other electronic certification system, dishonest issuers have the possibility to block a user from accessing a service without any legitimate reason by revoking her credentials. Therefore the users have to trust that the issuer has no interest in disrupting users activities and will not take any action in this regard as long as the terms of agreement are respected.

T6. *The users need to trust that the issuers do not take any action to block the use of credentials as long as the user complies with the agreements.*

It is conceivable that a user loses control over her credentials and therefore contacts the issuer requesting for revocation of that credentials. If the issuer delays processing the user's request the lost or stolen credentials can be misused to harm the owner.

T7. *The users need to trust that the issuers will promptly react and inform the revocation authorities when the users claim losing control over their credentials.*

One of the possible authentication levels using Privacy-ABCs is based on a so-called *scope-exclusive pseudonym* where the verifier is able to impact the generation of pseudonyms by the users and limit the number of partial identities that a user can obtain in a specific context. For example, in case of an online course evaluation system, the students should not be able to appear under different identities and submit multiple feedbacks even though they are accessing the system pseudonymously. In this case, the verifier imposes a specific *scope* to the pseudonym generation process so that every time a user tries to access the system, it has no choice other than showing up with the same pseudonym as the previous time in this context. In this situations a dishonest verifier can try to unveil the identity of a user in a pseudonymous context or correlate actives by imposing the "same" scope identifier in generation of pseudonyms in another context where the users are known to the system.

T8. *The users need to trust that the verifiers do not misbehave in defining policies in order to cross-link different domains of activities.*

If a revocation process exists in the deployment model the user needs to trust on the correct and reliable performance of the revocation authority. Delivering illegitimate information or hindrance to provide genuine data can disrupt granting user access to her desired services.

T9. *The users need to trust that the revocation authorities perform honestly and do not take any step towards blocking a user without legitimate grounds.*

Depending on the revocation mechanism, the user might need to show up with her identifier to the revocation authority in order to obtain the non-revocation evidence of her credentials for an upcoming transaction. If the revocation authority and the verifier collude, they might try to correlate the access timestamps and therefore discover the identity of the user who requested a service.

T10. *The users need to trust that the revocation authorities do not take any step towards collusion with the verifiers in order to profile the users.*

Embedding encrypted identifying information within an authentication token for inspection purposes makes the users dependent of the trustworthiness of the inspector. As soon as the token is submitted to the verifier, the inspector is able to lift the anonymity of the user and disclose her identity. Therefore the role of inspector must be taken by an entity that a user has established trust relationship with.

T11. *The users need to trust that the inspectors do not disclose their identities without making sure that the inspection grounds hold.*

5.4   Verifiers' Perspective

Provisioning of the users in the ecosystem is one of the major points where the verifiers have to trust the issuers to precisely check upon the attributes that they are attesting. The verifiers rely on the information that is certified by the issuers for the authentication phase so the issuers assumed to be trustful.

T12. *The verifiers need to trust that the issuers are diligent and meticulous when evaluating and attesting the users' attributes.*

When a user loses her credibility, it is the issuer's responsibility to take the appropriate action in order to block the further use of the respective credentials. Therefore, the verifiers rely on the issuers to immediately request revocation of the user's credentials when a user is not entitled anymore.

T13. *The verifiers need to trust that the issuers will promptly react to inform the revocation authorities when a credential loses its validity.*

In an authentication scenario where inspection is enabled, the only party who is able to identify a misbehaving user is the inspector. The verifier is not able to deal with the case if the inspector does not to cooperate. Therefore, similar to trust relationship T11 by the users, the verifiers dependent of the fairness and honesty of the inspector.

T14. *The verifiers need to trust that the inspectors fulfil their commitments and will investigate the reported cases fairly and deliver the identifiable information in case of verified circumstances.*

The validity of credentials without expiration information is checked through the information that the verifier acquires from the revocation authority. A compromised revocation authority can deliver outdated or illegitimate information to enable a user to get access to resources even with revoked credentials. Therefore the revocation authority needs to be a trusted entity from the verifiers' perspective.

T15. *The verifiers need to trust that the revocation authorities perform honestly and deliver the latest genuine information to the verifiers.*

Often user credentials are designed for individual use, and sharing is not allowed., Even though security measures such as hardware tokens can be employed to support this policy limit the usage of the credentials to the owners, the users can still share the tokens and let others benefit from services that they are not normally eligible for. The verifiers have no choice than trusting the users and the infrastructure on this matter.

T16. *The verifiers need to trust that the users do not share their credentials with the others, if this would be against the policy.*

5.5 Issuers' Perspective

As mentioned earlier T13, the issuer is responsible to take the appropriate steps to block further use of a credential when it loses its validity. The issuer has to initiates the revocation process with the revocation authority and trust that the revocation authority promptly reacts to it in order to disseminate the revocation status of the credential. A compromised revocation authority can delay or ignore this process to let the user benefit from existing services.

T17. *The Issuers need to trust that the revocation authorities perform honestly and react to the revocation requests promptly and without any delay.*

5.6 Inspectors' Perspective

In order to have a fair inspection process, the inspection grounds must be precisely and clearly communicated to the users in advance. In case of an inspection request, the inspector has to rely on the verifier that the users had been informed about these conditions properly.

T18. *The Inspector need to trust that the verifier has properly informed the users about the actual circumstances that entitle the verifier for de-anonymisation of the users.*

5.7 Revocation Authorities' Perspective

Revocation authorities are in charge of delivering up-to-date information about the credentials' revocation status to the users and the verifiers. However, they are not in a position to decide whether a credential must be revoked or not, without receiving revocation requests from the issuers. Therefore, their correct operations depends on the diligent performance of the issuers.

T19. *In order to provide reliable service, the revocation authorities need to trust that the issuers deliver legitimate and timely information of the revoked credentials.*

6   Added Complexity

In order to better illustrate the added complexity compared to the traditional authentication schemes without Privacy-ABCs, we analysed the case of passport documents to find out about the overhead for enhancing privacy in terms of trust relationships. In our analysis, we exclude the first three trust relationships (T1, T2, and T3) since they concern the theoretical and operational correctness of the crypto and the protocols.

From the rest, T11, T14 and T18 do not exist in the case of passport documents, as there is no *Inspector* role involved. Interestingly, there are only three more trust relationships that do not hold for passport documents and all of them are from the users' perspective. T5, T8 and T10 focus on the problem of privacy and profiling, thus they are not applicable for passports. Investigating the remaining 10 trust relationships, we concluded that all of them are valid for the passport document scenarios. As a result, the added complexity due to the privacy requirements is 6 trust relationships out of 16.

7   Conclusion

Privacy-ABCs are powerful techniques to cope with security and privacy requirements at the same time. Extensive research has been conducted to understand Privacy-ABCs and bring them into practice[12][13][1]. In order to deploy Privacy-ABCs in real application scenarios, a clear understanding of the trust relationships between the involved entities is unavoidable. In this work, we investigated the questions of *"who needs to trust whom on what?"* and introduced the necessary trust relationships between the architectural entities of the Privacy-ABCs' ecosystems. However, a particular application might potentially introduce further trust dependencies, and therefore, the proposed list might get extended.

In summary, nineteen trust relationships were identified, from which three of them considered to be generic trust in the correctness of the design, implementation and initialization of the crypto algorithms and the protocols. Furthermore, it turned out that the credential "Issuer" is the entity that has to be trusted the most and the "User" is the one who is putting the most trust in the others' correct performance. Comparing the trust relationships to the case of passport documents, as an example for traditional certificates, we identified six of them to be the additional requirements introduced by Privacy-ABCs.

Acknowledgements. The research leading to these results has received funding from the European Community's Seventh Framework Programme (FP7/2007-2013) under Grant Agreement no. 257782 for the project Attribute-based Credentials for Trust (ABC4Trust).

References

1. Attribute-based Crednetials for Trust (ABC4Trust) EU Project, https://abc4trust.eu/
2. Microsoft U-Prove, http://www.microsoft.com/uprove
3. Identity Mixer, http://idemix.wordpress.com/
4. Luna, J., Suri, N., Krontiris, I.: Privacy-by-design based on quantitative threat modeling. In: 2012 7th International Conference on Risk and Security of Internet and Systems (CRiSIS), pp. 1–8. IEEE (2012)
5. Hardin, R.: Trust and trustworthiness, vol. 4. Russell Sage Foundation (2004)
6. O'Hara, K.: Trust: From Socrates to Spin. Icon Books Ltd. (2004)
7. Mcknight, D.H., Chervany, N.L.: The meanings of trust. Tech. Rep (1996)
8. Jøsang, A., Presti, S.L.: Analysing the relationship between risk and trust. In: Jensen, C., Poslad, S., Dimitrakos, T. (eds.) iTrust 2004. LNCS, vol. 2995, pp. 135–145. Springer, Heidelberg (2004)
9. Delessy, N., Fernandez, E.B., Larrondo-Petrie, M.M.: A pattern language for identity management. In: Proceedings of the International Multi-Conference on Computing in the Global Information Technology, ICCGI 2007, p. 31. IEEE Computer Society, Washington, DC (2007), http://dx.doi.org/10.1109/ICCGI.2007.5
10. Kylau, U., Thomas, I., Menzel, M., Meinel, C.: Trust requirements in identity federation topologies. In: Proceedings of the 2009 International Conference on Advanced Information Networking and Applications, AINA 2009, pp. 137–145. IEEE Computer Society, Washington, DC (2009), http://dx.doi.org/10.1109/AINA.2009.80
11. D2.1 Architecture for Attribute-based Credential Technologies Version 1, https://abc4trust.eu/download/ABC4Trust-D2.1-Architecture-V1.pdf.
12. PRIME - Privacy and Identity Management for Europe, https://www.prime-project.eu/
13. PrimeLife EU Project, http://primelife.ercim.eu/

Android Malware Detection
Based on Software Complexity Metrics

Mykola Protsenko and Tilo Müller

Department of Computer Science
Friedrich-Alexander-Universität Erlangen-Nürnberg
mykola.protsenko@fau.de, tilo.mueller@cs.fau.de

Abstract. In this paper, we propose a new approach for the static detection of Android malware by means of machine learning that is based on software complexity metrics, such as *McCabe's Cyclomatic Complexity* and the *Chidamber and Kemerer Metrics Suite*. The practical evaluation of our approach, involving 20,703 benign and 11,444 malicious apps, witnesses a high classification quality of our proposed method, and we assess its resilience against common obfuscation transformations. With respect to our large-scale test set of more than 32,000 apps, we show a true positive rate of up to 93% and a false positive rate of 0.5% for unobfuscated malware samples. For obfuscated malware samples, however, we register a significant drop of the true positive rate, whereas permission-based classification schemes are immune against such program transformations. According to these results, we advocate for our new method to be a useful detector for samples within a malware family sharing functionality and source code. Our approach is more conservative than permission-based classifications, and might hence be more suitable for an automated weighting of Android apps, e.g., by the Google Bouncer.

1 Introduction

According to a recent security report [1], Android still remains the most popular platform for malware writers. About 99% of new mobile malware samples found in 2013 are targeting Android. Despite the attention this threat has drawn in both academia and industry, the explosive growth of known Android malware between 2011 and 2012 could not effectively be restricted. Quite the contrary, the number of Android malware samples was reported to have increased four times between 2012 and 2013, while the number of malware families increased by only 69% over the same period of time [2]. These numbers suggest that new malware samples most often belong to existing malware families, supporting the theory of broad code reuse among malware authors, and hence, reasoning our approach to classify malware based on software metrics. Moreover, these statistics confirm considerable flaws in current malware detection systems, e.g., inside the Google Bouncer. As a consequence, we must keep looking for efficient alternatives to detect Android malware without rejecting legitimate apps.

C. Eckert et al. (Eds.): TrustBus 2014, LNCS 8647, pp. 24–35, 2014.

1.1 Contributions

In this paper, we address the issue of static malware detection by proposing a new approach that utilizes machine learning applied on attributes which are based on software complexity metrics. Complexity metrics can be found in the classic literature for software engineering and are known as *McCabe's Cyclomatic Complexity* [3] and the *Chidamber and Kemerer Metrics Suite* [4], for example (see Sect. 2.1). Our selected set of metrics comprises control- and data-flow metrics as well as object-oriented design metrics. To assess the effectiveness of our proposed method, we perform a large-scale evaluation and compare it to Android malware classification based on permissions. As permission-based malware classification is well-known in the literature [5], and has already been applied in practice by sandboxes, we use its detection rate as a reference value.

In our first scenario, we involve more than 32,000 apps, including over 11,000 malicious apps, and demonstrate that the detection rate of our method is more accurate than its permission-based counterpart. For example, the true positive rate of our method reaches up to 93%, just like the permission-based approach, but its overall AUC value [6] is higher due to a better false positive rate, namely 0.5% rather than 2.5%. In a second scenario, which involves over 30,000 apps, we utilize strong obfuscation transformations for changing the code structure of malware samples in an automated fashion. This obfuscation step is based on *PANDORA* [7], a transformation system for Android bytecode without requiring the source code of an app. In consequence of this obfuscation, the metrics-based detection experiences a decrease of its accuracy, whereas the permission-based approach is independent from an app's internal structure. For example, the AUC value of our approach decreases to 0.95 for obfuscated malware, while the permission-based approach remains 0.98.

According to these results, we advocate for our new method to be a useful detector for "refurbished" malware in the first place, i.e., for malware samples within a family that shares functionality and source code. If the detection of shared code is intentionally destroyed by obfuscation, or if new malware families emerge, traditional permission-based methods outperform our approach. However, permission-based methods often misclassify social media apps and those that require an immense set of privacy-related permissions. With respect to these apps, our approach is more conservative and could hence be more practical for weighting systems like the Google Bouncer.

1.2 Background and Related Work

The classification of malware based on machine learning has a long history on Windows. In 2006, Kolter and Maloof [8] have applied machine learning on features such as *n-grams* of code bytes, i.e., sequences of n bytes of binary code. Since the number of distinct n-grams can be quite large, they applied an information gain attribute ranking to select most relevant n-grams. Their practical evaluation involved more than 3,500 benign and malicious executables and indicated a detection performance with a true positive rate of 0.98 and a false positive rate of 0.05. In 2013, Kong and Yan [9] proposed an automated classification of Windows malware based on function call graphs, extended with additional features such as API calls and I/O operations.

On Android, recently proposed malware classification based on static features utilizes attributes that can easily be extracted, such as permissions. *DroidMat*, presented by Dong-Jie et al. [10] in 2012, consults permissions, intents, intercomponent communication, and API calls to distinguish malicious apps from benign ones. The detection performance was evaluated on a data set of 1,500 benign and 238 malicious apps and compared with the Androguard risk ranking tool with respect to detection metrics like the accuracy. In 2013, Sanz et al. [5,11,12] performed an evaluation of machine learning approaches based on such static app properties as permissions [5], string constants [12], and uses-feature tags of Android manifest files [11]. Their evaluation involved two data sets, one with 357 benign and 249 malicious apps, the other with 333 benign and 333 malicious apps. In 2014, Arp et al. [13] presented *DREBIN*, an on-device malware detection tool utilizing machine learning based on features like requested hardware components, permissions, names of app components, intents, and API calls. The large-scale evaluation on the data set with nearly 130,000 apps demonstrated a detection performance of 94% with a false positive rate of 1%, outperforming the number of competing anti-virus scanners.

Besides static malware detection, machine learning is often used in combination with dynamic malware analysis. In 2011, the *Crowdroid* system by Burguera et al. [14] was proposed to perform the detection of malicious apps based on their runtime behavior, which is submitted to a central server rather than being processed on the device. This scheme aims to improve the detection performance by analyzing behavior traces collected from multiple users. In 2012, Shabtai et al. [15] proposed a behavioral based system named *Andromaly*, which also employs machine learning for the detection of malware based on dynamic events that are collected at an app's runtime.

2   Attribute Sets for Machine Learning

In this section, we introduce software complexity metrics known from the software engineering literature and define which of these metrics we pick for our attribute set (Sect. 2.1). Moreover, as our practical evaluation is based on the comparison of two attribute sets, we discuss Android-specific attributes such as permissions (Sect. 2.2).

2.1   Software Complexity Metrics

Software complexity metrics were traditionally used to ensure the maintainability and testability of software projects, and to identify code parts with potentially high bug density, in the field of software engineering. Our set of selected metrics reflects the complexity of a program's control flow, data flow, and object-oriented design (OOD). These metrics turned out to be also useful in the field of malware classification. In the following, we describe the selected metrics in more detail. To employ them in our detection system, we implemented their computation on top of the *SOOT* optimization and analysis framework [16].

Lines of Code. The first and the simplest metric we use is the number of Dalvik instructions, which we denote as the number of lines of code (LOC).

McCabe's Cyclomatic Complexity. One of the oldest and yet still most widely used metrics is the cyclomatic complexity first introduced by McCabe in 1976 [3]. This complexity measure is based on the cyclomatic number of a function's control flow graph (CFG), which corresponds to the number of the linearly independent paths in the graph. Grounding on McCabe's definition, we compute the control flow complexity of a function as $v = e - n + r + 1$, with e, n, and r being the number of edges, nodes, and return nodes of the control flow graph, respectively.

The Dependency Degree. As a measure for a function's data flow complexity, we use the dependency degree metric proposed by Beyer and Fararooy in 2010 [17]. This metric incorporates dependencies between the instructions using local variables and their defining statements. For a given CFG, its dependency graph $S_G = (B, E)$ is built by B, which is defined as the node set corresponding to a function's instruction set, and E, which is the set of directed edges that connect the instruction nodes with other instructions they depend on. The dependency degree of one instruction is defined as the degree of its corresponding node. The dependency degree of a whole function is defined as the sum of the dependency degrees of all its instructions, i.e., the total number of edges in a function's dependency graph.

The Chidamber and Kemerer Metrics Suite. The two previously described metrics both measure the complexity of a single function. The complexity of an app's object-oriented design can be evaluated with the metrics suite proposed by Chidamber and Kemerer in 1994 [4]. The six class complexity metrics of this suite are defined as follows:

- *Weighted Methods per Class (WMC)* is defined as a sum of all methods complexity weights. For the sake of simplicity, we assign each method a weight 1 yielding the *WMC* the total number of methods in a given class.
- *Depth of Inheritance Tree (DIT)* is the classes depth in the inheritance tree starting from the root node corresponding to `java.lang.Object`.
- *Number of Children (NOC)* counts all direct subclasses of a given class.
- *Coupling Between the Object classes (CBO)* counts all classes a given one is coupled to. Two classes are considered coupled, if one calls another's methods or uses its instance variables.
- *Response set For a Class (RFC)* is the sum of methods that is declared in a class and the methods called from those.
- *Lack of Cohesion in Methods (LCOM)*: For class methods $M_1, M_2, ..., M_n$, let I_j be the set of the instance variables used by method M_j, and define $P = \{(I_i, I_j) | I_i \cap I_j = \emptyset\}$ as well as $Q = \{(I_i, I_j) | I_i \cap I_j \neq \emptyset\}$. The LCOM metric is then computed as $LCOM = max\{|P| - |Q|, 0\}$.

Aggregation. Since all previously described metrics measure either the complexity of a single method or that of a single class, additional processing is required to convert those into whole-app attributes. In a first step, we convert method-level metrics into class-level metrics by aggregating the metrics of all classes methods with the following six functions: minimum (min), maximum (max), sum (sum), average (avg), median (med), and variance (var). In a second step, the class-level metrics, including those resulting from the first step, are aggregated in the same way for the whole app. For example, the app attribute `Cyclomatic.var.max` denotes the maximum variance of the cyclomatic complexity among all classes. According to these aggregation rules, for the three method-level and six class-level metrics described in the previous paragraphs, we obtain $3 \cdot 6 \cdot 6 + 6 \cdot 6 = 144$ complexity attributes in total.

2.2 Android-Specific Attributes

Our second attribute set is given by Android-specific attributes such as permissions. We investigated Android-specific features to compare them with software complexity metrics regarding their usefulness for malware detection. Note that in general, permissions requested in a manifest file often differ from the set of actually used permissions. Moreover, the number of available permissions varies with the Android API level [18]. In our study, we utilized the *Androguard* tool by Desnos and Gueguen [19], which supports a set of 199 permissions.

Aside from Android permissions, we also extracted eight features that are mostly specific to Android apps and can additionally be extracted by the Androguard tool, including the number of the app components, i.e., *Activities*, *Services*, *Broadcast Receivers* and *Service Providers*, as well as the presence of *native*, *dynamic*, and *reflective code*, and the ASCII obfuscation of *string constants*. Taking into account 144 complexity metrics, as described above, 199 permissions, and these eight attributes, gives us a total number of 351 app attributes serving as a basis for our evaluation. As explained in Sect. 4.3, however, the latter eight attributes were inappropriate for classification and discarded.

3 Obfuscation Transformations

Recent studies [7,20] confirm the low performance of commercial anti-virus products for Android in face of obfuscation and program transformations. To overcome such flaws in the future, new malware detection systems must compete with obfuscation. To evaluate the resilience of our detection system against common program transformations, we have applied various code obfuscation techniques to a set of malware samples. The obfuscation was performed by means of the *PANDORA* framework proposed by Protsenko and Müller [7]. The provided transformation set is able to perform significant changes to an app's bytecode without requiring its source code. These transformations strongly affect the complexity metrics described above, without affecting its Android-specific attributes like permissions. In Section 3.1 and 3.2, we give a brief description of all transformations we applied.

3.1   Data and Control Flow Obfuscation

The first group of obfuscation techniques we applied aims to disguise the usage of local variables by obfuscating the control and data flow of program methods. These transformations tend to increase the values of the method-level metrics such as the cyclomatic complexity and the dependency degree.

- *String Encryption*: We encrypt string constants by using the *Vigenere* encryption algorithm as well as a modification of the *Caesar* cipher with the key sequence generated the *Linear Congruential Method*. The decryption code is inserted after each string constant.
- *Integer Encoding*: Integer variables are obfuscated by splitting them into a quotient and a remainder for a constant divisor, and by applying a linear transformation to it, i.e., by multiplying a constant value and adding another constant value.
- *Array Index Shift*: The access to array elements is obfuscated by shifting their index values.
- *Locals Composition*: We unite some of the local variables of the same type into arrays and maps with random integer, character, and string keys.

3.2   Object-Oriented Design Obfuscation

The following obfuscation transformations modify and increase the complexity of an app's object-oriented design.

- *Encapsulate Field*: For a given instance or class variable, we create getter and setter methods and modify all usages and definitions of this variable to utilize these auxiliary methods.
- *Move Fields and Methods*: Both static and non-static methods and fields are occasionally moved from one class to another.
- *Merge Methods*: Two methods declared in the same class and having the same return type can be merged in one method, which has a combined parameter list plus one additional parameter to decide which of the code sequences is to be executed.
- *Drop Modifiers*: For classes, methods and fields, we discard access restriction modifiers, i.e., `private`, `protected`, and `final`, which allows for more obfuscation transformations.
- *Extract Method*: For methods with a signature that cannot be changed, e.g., app entry points, we outline method bodies to new methods. This enables other transformations to be applied on those methods, too.

4   Evaluation

In this section, we first describe the data sets and evaluation criteria we used to test our metrics-based classification scheme. We then summarize the results of two test scenarios, one with plain Android apps and the other with obfuscated apps, as described above. For the practical classification, we utilized the *WEKA* machine learning framework by Hall et al. [21]. WEKA is a collection of popular machine learning algorithms that can be applied to a given data set without the need to implement algorithms from-scratch.

4.1 Data Sets of Benign and Malicious Android Apps

The data sets we used during our evaluation were composed of Android apps collected for the Mobile-Sandbox by Spreitzenbarth et al. [22]. These apps were already classified into benign and malicious samples. Out of over 136,000 available apps from Google's official Play Store, and out of over 40,000 malicious samples identified by *VirusTotal*, representing 192 malware families, we randomly selected 32,147 distinct apps. In detail, we selected 20,703 benign apps and 11,444 malicious apps from 66 families, with at least 10 samples per family. We grouped the selected samples into the following data sets, each containing only distinct apps in their original or obfuscated form:

- *Dataset 1*: 32,147 apps; 20,703 benign and 11,444 malicious.
- *Dataset 2*: 16,104 apps; 10,380 benign and 5,724 malicious.
- *Dataset 3*: 14,221 apps; 10,323 benign and 3,898 obfuscated malicious.

Note that for each malicious sample from *Dataset 3*, there are samples in *Dataset 2* representing the same malware family.

4.2 Evaluation Criteria

During our evaluation, we have employed the usual metrics for classifying the quality of machine learning algorithms [23], outlined in the following:

- *True Positive Rate*: The ratio of correctly detected malicious samples.
- *False Positive Rate*: The ratio of misclassified benign samples.
- *Accuracy (ACC)*: The number of correctly classified samples.
- *Area under the ROC Curve (AUC)*: The probability that a randomly chosen malicious sample will be correctly classified [6].

AUC can be considered as the summary metric reflecting the classification ability of an algorithm. Hosmer et al. [23] propose the following guidelines for assessing the classification quality by the AUC value: For $AUC \geq 0.9$ they refer to an *outstanding* discrimination, $0.8 \geq AUC < 0.9$ yields an *excellent* discrimination, and for $0.7 \geq AUC < 0.8$ the discrimination is considered *acceptable*. AUC values below 0.7 witness poor practical usefulness of the classifier.

4.3 Attribute Ranking

As described in Sect 2, the attribute set of our evaluation includes 144 complexity metrics, 199 permissions, and eight other Android-specific features. For the resulting total number of app attributes, namely 351, we do not expect all attributes to be equally useful for the distinction of malicious and benign apps. For instance, some permissions do not occur in any app of our test sets, such as MANAGE_USB and WRITE_CALL_LOG. Additionally, some of the aggregated complexity metrics are expected to have high correlation, and hence induce attributes that can be dropped without significant loss of the prediction quality.

Table 1. No Obfuscation, 25 attributes

(a) Complexity Metrics

Algorithm	AUC	ACC	TPR	FPR
RandomForest -I 100	0.993	97.3186	0.934	0.005
RotationForest	0.988	96.6933	0.924	0.010
Bagging	0.985	95.3339	0.902	0.019
Decorate	0.977	94.7647	0.936	0.046
DTNB	0.970	93.1595	0.847	0.022
IBk -K 3	0.967	92.7303	0.918	0.068
PART	0.958	91.5855	0.863	0.055

(b) Permissions

Algorithm	AUC	ACC	TPR	FPR
RandomForest -I 50	0.969	93.9590	0.878	0.026
IBk -K 1	0.968	93.8812	0.880	0.029
Bagging	0.965	93.5173	0.875	0.031
DTNB	0.965	93.4831	0.858	0.023
RandomTree	0.964	93.8937	0.878	0.028
PART	0.962	93.7941	0.875	0.027
RotationForest	0.958	93.8346	0.877	0.028

To reduce the attributes to a small subset of the most relevant ones, we follow the example of Kolter and Maloof [8] and perform attribute ranking by means of the information gain. Note that the result of this ranking depends on the training set, so we obtained different ranking results for our two different scenarios. In both cases, however, the top-ranked permissions are SEND_SMS, READ_PHONE_STATE, RECEIVE_BOOT_COMPLETED, and READ_SMS. The top Android-specific features are represented by *number of services* and *broadcast receivers*.

Also note that in both scenarios, the complexity metrics clearly dominate in the Top-100 ranking, leaving place for only two Android-specific features, and four or two permissions in case of obfuscation disabled or enabled, respectively. Therefore, due to their low ranking, we decided to exclude Android-specific features other than permissions from further evaluation. From the remaining attributes, we analyzed two distinct attribute sets: complexity metrics and permissions. This decision was also supported by our goal to maintain comparability of the metrics with previous permission-based classification schemes from Sanz et al. [5].

4.4 Scenario 1: No Obfuscation

In the first evaluation scenario, we measure the qualities of metrics-based classification in comparison to permission-based classification without obfuscating apps. For this purpose, we performed a ten-fold cross-validation on *Testset 1* with different machine learning algorithms. The classification results for the top performing algorithms from the WEKA framework [21], namely *RandomForest, RotationForest, Bagging, Decorate, DTNB, IBk,* and *PART,* are summarized in Tab. 1 for the Top-25 attributes, and in Tab. 2 for the Top-50 attributes.

For both Top-25 and Top-50 selected attributes, the results demonstrated by the permission-based detection were slightly outperformed by our new approach based on complexity metrics. Among all attribute sets and classification algorithms, the overall leadership belongs to *RandomForest* with 100 trees trained on the Top-25 complexity metric-attributes with an outstanding AUC value of 0.993, and the true positive and false positive rates of 93.5% and 0.5% respectively. It is worth noting, that an increase from 25 to 50 attributes resulted in a slightly lower performance for the metrics-based scheme, whereas for the permission-based scheme the opposite was the case.

The result of our experiment for the permission-based classification is consistent with the results obtained by Sanz et al. [5], although they obtained slightly

Table 2. No Obfuscation, 50 attributes

(a) Complexity Metrics

Algorithm	AUC	ACC	TPR	FPR
RandomForest -I 100	0.992	97.1164	0.930	0.006
RotationForest	0.988	96.5596	0.925	0.012
Decorate	0.986	96.4196	0.931	0.017
Bagging	0.986	95.4273	0.903	0.017
IBk -K 3	0.972	93.2995	0.929	0.065
DTNB	0.969	93.2498	0.847	0.020
PART	0.958	92.6867	0.902	0.059

(b) Permissions

Algorithm	AUC	ACC	TPR	FPR
RandomForest -I 100	0.984	95.7725	0.930	0.027
IBk -K 3	0.983	95.0135	0.927	0.037
Bagging	0.978	94.7522	0.912	0.033
DTNB	0.976	94.8829	0.897	0.023
RotationForest	0.974	95.2873	0.914	0.026
PART	0.973	95.2219	0.922	0.031
Decorate	0.973	94.7118	0.913	0.034

Table 3. Obfuscation enabled, 25 attributes

(a) Complexity Metrics

Algorithm	AUC	ACC	TPR	FPR
RandomForest -I 50	0.867	72.2242	0.013	0.010
Bagging	0.808	71.9640	0.049	0.027
NaiveBayes	0.796	84.9589	0.758	0.116
DTNB	0.784	73.5532	0.144	0.041
RotationForest	0.691	71.8866	0.014	0.015
IBk -K 3	0.659	70.5858	0.146	0.083
Decorate	0.644	71.6476	0.068	0.039

(b) Permissions

Algorithm	AUC	ACC	TPR	FPR
RandomForest -I 50	0.963	94.4378	0.867	0.026
IBk -K 1	0.962	94.2761	0.870	0.030
Bagging	0.959	93.8190	0.862	0.033
DTNB	0.958	94.1706	0.847	0.023
PART	0.956	94.0721	0.860	0.029
RotationForest	0.947	94.0089	0.860	0.030
Decorate	0.941	93.7768	0.861	0.033

weaker results. Moreover, Sanz et al. did not perform attribute ranking but utilized complete permission set. In terms of AUC, the best algorithm in their evaluation was *RandomForest* with 10 trees, showing the AUC, true positive, and false positive rates of 0.92, 0.91, and 0.19, respectively.

4.5 Scenario 2: Obfuscation Enabled

In the second evaluation scenario, we tested the classification effectiveness of both approaches with the presence of obfuscated apps. Since we decided to put obfuscated samples only in the test set, but not in the training set, we had to refrain from employing cross-validation in this scenario. Instead, we used *Dataset 2* as a training set, and *Dataset 3* as an evaluation set. The results of our evaluation for the complexity metrics and permission-based approaches with the Top-25 and Top-50 attributes, respectively, are given in Tab. 3 and Tab. 4.

As expected, the classification performance of the permissions-based machine learning keeps the high level showed in the previous scenario, since obfuscation transformations do not affect app permissions. The complexity metrics-based classification, on the contrary, shows a significant drop of its detection quality. In case of Top-25 attributes, the results are not satisfactory at all, whereas for the Top-50 attributes, we can distinguish the *SimpleLogistic* classifier with more than acceptable values of AUC, and true positive and false positive rates, namely 0.947, 92.9%, and 0.055, respectively.

Since according to our results, the best performance for the Top-50 complexity metrics attributes was shown by *RandomForest* with 100 trees for no obfuscation and by *SimpleLogistic* in case of enabled obfuscation, we have tried to combine those classifiers in order to achieve good performance in both evaluation scenarios. For this purpose, we have used the *Voting* approach, which allows the combination of

Table 4. Obfuscation enabled, 50 attributes

(a) Complexity Metrics

Algorithm	AUC	ACC	TPR	FPR
SimpleLogistic	0.947	92.8908	0.885	0.055
RandomForest -I 100	0.940	75.5995	0.129	0.007
Bagging	0.921	84.9940	0.519	0.025
RotationForest	0.836	73.7993	0.083	0.015
LogitBoost	0.812	80.2686	0.461	0.068
Dagging	0.753	75.9581	0.144	0.008
Decorate	0.793	73.736	0.140	0.037

(b) Permissions

Algorithm	AUC	ACC	TPR	FPR
RandomForest -I 100	0.981	95.5629	0.916	0.029
IBk -K 1	0.979	95.2746	0.919	0.035
Bagging	0.975	94.6417	0.888	0.031
DTNB	0.971	95.2394	0.877	0.019
RandomTree	0.967	94.9300	0.915	0.038
Decorate	0.967	94.5292	0.894	0.035
PART	0.965	94.8878	0.909	0.036

Table 5. The Voting Approach, RandomForest -I 100 and SimpleLogistic

(a) 25 Attributes

	AUC	ACC	TPR	FPR
No Obfuscation	0.965	93.4955	0.873	0.031
Obfuscation Enabled	0.838	73.6165	0.061	0.009

(b) 50 Attributes

	AUC	ACC	TPR	FPR
No Obfuscation	0.990	96.2983	0.912	0.009
Obfuscation Enabled	0.965	92.3845	0.754	0.012

single classifiers. The evaluation results for the combination of the *RandomForest* with 100 trees and *SimpleLogistic* classifier are presented in Tab. 5.

According to the results of the voting-based approach, we were able to improve the detection for obfuscated apps without significantly loosing quality in the non-obfuscation scenario. The classification quality, however, is still only acceptable in case we use the Top-50 attributes. At this point, we want to emphasize that although the results showed by the permission-based detection outperform the proposed complexity metrics-approach, their results can still be considered high. Furthermore, the false positive rate for obfuscated samples is at most 1.2% and hence, consistently lower than the false positive rate of the permission-based approach. As a consequence, metrics-based classification can be considered more conservative than permission-based classification.

To substantiate our assertion, we have additionally investigated the classification of twelve popular social media and messaging apps, including Facebook, Google+, Skype, ChatOn, and more. This kind of apps is particularly interesting, as they are known for their extensive use of privacy-related permissions and regularly head the Play Store list of popular apps. Whereas the permission-based approach misclassified three out of twelve social media apps, which corresponds to a false positive rate of 25%, the metrics-based approach did not misclassify any of these apps.

5   Conclusion and Future Work

In this paper, we proposed a novel machine learning approach for static malware detection on Android that is based on software complexity metrics rather than permissions. Our large-scale evaluation, comprising data sets of more than 32,000 apps in total, has indicated a high detection quality for unobfuscated malware samples which outperforms the classic permission-based approach. In our evaluation scenario involving obfuscation transformations, however, the metrics-based detection has a lower true positive rate than the permission-based detection. As an advantage, also the false positive rate is lower and hence, we emphasize the usefulness of our method to detect new or refactored samples of known malware families. The metrics-based classification can be considered for conservative app weighting in automated analysis systems, such as the Google Bouncer. To substantiate our line of reasoning, we investigated twelve popular social media apps showing a high false positive rate for permission-based classification but none for metrics-based classification. Investigating this effect in more detail, and limiting our false positive rate further, remains an important subject of future work.

Acknowledgments. The research leading to these results was supported by the "Bavarian State Ministry of Education, Science and the Arts" as part of the FORSEC research association. Furthermore, we want to thank Johannes Götzfried and Dominik Maier for proofreading our paper and giving us valuable hints for improving it. A special thanks goes to Michael Spreitzenbarth for giving us access to a large set of benign and malicious Android apps.

References

1. Cisco Systems Inc.: Cisco 2014 Annual Security Report. `https://www.cisco.com/web/offer/gist_ty2_asset/Cisco_2014_ASR.pdf` (accessed: March 18, 2014)
2. Bartlomiej Uscilowski: Symantec Security Response (Mobile Adware and Malware Analysis),
   `http://www.symantec.com/content/en/us/enterprise/media/security_response/whitepapers/madware_and_malware_analysis.pdf` (accessed: March 18, 2014)
3. McCabe, T.J.: A Complexity Measure. IEEE Transactions on Software Engineering SE-2(4), 308–320 (1976)
4. Chidamber, S.R., Kemerer, C.F.: A Metrics Suite for Object Oriented Design. IEEE Transactions on Software Engineering 20(6), 476–493 (1994)
5. Sanz, B., Santos, I., Laorden, C., Ugarte-Pedrero, X., Bringas, P.G., Álvarez, G.: PUMA: Permission Usage to Detect Malware in Android. In: Herrero, Á., et al. (eds.) Int. Joint Conf. CISIS 2012-ICEUTE 2012-SOCO 2012. AISC, vol. 189, pp. 289–298. Springer, Heidelberg (2013)
6. Hanley, J.A., McNeil, B.J.: The meaning and use of the area under a receiver operating characteristic (ROC) curve. Radiology 143(1), 29–36 (1982)
7. Protsenko, M., Müller, T.: PANDORA Applies Non-Deterministic Obfuscation Randomly to Android. In: Osorio, F.C. (ed.) 8th International Conference on Malicious and Unwanted Software (Malware 2013) (October 2013)
8. Kolter, J.Z., Maloof, M.A.: Learning to Detect and Classify Malicious Executables in the Wild. Journal of Machine Learning Research 7, 2721–2744 (2006)
9. Kong, D., Yan, G.: Discriminant Malware Distance Learning on Structural Information for Automated Malware Classification. In: Proceedings of the International Conference on Measurement and Modeling of Computer Systems, SIGMETRICS 2013, pp. 347–348. ACM, New York (2013)
10. Wu, D.J., Mao, C.H., Wei, T.E., Lee, H.M., Wu, K.P.: DroidMat: Android Malware Detection through Manifest and API Calls Tracing. In: Seventh Asia Joint Conference on Information Security (Asia JCIS 2012), Tokyo, Japan (August 2012)

11. Sanz, B., Santos, I., Laorden, C., Ugarte-Pedrero, X., Nieves, J., Bringas, P.G., lvarez Maran, G.: MAMA: Manifest Analysis for Malware detection in Android. Cybernetics and Systems 44(6-7), 469–488 (2013)
12. Sanz, B., Santos, I., Nieves, J., Laorden, C., Alonso-Gonzalez, I., Bringas, P.G.: MADS: Malicious Android Applications Detection through String Analysis. In: Lopez, J., Huang, X., Sandhu, R. (eds.) NSS 2013. LNCS, vol. 7873, pp. 178–191. Springer, Heidelberg (2013)
13. Arp, D., Spreitzenbarth, M., Hubner, M., Gascon, H., Rieck, K.: DREBIN: Effective and Explainable Detection of Android Malware in Your Pocket. In: Proceedings of the ISOC Network and Distributed System Security Symposium (NDSS), San Diego, CA (February 2014)
14. Burguera, I., Zurutuza, U., Nadjm-Tehrani, S.: Crowdroid: Behavior-based Malware Detection System for Android. In: Proceedings of the 1st ACM Workshop on Security and Privacy in Smartphones and Mobile Devices, New York, NY, USA, pp. 15–26 (2011)
15. Shabtai, A., Kanonov, U., Elovici, Y., Glezer, C., Weiss, Y.: Andromaly: A Behavioral Malware Detection Framework for Android Devices. Journal of Intelligent Information Systems 38(1), 161–190 (2012)
16. Vallée-Rai, R., Co, P., Gagnon, E., Hendren, L., Lam, P., Sundaresan, V.: Soot - A Java Bytecode Optimization Framework. In: Proceedings of the Conference of the Centre for Advanced Studies on Collaborative Research, CASCON 1999. IBM Press (1999)
17. Beyer, D., Fararooy, A.: A Simple and Effective Measure for Complex Low-Level Dependencies. In: Proceedings of the 8th International Conference on Program Comprehension, ICPC 2010. IEEE Computer Society, Washington, DC (2010)
18. Wei, X., Gomez, L., Neamtiu, I., Faloutsos, M.: Permission Evolution in the Android Ecosystem. In: Proceedings of the 28th Annual Computer Security Applications Conference, ACSAC 2012, pp. 31–40. ACM, New York (2012)
19. Desnos, A., Gueguen, G.: Android: From Reversing to Decompilation. In: Proceedings of the Black Hat Conference, Operational Cryptology and Virology Laboratory, Abu Dhabi (July 2011)
20. Rastogi, V., Chen, Y., Jiang, X.: Droidchameleon: Evaluating android anti-malware against transformation attacks. In: Proceedings of the 8th ACM SIGSAC Symposium on Information, Computer and Communications Security, ASIA CCS 2013, pp. 329–334. ACM, New York (2013)
21. Hall, M., Frank, E., Holmes, G., Pfahringer, B., Reutemann, P., Witten, I.H.: The WEKA Data Mining Software: An Update. ACM SIGKDD Explorations Newsletter 11(1), 10–18 (2009)
22. Spreitzenbarth, M., Freiling, F., Echtler, F., Schreck, T., Hoffmann, J.: Mobile-Sandbox: Having a Deeper Look into Android Applications. In: Proceedings of the 28th Annual ACM Symposium on Applied Computing (SAC 2013), pp. 1808–1815. ACM, New York (2013)
23. Hosmer, D., Lemeshow, S., Sturdivant, R.: Applied Logistic Regression, 2nd edn. Wiley Series in Probability and Statistics. John Wiley & Sons (2013)

A Decision Support System
for IT Security Incident Management

Gerhard Rauchecker, Emrah Yasasin, and Guido Schryen

Department of Management Information Systems, University of Regensburg,
Universitätsstraße 31, 93053 Regensburg, Germany
{gerhard.rauchecker,emrah.yasasin,guido.schryen}@wiwi.uni-regensburg.de
http://www.winfor.uni-regensburg.de/Home/index.html.en

Abstract. The problem of processing IT security incidents is a key task
in the field of security service management. This paper addresses the
problem of effectively assigning and scheduling security incidents to the
members of the IT staff. To solve this problem, we propose an innovative approach to assign staff members to security incidents by applying
mathematical programming to the field of IT security management. We
formulate an optimization model and propose efficient solution methods.
The numerical simulations show that our approach improves current best
practice behaviour significantly.

Keywords: IT Security Incidents, IT Security Services, Decision Support System, Heuristics, Optimization, Computational Experiment.

1 Introduction

According to a report by [3], Dun & Bradstreet refered that 59 % of Fortune
500 companies experience at least 1.6 hours of downtime of IT systems per week
(about 83 hours per year). To illustrate the dimension of potential costs, [3]
gives the following example: "Assume that an average Fortune 500 company has
10,000 employees who are paid an average of $56 per hour, including benefits
($40 per hour salary + $16 per hour in benefits). Just the labour component of
downtime costs for such a company would be $896,000 weekly, which translates
into more than $46 million per year." From these figures it can be concluded
that severe downtimes of IT systems often cost a significant amount of money.

Therefore, IT security incidents or outages of possibly different types (e.g.
server failure due to hijacking) require processing as soon as possible by the IT
staff members. Thus, effective and efficient scheduling of their staff is regarded
as one of the critical tasks for an organization's IT support. Interestingly, this
challenge has only rarely been addressed in the literature (see section 2).

We address this identified research gap and propose an innovative approach by
introducing methods of operations research (OR) to solve questions arising in the
field of IT security management. To the best of our knowledge, there is no work
including the powerful methods of OR to IT security management, although this

C. Eckert et al. (Eds.): TrustBus 2014, LNCS 8647, pp. 36–47, 2014.

is a very promising symbiosis in our opinion. Hence, we propose an optimization model for optimally assigning and scheduling security incidents to IT staff members. A strong advantage of our approach is its widespread applicability, because the model can also be established in general IT incident management frameworks which are not security related. We show that our approach improves current best practice significantly. When designing our model, we were highly influenced by ITIL [6]. In ITIL there are several processes defined, one of them being "Incident Management" that manages the life cycle of all incidents. The main purpose of incident management is to return the IT service as soon as possible. In this investigation, we concentrate on the "Incident Resolution Time" that is the average time for resolving an incident grouped into severity priorities. Thereby, we focus on a first level support. Our paper contributes to the usability of security services in the form of decision analytics in the area of IT security management.

The paper is organized as follows: the next section introduces related work. The third section outlines the methodology. We propose our optimization model of the decision support problem and develop two heuristic algorithms to solve this model efficiently. In section 4, we explain our computational experiments and present our results in section 5. Finally, we outline our contribution and close with an outlook on future research.

2 Related Work

When researching about IT incident management, three main directions can be identified: conceptual, prototypical and quantitative approaches. Lots of investigations are conceptual like ITIL, CoBIT and other frameworks for incident management [4, 6, 7, 8]. The prototypical approaches describe the development and prototypic implementation of a documentation system for IT incidents. In [9], occurring IT incidents are documented within an prototypic implementation for saving efforts for the employees involved and supporting the adaptability of the resulting system. [11], for instance, present an approach to diagnose application incidents by effectively searching relevant co-occurring and re-occcurring incidents.

Regarding the context of quantitative approaches, there is only limited work existing. An algorithm to assign IT incidents is provided by [10]. Main shortcomings of this approach are that it neither takes account for the fact that incidents may have different levels of severity, nor give they a benchmark of their algorithm. Although [12, 13] consider an assignment of developers in the context of bug fixing and feature developement, they do not solve a combinated assignment and scheduling problem, which would be a more complicated problem class. In [1, 2], semi-automated approaches for the assignment of bug reports to a developer are considered using machine learning algorithms based on text classification. However, these approaches need "an open bug repository for some period of time from which the patterns of who solves what kinds of bugs can be learned" [2] or a lot of contextual knowledge [1] which, in practice, both often do not exist. Hence, these investigations are probably suitable when focussing on large open source projects.

Thus, we integrate the quantitative methods of OR by giving a mathematical programming formulation for the assignment and scheduling of security incidents to IT staff members. We further develop and computationally evaluate heuristics to solve the mathematical program efficiently.

3   Optimization Model and Heuristics

In this section, we propose a linear programming model for optimally assigning and scheduling trouble tickets to members of the IT support, mainly influenced from [15] who propose a mathematical program for the allocation and scheduling of rescue units in the aftermath of natural disasters. In our formulation, a set of n tickets is available at time zero and tickets are assigned to staff members by one central agent at time zero. Tasks are non-preemptive, i.e., if a staff member starts to process an incident, he has to finish this incident without interruption. For tickets with similar resolution times, it is more convenient to solve tickets with higher priority first. Therefore, we introduce ticket weights (see subsection 3.2) and minimize the total weighted completion time of all tickets. Finally, this section closes with the proposition of two heuristic algorithms to solve the optimization model efficiently.

3.1   Dynamics of Ticket Occurrence

The fact that all tickets are available at time zero, while in real world scenarios we have a dynamic situation where tickets occur at different points of time, seems to be a shortcoming of our approach. But this, in fact, is not true and we will give a simple example why it can be better to wait a certain time until a bunch of tickets has arrived instead of myopically assigning tickets to staff members at the time of their occurrence. One reason surely is that often all staff members are currently occupied and therefore there is no loss of time when collecting a set of tickets before assigning them to the staff members. But even in the case that some of the staff members are ready to process a ticket immediately, it can be better (by means of the total weighted completion time) to collect some tickets and then assign them to the staff. We give a simple example of that by considering a scenario where the staff consists only of one member.

Assume that the first ticket arrives at time 0. The ticket has a moderate priority and a corresponding ticket weight $w_1 = 4$. The response time is $p_{\overline{t_1}} = 5$, the resolution time is $p_{t_1} = 20$ and the ticket has no setup time (remote ticket). The second ticket arrives at time 10. It has a critical priority and a corresponding ticket weight $w_2 = 16$. The response time is $p_{\overline{t_2}} = 5$, the resolution time is $p_{t_2} = 30$ and the ticket has no setup time (remote ticket). If we assign the first ticket immediately to the staff, then he needs a total time of 25 to respond to and solve the ticket. After that[1], he can respond to and solve the second ticket. Therefore, we have a total weighted completion time of $4 \cdot 25 + 16 \cdot (25 - 10 + 35) = 900$. If we wait until the occurrence of the second ticket and choose the schedule (*respond to second ticket, solve second ticket, respond to first ticket, solve first ticket*), we get a total weighted completion time of $16 \cdot 35 + 4 \cdot (35 + 25) = 800$. Even if we add up the waiting time 10 for the first ticket with its weight 4, we still get a better total weighted completion time of 840 in the second schedule. Of course, this example can be adopted to much more complex scenarios.

Furthermore, we account for both the dynamics of the situation and the need for timely decisions by suggesting that the optimization model is applied in an iterative manner: if the central agent determines to update the current assignment and scheduling plan based on new incoming tickets, a new instance of the optimization problem is created and solved taking into account current assignments.

3.2   Model Setup

Before introducing our mathematical program, we have to give the definitions which are necessary for its formulation.

We have a set of staff members $K := \{1, ..., m\}$, a set of tickets $\{1, ..., n\}$, a set of incidents $T := \{t_1, \ldots, t_n\}$ that represent the solutions of the tickets and a set of incidents $\overline{T} := \{\overline{t_1}, \ldots, \overline{t_n}\}$ which represent the responses to the tickets. Furthermore, we use fictitious incidents t_0 and t_{n+1} for modeling purposes. We will further need the sets $I_0 := \{t_0\} \cup T \cup \overline{T}$, $I_{n+1} := T \cup \overline{T} \cup \{t_{n+1}\}$ and the set of real (non-fictitious) incidents $I_{real} := T \cup \overline{T}$.

Next, we will propose our models decision variables. For incidents $\alpha \in I_0$, $\beta \in I_{n+1}$ and a staff member $k \in K$ we define

$$X_{\alpha\beta}^k := \begin{cases} 1, \text{ if } \alpha \text{ is executed directly before } \beta \text{ by } k \\ 0, \text{ else} \end{cases}$$

$$Y_{\alpha\beta}^k := \begin{cases} 1, \text{ if } \alpha \text{ is executed before } \beta \text{ by } k \\ 0, \text{ else} \end{cases}$$

In the following, we introduce the parameters used in our formulation. For a ticket $j = 1, \ldots, n$ and a staff member $k \in K$, $p_{t_j}^k \in \mathbb{R}_{\geq 0}$ (respectively $p_{\overline{t_j}}^k \in \mathbb{R}_{\geq 0}$) represents the time required by k to solve ticket j (respectively to respond to ticket j). Similarly, the parameters s_γ^k for $k \in K$ and $\gamma \in I_{real}$ denote the setup times, i.e., the time required to reach the location where the incident can be processed. Of course, this time is 0 if γ is a response to a ticket or a solution that can be executed remotely which means that the ticket can be solved by a staff member directly from its workplace. Note that the setup times do not

---

[1] Note that it would be possible to respond to the second ticket between the response to and the solution of the first ticket, but because of the non-preemptiveness of tasks, the staff member cannot respond to the second ticket before time 25, because the solution of the first ticket happens in the time window between time 5 and time 25 while the second ticket occurs at time 10.

depend on the incident which was processed before γ, because we assume that the staff member always returns to his office to catch the next incident from his computer. We also use a capability parameter cap_j^k which is 1 if staff member k is capable of processing ticket j and 0 otherwise.

We further have different priority levels (e.g. critical, high, medium, low, very low) that indicate the priority of the tickets. For each ticket $j = 1, \ldots, n$ we have a corresponding ticket weight w_j, a target response time r_j^{max} and a target resolution time c_j^{max}, each of them depending solely on the priority level of the ticket. Such times were suggested by ITIL [6] for example. The ticket weights w_j, assigned by the central agent, are based on the priority level which means the more urgent the priority level is, the higher is its ticket weight. The target response time represents the maximum acceptable time until the beginning of the response to a ticket whereas the target resolution time denotes the maximum acceptable time until the end of the solution of a ticket.

3.3 Model

With the above notations we can introduce the following linear programming model.

$$\min_{X,Y} \sum_{j=1}^{n} w_j \sum_{k=1}^{m} \left(\sum_{\alpha \in I_0} (p_{t_j}^k + s_{t_j}^k) X_{\alpha t_j}^k + \sum_{\gamma \in I_{real}} (p_\gamma^k + s_\gamma^k) Y_{\gamma t_j}^k \right) \tag{1}$$

$$s.t. \sum_{\alpha \in I_0} \sum_{k=1}^{m} X_{\alpha \gamma}^k = 1, \quad \gamma \in I_{real} \tag{2}$$

$$\sum_{\beta \in I_{n+1}} X_{t_0 \beta}^k = 1, \quad k = 1, \ldots, m \tag{3}$$

$$\sum_{\alpha \in I_0} X_{\alpha \gamma}^k = \sum_{\beta \in I_{n+1}} X_{\gamma \beta}^k, \quad \gamma \in I_{real}; k = 1, \ldots, m \tag{4}$$

$$\sum_{k=1}^{m} \sum_{\gamma \in I_{real}} Y_{\gamma \gamma}^k = 0 \tag{5}$$

$$Y_{\alpha \gamma}^k + Y_{\gamma \beta}^k - 1 \le Y_{\alpha \beta}^k, \quad \alpha \in I_0; \beta \in I_{n+1}; \gamma \in I_{real}; k = 1, \ldots, m \tag{6}$$

$$X_{\alpha \beta}^k \le Y_{\alpha \beta}^k, \quad \alpha \in I_0; \beta \in I_{n+1}; k = 1, \ldots, m \tag{7}$$

$$\sum_{\gamma \in I_0} X_{\gamma \beta}^k + \sum_{\gamma \in I_{n+1}} X_{\alpha \gamma}^k \ge 2 \cdot Y_{\alpha \beta}^k, \quad \alpha \in I_0; \beta \in I_{n+1}; k = 1, \ldots, m \tag{8}$$

$$\sum_{k=1}^{m} \left(\sum_{\alpha \in I_0} (p_{t_j}^k + s_{t_j}^k) X_{\alpha t_j}^k + \sum_{\gamma \in I_{real}} (p_\gamma^k + s_\gamma^k) Y_{\gamma t_j}^k \right) \le c_j^{max}, \quad j = 1, \ldots, n \tag{9}$$

$$\sum_{k=1}^{m} \sum_{\gamma \in I_{real}} p_\gamma^k Y_{\gamma t_j}^k \le r_j^{max}, \quad j = 1, \ldots, n \tag{10}$$

$$\sum_{\beta \in I_{n+1}} \left(X_{t_j\beta}^k + X_{\overline{t_j}\beta}^k \right) \le 2 \cdot cap_j^k, \quad j = 1, \ldots, n \tag{11}$$

$$\sum_{k=1}^{m} Y_{\overline{t_j}t_j}^k = 1, \quad j = 1, \ldots, n \tag{12}$$

$$X_{\alpha\beta}^k, Y_{\alpha\beta}^k \in \{0, 1\}, \quad \alpha \in I_0; \beta \in I_{n+1}; k = 1, \ldots, m \tag{13}$$

The objective function (1) aims at minimizing the total weighted completion time. Constraint (2) guarantees that for each real incident there is exactly one incident processed immediately before. Constraint (3) ensures that each staff member k starts with the fictitious incident t_0 and then processes some incident β. Constraint (4) indicates for every staff member k that if there is an immediate predecessor for a specific real incident, there must be an immediate successor as well. Constraint (5) prohibits loops and constraint (6) is a transitivity constraint which assures that a staff member k, who processes incident α before a real incident γ and γ before incident β, also processes α before β. Constraint (7) means that any immediate predecessor is also a general predecessor. Constraint (8) secures that if a staff member k processes an incident α before an incident β, there has to be an incident which is processed by k immediately before β and an incident which is processed by k immediately after α. Constraints (9) and (10) list the target times of the tickets. Constraint (11) guarantees that tickets are only assigned to staff members that have the ability to solve them. Constraint (12) assures that before solving a ticket, the same staff member k has to respond to this.

3.4   Heuristics

The problem stated in this paper is computationally intractable and NP-hard. We will briefly explain this. If we drop a) the assumption that the response to a ticket has to be performed before the solution of a ticket and b) the target time constraints, we get a problem which is more simple than our problem but still a strong generalization of the 2-machine identical parallel machine scheduling problem with total weighted completion time as the objective function, which is known to be NP-hard. This fact has been proven by [5]. Furthermore, even for moderate instance sizes (e.g. 20 tickets and 10 staff members), we were not able to obtain optimal solutions within 12 hours. Therefore, we need to develop efficient solution heuristics to apply our approach in practical contexts.

Greedy Heuristic. Greedy heuristics are an often used technique in the context of IT incidents assignment in various contexts (e.g. [12, 13]). These heuristics make decisions about the construction of a solution based on local considerations such as preferring the choice that gives immediate best reward. In our context, this is a "first-come-first-serve" technique which is also current best practice to assign IT incidents to staff members [16]. The first heuristic we present is therefore a greedy heuristic, referred by **Greedy**, that models current best practice. The heuristic first sorts the tickets in descending order of their ticket weights and then consecutively assigns the tickets to that staff member who has the shortest queue by means of current completion time. The response and resolution of the current ticket are both assigned in this succession to the end of that staff members current queue. The pseudocode is presented in table 1.

Table 1. Greedy pseudocode

1	sort the incidents in descending order of their ticket weights $w_1 \geq \ldots \geq w_n$
2	initialize the current completion time $curr_k := 0$ and the current schedule
	$\sigma_k := \emptyset$ of every staff member $k \in K$
3	**for** $i = 1, \ldots, n$ **do**
4	define the set of feasible staff members to process i by
	$K^* := \{k \in K \mid cap_i^k = 1 \wedge curr_k \leq r_i^{max} \wedge curr_k + p_{\overline{t_i}}^k + s_{t_i}^k + p_{t_i}^k \leq c_i^{max}\}$
5	**if** $K^* \neq \emptyset$ **then**
6	choose staff member k^* with the lowest current completion time
	$k^* := \arg\min_{k \in K^*}\{curr_k\}$ to response to and solve ticket i
7	update $curr_{k^*} := curr_{k^*} + p_{\overline{t_i}}^{k^*} + s_{t_i}^{k^*} + p_{t_i}^{k^*}$ and $\sigma_{k^*} := (\sigma_{k^*}, \overline{t_i}, t_i)$
8	**else return** infeasible
9	**endfor**
10	**return** the list of feasible schedules $(\sigma_1, \ldots, \sigma_m)$

Scheduling Heuristic. Although **Greedy** models best practice behaviour, it follows a very myopic assignment rule, because the staff member selection does not depend on the specific response times, the setup times or the resolution times of a ticket. Therefore, we suggest a scheduling heuristic, referred by **Sched**, which takes account for all of these times. We developed this heuristic based on the best performing algorithm in [14], referred to there as "Heuristic algorithm 7", which addresses a related problem from the scheduling literature. The pseudocode of the **Sched** heuristic is presented in table 2.

The main idea of this procedure is to select that pair of remaining tickets and staff members that minimizes the ratio of the total time to complete the ticket and its corresponding ticket weight. The response to that ticket (or the solution if a response has been given yet) is added to the end of the queue of the selected staff member. The selection criterion also takes care of the fact that before solving a ticket, a response to this ticket has to be performed by the same staff member (lines 8 and 14). We take account for keeping the timeframes (see table 4) for both the response to and the solution of a ticket with the use of the while-loop in lines 12 to 22. This loop addresses the case that the current assignment (i^*, k^*) makes it impossible to keep the timeframes for the remaining tickets. In this case we drop the current assignment (by setting $check := 1$ in line 13) and process urgent tickets first which are risky to miss their target times. In lines 15 to 21 (analogously in lines 23 to 29) we apply the current assignment by responding to the selected ticket or by solving the ticket (if the response has been given yet). At this point, we update the current completion time and the current schedule of the selected staff member and add a response marker to the ticket (or remove the ticket from the remaining tickets if the ticket has been solved right now).

Table 2. Sched pseudocode

1	initialize the current completion time $curr_k := 0$, the updated completion time $\widetilde{curr_k}$ and the current schedule $\sigma_k := \emptyset$ of every staff member $k \in K$
2	initialize the remaining tickets $RT := \{1, \ldots, n\}$, the tickets yet responded to $Resp := \emptyset$ and a check parameter $check := 0$
3	**while** $RT \neq \emptyset$ **do**
4	reset $check := 0$
5	define the set of possible combinations by $F := \{(i,k) \in RT \times K \mid cap_i^k = 1\}$
6	**if** $F \neq \emptyset$ **then**
7	set $F_{res} := \{(i,k) \in F \mid i \notin Resp\}$ and $F_{sol} := \{(i,k) \in F \mid$ staff member k has yet responded to ticket $i\}$
8	select the current ticket i^* and its processing staff member k^* as the best argument from the two minimization problems $\min_{(i,k) \in F_{res}} \left\{ \frac{curr_k + p_{t_i}^k + s_{t_i}^k + p_{t_i}^k}{w_i} \right\}$ and $\min_{(i,k) \in F_{sol}} \left\{ \frac{curr_k + s_{t_i}^k + p_{t_i}^k}{w_i} \right\}$
9	set $\widetilde{curr_k} := curr_k$ for all $k \in K$
10	**if** $(i^*, k^*) \in F_{res}$ **then** update $\widetilde{curr_{k^*}} := \widetilde{curr_{k^*}} + p_{t_{i^*}}^{k^*}$
11	**else** update $\widetilde{curr_{k^*}} := \widetilde{curr_{k^*}} + s_{t_{i^*}}^{k^*} + p_{t_{i^*}}^{k^*}$ **endif**
12	**while** exists $(i,k) \in F_{sol}$ with $\widetilde{curr_k} + s_{t_i}^k + p_{t_i}^k > c_i^{max}$ **or** exists $i \notin Resp$ with $\min_{k \in K \mid cap_i^k = 1} \{\widetilde{curr_k}\} > r_i^{max}$ **do**
13	set $check := 1$
14	select the current ticket i^* and its processing staff member k^* as the best argument from the two minimization problems $\min_{(i,k) \in F_{sol}} \left\{ c_i^{max} - (curr_k + s_{t_i}^k + p_{t_i}^k) \right\}$ (to select (i^*, k^*)) and $\min_{i \notin Resp} \max_{k \in K \mid cap_i^k = 1} \left\{ r_i^{max} - curr_k \right\}$ (to select i^*) along with $\min_{k \in K \mid cap_{i^*}^k = 1} \{curr_k\}$ (to select k^*)
15	**if** $i^* \notin Resp$ **then**
16	**if** $curr_{k^*} > r_{i^*}^{max}$ **then return** infeasible **endif**
17	update $Resp := Resp \cup \{i^*\}$, $\sigma_{k^*} := (\sigma_{k^*}, \overline{t_{i^*}})$, $F_{sol} := F_{sol} \cup \{(i^*, k^*)\}$ and $curr_{k^*} := curr_{k^*} + p_{t_{i^*}}^{k^*}$
18	**else**
19	update $RT := RT \setminus \{i^*\}$, $\sigma_{k^*} := (\sigma_{k^*}, t_{i^*})$, $F_{sol} := F_{sol} \setminus \{(i^*, k^*)\}$ and $curr_{k^*} := curr_{k^*} + s_{t_{i^*}}^{k^*} + p_{t_{i^*}}^{k^*}$
20	**if** $curr_{k^*} > c_{i^*}^{max}$ **then return** infeasible **endif**
21	**endif**
22	**endwhile**
23	**if** $check = 0$ **then**
24	**if** $i^* \notin Resp$ **then**
25	update $Resp := Resp \cup \{i^*\}$, $\sigma_{k^*} := (\sigma_{k^*}, \overline{t_{i^*}})$ and $curr_{k^*} := curr_{k^*} + p_{t_{i^*}}^{k^*}$
26	**else**
27	update $RT := RT \setminus \{i^*\}$, $\sigma_{k^*} := (\sigma_{k^*}, t_{i^*})$ and $curr_{k^*} := curr_{k^*} + s_{t_{i^*}}^{k^*} + p_{t_{i^*}}^{k^*}$
28	**endif**
29	**endif**
30	**else return** infeasible
31	**endwhile**
32	**return** the list of feasible schedules $(\sigma_1, \ldots, \sigma_m)$

4   Computational Experiments

In order to evaluate the performance of our **Sched** heuristic, we investigated different problem sizes and randomly generated 10 instances per size. Our aim is to document the improvement of current best practice, which was modeled as **Greedy** heuristic. In order to reach this, we calculated the solutions of both heuristics in all instances.

We generated scenarios with 5, 10, 20, 40, 60 and 80 staff members, which should cover medium sized companies as well as large enterprises. We assume that there are at least as many and at most twice as many tickets as staff members. All times are expressed in minutes. The priority levels of a ticket can take one of the values *critical, high, medium, low* and *very low*. The target times for each priority level are presented in table 4 and are inspired by ITIL [6]. We have chosen normal distributions for generating the time parameters in our instances which is a common used approach in the academic literature, e.g. [15]. The response and setup times seem to be independent from the specific priority level of a ticket and are presented in table 3. We have chosen a 50% probability for a ticket to be solved remotely. Otherwise the normal distribution for the setup time is applied.

Table 3. Data independent from priorities

Input parameter	Value, distribution
Setup times	$s_j^k \sim N(5,1)$ or $s_j^k = 0$ if remote
Response times	$p_{t_j}^k \sim N(5,1)$

In contrast to the response and setup times, the solution times are indeed dependent on the specific priority level, see table 4. This is obvious because a critical ticket, such as a server blackout, tends to require more time to be solved than a lower priority ticket, such as a crashed virus scanner at a single workplace.

Table 4. Data dependent from priorities

Priority level	critical	high	moderately	low	very low
Resolution times $p_{t_j}^k \sim$	$N(30,10)$	$N(25,10)$	$N(20,10)$	$N(15,10)$	$N(10,10)$
Occurrence probability	5%	10%	15%	30%	40%
Corresp. ticket weight	16	8	4	2	1
Target response time	0	10	60	240	1440
Target resolution time	60	240	480	1440	10080

We also consider the fact that tickets with a higher priority tend to occur more seldomly than tickets with a lower priority, see table 4. The probalibility of a staff member to be capable of processing a certain ticket was set to 50%.

5   Results

In this section, we evaluate the results drawn from our computational experiments. The results are presented in table 5. The first and fourth row contain the ratio #Staff/#Tickets of the number of staff members to the number of tickets. For every instance size, we average the ratios $SchedSol_i/GreedySol_i$ for all ten instances $i = 1, \ldots, 10$, which results in the values $Sched/Greedy$ listed in rows 2 and 5 (where $SchedSol_i$ and $GreedySol_i$ denote the total weighted completion time of the **Sched** and the **Greedy** heuristic solution for instance i). The numbers $CoeffVar$ stand for the coefficients of variance of the ratios $(SchedSol_i/GreedySol_i)_{i=1,\ldots,10}$ and are a measure for robustness.

Table 5. Results of computations

#Staff/#Tickets	5/5	5/10	10/10	10/15	10/20	20/20	20/30	20/40	
Sched/Greedy	0.91	0.86	0.72	0.68	0.66	0.61	0.59	0.56	
CoeffVar	0.15	0.15	0.15	0.13	0.08	0.09	0.10	0.06	
#Staff/#Tickets	40/40	40/60	40/80	60/60	60/90	60/120	80/80	80/120	80/160
Sched/Greedy	0.52	0.49	0.49	0.46	0.47	0.44	0.40	0.43	0.43
CoeffVar	0.10	0.10	0.06	0.11	0.06	0.07	0.10	0.07	0.06

The computational results show that our developed heuristic **Sched** improves the current best practice behavior (modeled as **Greedy** heuristic) from 9% up to 60%. In larger companies, with an IT support consisting of 20 or more staff members, the improvement is even greater than 39%. The reason for the **Sched** heuristic being more dominant over the **Greedy** heuristic in larger instance sizes is explained in the following. If we have a small IT support with about 5 or 10 staff members, the number of employees that can solve a specific ticket is rather low. This number increases with the size of the IT support staff and therefore the response, setup and solution times of a ticket, that depend not only on tickets but also on the staff members, become more relevant. This is the point where our **Sched** heuristic performs much better than the **Greedy** heuristic which does not account for any of these times. The coefficient of variation is a measure for the relative dispersion of data. In our context, this parameter describes the average percentile deviation of the ratios $SchedSol_i/GreedySol_i, i = 1, \ldots, 10$, from the mean value Sched/Greedy. This relative spread reaches from 6% in the best to 15% in the worst scenario. These values are thus at a good range. Further, runtimes show that the developed **Sched** heuristic needs only few seconds in all tested cases and is thus very applicable in practice.

6   Conclusion and Future Work

In this paper, we address the problem of effectively assigning IT security incidents to IT staff members, which is a crucial task in IT security management. First, we introduced a mathematical programming model to optimally assigning and scheduling these incidents. By doing this, we bridged the gap between the quantitative methods of OR and the field of IT security management. Although we could not solve relevant scenarios optimally due to the model complexity, we showed the practical applicability of our approach by developing efficient solution heuristics. Second, we showed that our **Sched** heuristic improves current best practice, modeled as **Greedy** heuristic, by up to 60% and at the same time can be used in practice because of the very low execution times of the algorithm.

As future work, we are going to extend our approach by considering dependencies between the tickets. For instance, some tickets cannot be solved before having solved other tickets first. We will also expand our approach to higher support levels. Further, our current approach assumes to wait a certain time until a bunch of tickets has arrived. This tradeoff between waiting time and immediate assignment requires further research with real data. In further researches, the assumption that tasks are non-preemptive can be dropped in order to pause the task when appropriate. For example, this is likely to become necessary when all staff members are currently occupied and a critical ticket arrives. Finally, we will develop other heuristics and adopt metaheuristics to cover these extensions and to gain further benchmarks for the quality of the heuristics.

Acknowledgments. The research leading to these results was supported by the "Bavarian State of Ministry, Education, Science and the Arts" as part of the FORSEC research association (https://www.bayforsec.de) and by the "Regionale Wettbewerbsfähigkeit und Beschäftigung", Bayern, 2007-2013 (EFRE) as part of the SECBIT project (http://www.secbit.de).

References

[1] Anvik, J.: Automating Bug Report Assignment. In: ICSE 2006 Proceedings of the 28th International Conference on Software Engineering, pp. 937–940 (2006)

[2] Anvik, J., Hiew, L., Murphy, G.: Who should fix this bug? In: ICSE 2006 Proceedings of the 28th International Conference on Software Engineering, pp. 361–370 (2006)

[3] Arnold, A.: Assessing the Financial Impact of Downtime. Vision Solutions, White Paper (2010),
http://www.strategiccompanies.com/pdfs/Assessing%20the
%20Financial%20Impact%20of%20Downtime.pdf

[4] Bernard, P.: COBIT 5 - A Management Guide. Van Haren Publishing (2012)

[5] Bruno, J., Coffman Jr., E.G., Sehti, R.: Scheduling Independent Tasks to Reduce Mean Finishing Time. Communications of the ACM 17(7), 382–387 (1974)

[6] Office, C., Steinberg, R., Rudd, C., Lacy, S., Hanna, A.: ITIL Service Operation, 2nd edn. TSO, London (2011)

[7] Cichonski, P., Millar, T., Grance, T., Scarfone, K.: Computer Security Incident Handling Guide. National Institute of Standards and Technology Special Publication 800-61, Revision 2 (2012)

[8] ISO/IEC: ISO/IEC 27035 - Information Technology - Security Techniques - Information Security Incident Management (2011)

[9] Kurowski, S., Frings, S.: Computational Documentation of IT Incidents as Support for Forensic Operations. In: Proceedings of the 2011 Sixth International Conference on IT Security Incident Management and IT Forensics, pp. 37–47. IEEE Computer Society, Washington, DC (2011)

[10] Li, X., Zhan, Z., Guo, S., Zhang, L.: IT Incident Assign Algorithm Based on the Difference Between Support Groups. In: International Conference on Advanced Intelligence and Awarenss Internet (AIAI), pp. 319–323 (2010)

[11] Liu, R., Lee, J.: IT Incident Management by Analyzing Incident Relations. In: Liu, C., Ludwig, H., Toumani, F., Yu, Q. (eds.) Service Oriented Computing. LNCS, vol. 7636, pp. 631–638. Springer, Heidelberg (2012)

[12] Rahman, M., Ruhe, G., Zimmermann, T.: Optimized Assignment of Developers for Fixing Bugs: An Initial Evaluation for Eclipse Projects. In: IEEE International Symposium on Empirical Software Engineering and Measurement, pp. 439–442 (2009)

[13] Rahman, M., Sohan, S.M., Maurer, F., Ruhe, G.: Evaluation of Optimized Staffing for Feature Development and Bug Fixing. In: Proceedings of the 2010 ACM-IEEE International Symposium on Empirical Software Engineering and Measurement (2010)

[14] Weng, M.X., Lu, J., Ren, H.: Unrelated Parallel Machine Scheduling with Setup Consideration and a Total Weighted Completion Time Objective. International Journal of Production Economics 70(3), 215–226 (2001)

[15] Wex, F., Schryen, G., Feuerriegel, S., Neumann, D.: Emergency Response in Natural Disaster Management: Allocation and Scheduling of Rescue Units. European Journal of Operational Research 235(3), 697–708 (2014)

[16] Zitek, N.: ITIL Incident Management - How to separate roles at different support levels. ITIL & ISO 20000 Blog (2013),
http://www.20000academy.com/Blog/November-2013/
ITIL-Incident-Management-How-to-separate-roles-at-different-support-levels

Trust Evaluation of a System for an Activity with Subjective Logic

Nagham Alhadad[1,2], Yann Busnel[1],
Patricia Serrano-Alvarado[1], and Philippe Lamarre[3]

[1] LINA/Université de Nantes – France
[2] LIG/Université de Grenoble Alpes – France
[3] LIRIS/INSA Lyon – France

Abstract. Recently, *trust* emerged as a momentous aspect to evaluate resources, services or persons. In our work, the trust notion focuses on a system as a whole and from the point of view of a particular user to do a particular digital activity as editing a document, mailing, chatting, *etc*. Our general goals are *(i)* to enable users to have a personal comparison of applications allowing them to do an activity such that they can choose the one satisfying their personal expectations and *(ii)* to know how trustworthy their system is to do a particular activity (all applications together). We consider a system as a graph composed of paths where the source is a person and the target is a final application or data. We consider that trust in a system depends on its architecture and we identify two problems *(i)* how to evaluate trust in a graph having dependent paths *i.e.*, paths having common nodes, and *(ii)* how to express and deal with uncertainty in evaluating trust in a system. Concerning the first problem, trust approaches based on graphs have been proposed in the domain of social networks. Their solution for dependent paths is either removing paths or just choosing one of them what causes loss of information. Considering the second problem, *subjective logic* emerged to express trust as a subjective opinion with a degree of uncertainty. In this paper we present SUBJECTIVETRUST, an approach that relies on subjective logic to evaluate trust in distributed systems. It proposes two solutions to treat dependent paths and takes into account the shape of the system architecture in trust evaluation. We analyze SUBJECTIVETRUST in a series of experiments that show its accuracy.

1   Introduction

When users need to choose a system to perform a digital activity, like editing a document or mailing, they face several available options. To choose a system, they evaluate many criteria as functionality, ease of use, QoS, or economical aspects. *Trust* also emerged as a momentous aspect of choice [13]. Evaluating trust in a system is complex and becomes more challenging when systems use distributed architectures. Our general goals are *(i)* to enable users to have a personal comparison of applications allowing them to do an activity such that they can choose the one satisfying their personal expectations and *(ii)* to know how trustworthy their system is to do a particular activity (all applications together). We argue that studying trust in the separate entities that compose a system does not give a picture of how trustworthy a system is as a whole. Indeed, the

C. Eckert et al. (Eds.): TrustBus 2014, LNCS 8647, pp. 48–59, 2014.

trust in a system depends on its entities but also on its architecture. More precisely, on the way the entities, the users depends on to do their activities, are organized.

Trust has been studied from different points of views [5,6,17] and to evaluate it metrics vary from binary, scalar to probabilistic approaches [13,18]. As users hardly have all information to provide a dogmatic opinion on something or someone, *subjective logic* [10], an extension of classical probability, emerged to express trust as a subjective opinion with a degree of uncertainty.

We consider a system as a graph [3] composed of paths where the source is a person and the target a final application or data. Intermediary nodes are entities (software) allowing to achieve the activity. Each path is a way to do a given activity. Trust approaches based on graphs [7,9,11,12,14,16] are especially used in the context of social networks where the main idea to derive trust is to propagate it *through a path* then *through a social graph* [1]. Their solution for dependent paths is either removing paths or just choosing one of them in such a way the obtained graph has only independent paths what causes loss of information.

In a former work, we proposed SOCIOTRUST, an approach to evaluate trust based on probability theory [4]. In this paper, we aim to take advantage of the benefits of subjective logic and we present SUBJECTIVETRUST, an approach to evaluate trust in distributed system architectures that relies on subjective logic. The goal is to allow a person to evaluate her trust in a system for an activity from her *potentially uncertain* trust in each node of the system graph. Although our approach relies on a graph, like in the social network domain, the interpretation of the graph is different. For us, a graph represents *a system for a digital activity* and not *a social network*. This assumption plays an important role in the operations we apply and in the results we interpret. SUBJECTIVETRUST estimates trust at two levels of granularities, namely, *trust in a path* and *trust in a system*. We address the problem of *dependent paths* in a graph and we propose two solutions. We evaluate SUBJECTIVETRUST in a series of experiments that compare the proposed solutions and analyze their accuracy.

This paper is organized as follows. Section 2 gives a quick overview of subjective logic and presents related works. Section 3 introduces SUBJECTIVETRUST. We present the experiments that validate our approach in Section 4 before concluding in Section 5.

2   Background and Related Works

Subjective logic has been proposed recently as a formalism to express uncertainty [10]. In this paper we do not propose enhancements to this logic, we just adopt it to the context of personal evaluation of trust in a system for an activity. Next section gives an overview of subjective logic (*cf.* Section 2.1). We then explicit the problem of dependent paths in graph-based trust approaches and present related works (*cf.* Section 2.2).

2.1   Overview of Subjective Logic

Several metrics have been proposed to evaluate trust. In binary metrics, trust values are only *trust* or *distrust* [8]. In simple metrics, trust values are scaled intervals formed from relatively simple methods of computation like a multiplication or a weighted average [7]. In probabilistic metrics, a trust value represents the probability of how much likely a trustor will perform actions as the trustee expects. In these metrics, a given person cannot express her ignorance or her degree of uncertainty about a proposition because there is no value that means "I do not know" or "I am not sure". This idea led researchers to look for mathematical formalisms to express uncertainty.

Subjective logic [10], an extension of classical probability, proposes a solution to this problem. It is a probabilistic logic that uses *opinions* as input and output variables. Opinions explicitly express uncertainty about probability values, and can express degrees of ignorance about a proposition. In the terminology of subjective logic, an opinion held by an individual P about a proposition x is the ordered quadruple $O_x = (b_x, d_x, u_x, a_x)$, where b_x (belief) is the belief that x is true, d_x (disbelief) is the belief that x is false, and u_x (uncertainty) is the amount of uncommitted belief, $b_x, d_x, u_x \in [0..1]$ and $b_x + d_x + u_x = 1$. The last value $a_x \in [0..1]$ is called the base rate. In the absence of any specific evidence about a given party, the base rate determines the default trust. An opinion's probability expectation value, which can be determined as $E(O_x) = b_x + a_x u_x$, is interpreted as a probability measure indicating how x is expected to behave in the future. More precisely, a_x determines how uncertainty shall contribute to the probability expectation value $E(O_x)$. Subjective logic consists of a set of logical operations which are defined to combine opinions.

- Conjunction operator ($\wedge$) represents the opinion of a person on several propositions.
- Disjunction operator ($\vee$) represents the opinion of a person on one of the propositions or any union of them.
- Discounting operator ($\otimes$) represents the transitivity of the opinions.
- Consensus operator ($\oplus$) represents the consensus of opinions of different persons.

In this work, we use subjective logic to evaluate trust.

2.2 Graph-Based Trust Approach

Trust approaches based on graphs [1,8,11,12,15,16] are especially used in social networks where the main idea of trust derivation is to propagate it between two nodes in a graph that represents the social network. A social network is a social structure composed of a set of persons (individuals or organizations) and a set of relations among these persons. It can be represented as a graph where the nodes are the persons and the edges are the relations between them. Trust between two persons in a social network can be evaluated based on this graph where the source node is the trustor, the target node is the trustee and the other nodes are the intermediate nodes between the trustor and the trustee. Values are associated with the edges to represent the trust value attributed by the edge source node towards the edge target node. Figure 1 shows an example of trust relationships in a social network. For instance, B trusts C with the value 0.8.

Trust propagation focuses on finding a trust value from a person towards another given person through the multiple paths that relate them. For instance, in Figure 1, how much A trusts E knowing that there are two paths that relate A with E? The paths are: $path_1 = \{A, B, C, E\}$, and $path_2 = \{A, B, D, E\}$. In [1], authors propose a general approach for graph-based trust. They divide the process of trust evaluation into two steps:

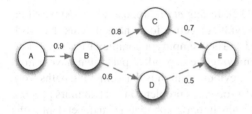

⊗ average	⊗ multiplication
⊕ maximum	⊕ comultiplication
Relation 1:	Relation 1:
$T_E^A = 0.825$	$T_E^A = 0.623$
Relation 2:	Relation 2:
$T_E^A = 0.8$	$T_E^A = 0.64$

Fig. 1. The different obtained results of Relations 1, 2 by applying an example of discrete metrics and continuous metrics on a simple graph

1. Trust combination through a path: the main idea is to combine the trust values among the intermediate edges of a path to obtain a trust value though this path. Several operators are employed ranging from basic operators like the minimum to new operators like the *discounting* operator of subjective logic.
2. Trust combination through a graph: the main idea is to combine the several trust values through the multiple paths, which relate the source with the target, to obtain a single trust value through the whole graph. Several operators are employed to combine trust through a graph, ranging from basic operators like the average to new ones like the *consensus* operator of subjective logic.

   In [11,12], Jøsang *et al.* raised a problem of graph-based trust approaches if trust is evaluated through the previous two steps. They argue that some metrics do not give exact results when there are dependent paths *i.e.,* paths that have common edges in the graph. To explain this problem, we give a simple example shown in Figure 1. We need to evaluate T_E^A corresponding to A's trust value in E. The paths between A and E are: $path_1 = \{A, B, C, E\}$ and $path_2 = \{A, B, D, E\}$. There is a common edge between these two paths which is $A \longrightarrow B$. Let $\otimes$ be the operator of trust combination through a path and $\oplus$ be the operator of trust combination through a graph. To evaluate T_E^A, the A's trust value in E:

$$T_E^A = T_B^A \otimes ((T_C^B \otimes T_E^C) \oplus (T_D^B \otimes T_E^D)) \tag{1}$$

However, if we apply the previous two steps, T_E^A is computed as follows:

$$T_E^A = (T_B^A \otimes T_C^B \otimes T_E^C) \oplus (T_B^A \otimes T_D^B \otimes T_E^D) \tag{2}$$

   Relations 1, 2 consist of the same two paths $path_1$ and $path_2$, but their combined structures are different. T_B^A appears twice in Relation 2. In some metrics, the previous two equations produce different results. For instance, when implementing $\otimes$ as binary logic "AND", and $\oplus$ as binary logic "OR", the results would be equal. However, when implementing $\otimes$ and $\oplus$ as probabilistic multiplication and comultiplication respectively, the results would be different. If $\otimes$ is the minimum function and $\oplus$ is the average function, the results are also different. Figure 1 shows the application of different operators on the example of our simple graph and the different obtained results of Relations 1 and 2.

   In graph-based trust approaches, this problem is either ignored [16], either simple solutions are proposed like choosing one path in a graph [15], or removing the paths that are considered unreliable [8,12]. In [12], Jøsang *et al.* propose a method based on graph simplification and trust derivation with subjective logic named, Trust Network Analysis with Subjective Logic (TNA-SL). They simplify a complex trust graph into a graph having independent paths by removing the dependent paths that have a high value of *uncertainty*. The problem of the previous solution is that removing paths from a graph could cause loss of information. To solve this problem, in [11], authors propose to transform a graph that has dependent paths into a graph that has independent paths by duplicating the edges in common and splitting the associated opinions to them.

In SOCIOTRUST [4], a graph-based trust approach based on probability theory to evaluate trust in a system for an activity, the problem of dependent paths is solved using *conditional probability*. In SOCIOTRUST, trust values are considered as the probability by which a trustor believes that a trustee behaves as expected [13]. SOCIOTRUST is an approach that works perfectly in full-knowledge environments. However, in uncertain environments, users might not be in possession of all the information to provide a dogmatic opinion and traditional probability cannot express uncertainty.

In this work, we rely on a graph to evaluate trust like in the social network domain, but our interpretation of the graph is different. For us, a graph represents *a system for a digital activity* and not *a social network*. This assumption plays an important role in the operations we apply for trust evaluation. For instance, in a social network, to evaluate trust through a path using subjective logic, the operator of discounting ($\otimes$) is used to compute the transitivity through a path, whereas, in our work, evaluating trust in a path is the trust in the *collection* of the nodes that form this path. In the same manner, to evaluate trust through a graph in a social network, the operator of consensus ($\oplus$) is used to evaluate the consensus of opinions of different persons through the different paths that form the graph, whereas, in our work, paths represent the ways one person disposes to achieve an activity, so evaluating trust in a graph is the trust in one of the paths or any union of them.

Next Section presents SUBJECTIVETRUST, the contribution of this paper that is based on subjective logic to deal with uncertainty. It faces the problem of dependent paths by proposing two methods, **Copy** and **Split**. We provide these methods with the necessary formalisms and algorithms to be applied to the context of our work.

3   SUBJECTIVETRUST

In this approach, the graph represents an architecture allowing an activity to be achieved. The source node in a graph is the user who performs an activity and the target node is a data instance or an application that is related to this activity [3]. Each path between the source node and the target node represents a way to achieve the activity through a system. User's opinions are associated with the nodes and not the edges as in social networks because they represent the local user's opinions on these nodes. Whereas in social networks the associated values to the edges represent the trust between the nodes related by the edges[1].

---

[1] For more details about obtaining a graph of a system allowing an activity to be achieved, see our previous work SOCIOTRUST [4].

We aim to evaluate trust towards a whole graph that represents an activity achieved through a system. To do that, we pass through two steps *opinion on a path* (*cf.* Section 3.1) and *opinion on a system* (*cf.* Section 3.2), both for an activity achieved by a user. In our graph, dependent paths are the ones that have **common nodes** and not common edges because opinions are associated with nodes in our approach. To solve the problem of dependent paths, we propose two methods named, **Copy** and **Split** with their necessary formalisms and algorithms to be applied to the context of our work. In both, we consider duplicating the common nodes in order to obtain two independent opinions associated with them. In **Copy**, we also duplicate the opinions associated with the common nodes. **Split** is inspired from [11], after duplicating the common nodes, the associated opinions to them are also split. In the following sections, we denote a path by σ and a system by α. A path in our graph does not consider the source and the target node.

3.1 Opinion on a Path for an Activity

When a user needs to achieve an activity through a path, she needs to pass through all the nodes composing this path. Hence, an opinion on a path is a composition of the opinions on all the nodes composing this path.

The conjunction operator in subjective logic represents the opinion of a person on several propositions. If $O_x^P = (b_x^P, d_x^P, u_x^P, a_x^P)$ is P's opinion on x and $O_y^P = (b_y^P, d_y^P, u_y^P, a_y^P)$ is P's opinion on y, $O_{x \wedge y}^P$ represents P's opinion on both x and y. Thus, the conjunction operator is the appropriate operator to compute an opinion on a path from the opinions on the nodes.

Let $\sigma = \{N_1, N_2, \ldots, N_n\}$ be a path that enables a user P to achieve an activity. P's opinion on the nodes $\{N_i\}_{i \in [1..n]}$ for an activity are denoted by $O_{N_i} = (b_{N_i}, d_{N_i}, u_{N_i}, a_{N_i})$. P's opinion on the path σ for achieving an activity, denoted by $O_\sigma = (b_\sigma, d_\sigma, u_\sigma, a_\sigma)$ can be derived by the conjunction of P's opinions on $\{N_i\}_{i \in [1..n]}$. $O_{\sigma = \{N_1,\ldots,N_n\}} = \bigwedge \{O_{N_i}\}_{i \in [1..n]}$. Given the following relations from [10], we have:

$$O_{x \wedge y} = \begin{cases} b_{x \wedge y} = b_x b_y \\ d_{x \wedge y} = d_x + d_y - d_x d_y \\ u_{x \wedge y} = b_x u_y + u_x b_y + u_x u_y \\ a_{x \wedge y} = \frac{b_x u_y a_y + b_y u_x a_x + u_x a_x u_y a_y}{b_x u_y + u_x b_y + u_x u_y} \end{cases} \tag{3}$$

We obtain the following generalization for the opinion on a path σ:

$$O_{\sigma = \{N_1,\ldots,N_n\}} = \begin{cases} b_{\sigma = \{N_1,\ldots,N_n\}} = b_{\wedge \{N_i\}_{i \in [1..n]}} = \prod_{i=1}^{n} b_{N_i} \\ d_{\sigma = \{N_1,\ldots,N_n\}} = d_{\wedge \{N_i\}_{i \in [1..n]}} = 1 - \prod_{i=1}^{n} (1 - d_{N_i}) \\ u_{\sigma = \{N_1,\ldots,N_n\}} = u_{\wedge \{N_i\}_{i \in [1..n]}} = \prod_{i=1}^{n} (b_{N_i} + u_{N_i}) - \prod_{i=1}^{n} (b_{N_i}) \\ a_{\sigma = \{N_1,\ldots,N_n\}} = a_{\wedge \{N_i\}_{i \in [1..n]}} = \frac{\prod_{i=1}^{n} (b_{N_i} + u_{N_i} a_{N_i}) - \prod_{i=1}^{n} (b_{N_i})}{\prod_{i=1}^{n} (b_{N_i} + u_{N_i}) - \prod_{i=1}^{n} (b_{N_i})} \end{cases} \tag{4}$$

Due to space constrains, proofs of Relation 4 and the verifications of the correction (*i.e.*, $b_\sigma + d_\sigma + u_\sigma = 1, 0 < b_\sigma, d_\sigma, u_\sigma, a_\sigma < 1$) are not presented here. The interested reader is invited to read the companion paper to the present work where all our proofs are developed [2].

3.2 Opinion on a System for an Activity

A system, which often contains several paths, represents the several ways a user can achieve her activity. After building opinions on all paths, an opinion on a system can be built. An opinion on a system is the opinion of a person on one of the paths or any union of them.

The disjunction operator in subjective logic represents the opinion of a person on one or several propositions. If $O_x^P = (b_x^P, d_x^P, u_x^P, a_x^P)$ is P's opinion on x and $O_y^P = (b_y^P, d_y^P, u_y^P, a_y^P)$ is P's opinion on y, $O_{x \vee y}^P$ represents P's opinion on x or y or both. Thus, the disjunction operator is the appropriate operator to evaluate an opinion on a system. In the following, we show how to build an opinion on a system when *(i)* there are not common nodes among paths and *(ii)* there are common nodes among paths.

Opinion on a System Having Independent Paths: let $\{\sigma_1, \sigma_2, \ldots, \sigma_m\}$ be the paths that enable a user P to achieve an activity. The user opinion on the paths $\{\sigma_i\}_{i \in [1..m]}$ for an activity are denoted by $O_{\sigma_i} = (b_{\sigma_i}, d_{\sigma_i}, u_{\sigma_i}, a_{\sigma_i})$. The user opinion on the system α for achieving the activity, denoted by $O_\alpha = (b_\alpha, d_\alpha, u_\alpha, a_\alpha)$ can be derived by the disjunction of P's opinions on $\{\sigma_i\}_{i \in [1..m]}$. $O_\alpha = \bigvee \{O_{\sigma_i}\}_{i \in [1..m]}$. Given the following relations from [10]:

$$O_{x \vee y} = \begin{cases} b_{x \vee y} = b_x + b_y - b_x b_y \\ d_{x \vee y} = d_x d_y \\ u_{x \vee y} = d_x u_y + u_x d_y + u_x u_y \\ a_{x \vee y} = \frac{u_x a_x + u_y a_y - b_x u_y a_y - b_y u_x a_x - u_x a_x u_y a_y}{u_x + u_y - b_x u_y - b_y u_x - u_x u_y} \end{cases} \tag{5}$$

We obtain the following generalization for the opinion on a system α::

$$O_{\alpha = \{\sigma_1, \ldots, \sigma_m\}} = \begin{cases} b_{\alpha = \{\sigma_1, \ldots, \sigma_m\}} = b_{\vee \{\sigma_i\}} = 1 - \prod_{i=1}^m (1 - b_{\sigma_i}) \\ d_{\alpha = \{\sigma_1, \ldots, \sigma_m\}} = d_{\vee \{\sigma_i\}} = \prod_{i=1}^m d_{\sigma_i} \\ u_{\alpha = \{\sigma_1, \ldots, \sigma_m\}} = u_{\vee \{\sigma_i\}} = \prod_{i=1}^m (d_{\sigma_i} + u_{\sigma_i}) - \prod_{i=1}^m (d_{\sigma_i}) \\ a_{\alpha = \{\sigma_1, \ldots, \sigma_m\}} = a_{\vee \{\sigma_i\}} = \frac{\prod_{i=1}^m (d_{\sigma_i} + u_{\sigma_i}) - \prod_{i=1}^m (d_{\sigma_i} + u_{\sigma_i} - u_{\sigma_i} a_{\sigma_i})}{\prod_{i=1}^m (d_{\sigma_i} + u_{\sigma_i}) - \prod_{i=1}^m (d_{\sigma_i})} \end{cases} \tag{6}$$

The proofs of Relation 6 and the verifications of the relations: $b_\alpha + d_\alpha + u_\alpha = 1$, $0 < b_\alpha < 1, 0 < d_\alpha < 1, 0 < u_\alpha < 1$ and $0 < a_\alpha < 1$ are developed in [2].

Opinion on a System Having Dependent Paths: in subjective logic as in probabilistic logic, the disjunction is not distributive over the conjunction, *i.e.,* we have $O_x \wedge (O_y \vee O_z) \neq (O_x \wedge O_y) \vee (O_x \wedge O_z)$. This is due to the fact that opinions must be assumed to be independent, whereas distribution always introduces an element of dependence. In SOCIOTRUST [4], this problem has been resolved by using conditional probability. Then when there are common nodes among paths, Relations 4 and 6 cannot be applied directly. In order to apply subjective logic for evaluating trust in a system, we propose to transform a graph having dependent paths to a graph having independent paths. Once this transformation is made, we can apply the Relations 4 and 6. To do that, two methods are proposed **Copy** and **Split**.

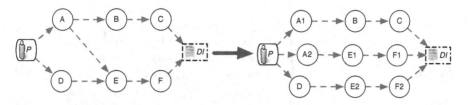

Fig. 2. Graph transformation using node splitting

1 Find all the paths $\sigma_{i:i\in[1..n]}$ for an activity performed by a person
2 **foreach** $\sigma_{i:i\in[1..n]}$ **do**
3   **foreach** $N_{j:j\in[1..length(\sigma_i)]} \in \sigma_i$ **do**
4   **if** $\exists k \neq j: N_j \in \sigma_k$ **then**
5   **foreach** $k_{l:l\in[1..num(\sigma_k)]}$ **do**
6   Create a node N_l
7                  $O_{N_l} \leftarrow O_{N_j}$
8   Replace N_j by N_l in σ_{k_l}
9   **end**
10   **end**
11   **end**
12 **end**

Algorithm 1. Copy algorithm

Copy: this method is achieved by duplicating a common node into several different nodes as illustrated in Figure 2. The left side of this figure shows an example of a graph that has three dependent paths. The source node is P and the target node is DI. The dependent paths are: $\sigma_1 = \{A, B, C\}$, $\sigma_2 = \{A, E, F\}$ and $\sigma_3 = \{D, E, F\}$. The common nodes are A, E and F. For instance, A is a common node between σ_1 and σ_2. By applying **Copy**, A becomes A_1, A_2 such that in the new graph, $A_1 \in \sigma'_1 = \{A1, B, C\}$ and $A_2 \in \sigma'_2 = \{A2, E, F\}$, so is the case for the nodes E and F. The right part of Figure 2 shows the new graph after duplicating the common nodes. The new graph contains the paths $\sigma'_1 = \{A1, B, C\}$, $\sigma'_2 = \{A2, E1, F1\}$ and $\sigma'_3 = \{D, E2, F2\}$. Concerning opinions, we keep the same opinion associated with the original node on the duplicated nodes. This method is based on the idea that the new produced path σ' maintains the same opinion of the original path σ. In this case $O_{\sigma_1} = O_{\sigma'_1}$ and $O_{\sigma_2} = O_{\sigma'_2}$. This method is shown in Algorithm 1.

Split: similar to **Copy**, nodes are duplicated to obtain independent paths as shown in Figure 2. In order to maintain the opinion on the global system, we split the opinion on the dependent node into independent opinions, such that their disjunction produces the original opinion. Formally speaking, if node A is in common between σ_1 and σ_2 and the opinion on A is O_A, A is duplicated into $A_1 \in \sigma'_1$ and $A_2 \in \sigma'_2$ and the opinion O_A is split into O_{A_1} and O_{A_2} where O_{A_1} and O_{A_2} satisfy the following relations: $O_{A_1} = O_{A_2}$ and $O_{A_1} \vee O_{A_2} = O_A$.

$$\bigwedge \left\{ \begin{array}{l} O_{A_1} \vee \ldots \vee O_{A_n} = O_A \\ O_{A_1} = \ldots = O_{A_n} \end{array} \right. \Rightarrow \left\{ \begin{array}{l} b_{A1} = b_{A2} = \ldots = b_{An} = 1 - (1 - b_A)^{\frac{1}{n}} \\ d_{A1} = d_{A2} = \ldots = d_{An} = d_A^{\frac{1}{n}} \\ u_{A1} = u_{A2} = \ldots = u_{An} = (d_A + u_A)^{\frac{1}{n}} - d_A^{\frac{1}{n}} \\ a_{A1} = a_{A2} = \ldots = a_{An} = \frac{(1-b_A)^{\frac{1}{n}} - (1-b_A - a_A u_A)^{\frac{1}{n}}}{(d_A+u_A)^{\frac{1}{n}} - d_A^{\frac{1}{n}}} \end{array} \right. \quad (7)$$

The proofs of Relation 7 are developed in [2]. **Split** algorithm is made by replacing Line 7 in **Copy** Algorithm by: "$O_{N_{jk}} \leftarrow$ opinion resulted from Relation 7".

4   Experimental Evaluation

In this section, we compare **Copy** and **Split** to a modified version of TNA-SL [12], that is based on simplifying the graph by deleting the dependent paths that have high value of uncertainty (*cf.* Section 2.2). In TNA-SL, after the graph simplification, trust is propagated. In our work, trust is not propagated and a comparison to a propagation approach has no sense. Thus, we modify TNA-SL such that trust evaluation is made by applying Relations 4 and 6 introduced in Section 3. We call this method a modified TNA-SL (**mTNA**).

The objectives of the experiments are *(i)* to compare **Copy** and **Split** to **mTNA** to verify their behavior and observe the differences among the results, and *(ii)* to evaluate their accuracy. Next sections present the experiments, their results, analysis and interpretation.

4.1   Comparing the Proposed Methods

To tackle the first objective, we experiment with a graph that contains only independent paths. The three methods, **mTNA**, **Copy** and **Split** give the same exact results as expected because the three of them follow the same computational model when graphs contain only independent paths. Then, we experiment on a graph that has relatively high rate of common nodes and dependent paths. 75% of the paths of the chosen graph are dependent paths and 60% of nodes are common nodes.

In our experiments, random opinions $O_N = (b_N, d_N, u_N, a_N)$ are associated with each node, and the opinion's probability expectation value of the graph, $\mathbb{E}(O_\alpha) = b_\alpha + a_\alpha u_\alpha$ is computed using the three methods, **mTNA**, **Copy** and **Split**. This experiment is repeated 50 times where each time represents random opinions of a person associated with the different nodes that compose the graph. We analyze the opinion's probability expectation values of the graph, $\mathbb{E}(O_\alpha) = b_\alpha + a_\alpha u_\alpha$ and not all the opinion parameters $O_\alpha = (b_\alpha, d_\alpha, u_\alpha, a_\alpha)$.

Figure 3 shows obtained results. We notice that the three methods almost have the same behavior, when the $\mathbb{E}(O_\alpha)$ increases in one method it increases in the other methods, and vice versa. We also observe some differences among the three methods that are not always negligible like at experience 9 and 40 in Figure 3. This observation led us to the question: which of these methods give the most accurate results? To evaluate the accuracy of **Split**, **Copy** and **mTNA**, we conduct other experiments explained in the next section.

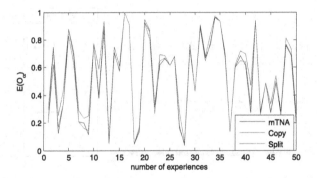

Fig. 3. Value of $\mathbb{E}(O_\alpha)$ for 50 persons using the three methods **mTNA**, **Copy** and **Split**

4.2   Studying the Accuracy of the Proposed Methods

SOCIOTRUST [4], that uses theory of probability to evaluate trust in a system, has the advantages that it has no approximations in case there are dependent paths thanks to conditional probability (*cf.* Section 2.2). Thus it works perfectly if users are sure of their judgments of trust *i.e.,* the values of uncertainty are equal to 0.

Subjective logic is equivalent to traditional probabilistic logic when $b + d = 1$ such that $u = 0$, *i.e.,* the value of uncertainty is equal to 0. When $u = 0$, the operations in subjective logic are directly compatible with the operations of the traditional probability. In this case the value of $\mathbb{E}(O) = b + au = b$ corresponds to the value of probability.

Since SOCIOTRUST is based on probability theory, the obtained results by applying subjective logic if $u = 0$ should be equal to the ones using probability theory. We can evaluate the accuracy of the proposed methods by setting $u = 0$ and comparing the value of $b_\alpha = \mathbb{E}(O_\alpha)$ resulted from applying the three methods to the trust value obtained by applying SOCIOTRUST.

The experiments are conducted on the graph of Section 4.1. Random opinions $O_N = (b_N, d_N, 0, a_N)$ are associated with each node, and the probability expectation of the graph $\mathbb{E}(O_\alpha) = b_\alpha + a_\alpha u_\alpha = b_\alpha$ is computed.

For simplicity, the notations T_{ST}, T_{MTNA}, T_{COPY}, T_{SPLIT} respectively denote system's trust value resulting from applying SOCIOTRUST and system's opinion probability expectation resulting from applying **mTNA**, **Copy** and **Split**.

To make our comparision of T_{ST} versus T_{MTNA}, T_{COPY}, T_{SPLIT}, we simply compute the subtractions between them *i.e.,* $T_{ST} - T_{\text{MTNA}}$, $T_{ST} - T_{\text{COPY}}$, $T_{ST} - T_{\text{SPLIT}}$. The average of each of the previous values are computed through 10000 time to give a reliable average. The standard deviation (SD) is also computed to show how much variation from the average exists in the three cases. Figure 4 shows obtained results.

As we notice from Figure 4, **Copy** is the method that gives the closest results to SOCIOTRUST, the average of the difference of its result when $u = 0$ and the result of traditional probability over 10000 times is equal to 0.014, which is an indication that this method gives the nearest result to the exact result and its average error rate is around 1.4%.

The average error rate of **mTNA** (2.4%) is less than **Split** (3.2%), but the standard deviation of **mTNA** is 0.045 where in **Split**, it is 0.037. That means that in some cases,

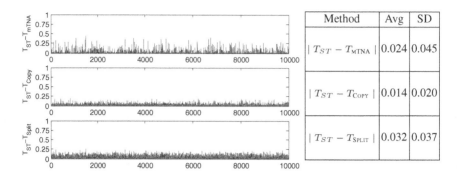

Method	Avg	SD
$\mid T_{ST} - T_{\mathrm{MTNA}} \mid$	0.024	0.045
$\mid T_{ST} - T_{\mathrm{COPY}} \mid$	0.014	0.020
$\mid T_{ST} - T_{\mathrm{SPLIT}} \mid$	0.032	0.037

Fig. 4. The difference between the opinion's probability expectation of a graph $\mathbb{E}(O_\alpha)$ using **mTNA**, **Copy** and **Split** when $u = 0$ and the trust value resulting from using SOCIOTRUST

mTNA can give results that are farther than **Split** from the exact results. Thus, **Split** shows a more stable behavior than **mTNA**.

Copy shows the most convincing result. The average error rate is around 0.014 and the standard deviation is 0.02.

The objective of this experiment is not criticizing the proposed methods in the literature for the problem of dependent paths. These methods are proposed to deal with the problem of trust propagation through a graph, whereas, in our work we focus on evaluating trust towards the whole graph. The employed operators in our case are different from the employed operators in trust propagation. TNA-SL or any proposed method in the literature can work properly in their context.

In this experiment, we show that **Copy**, our new proposed method, is the method the more adaptable to be used with respect to the context of our work. Extensive simulations on different types of graphs are provided in [2] and follow the same behavior presented above.

5   Conclusion and Perspectives

This paper presents SUBJECTIVETRUST, a graph-based trust model to evaluate user's trust in a system for an activity from their trust in nodes in the system graph. SUBJECTIVETRUST uses subjective logic to allow users to express their uncertainties in their jugement of trust. We propose two methods to face the problem of dependent paths in a graph for evaluating trust and through our experiments we show their accuracy in our contexte.

Our previous work [4], named SOCIOTRUST, that uses traditional probability, was confronted to real users through a real case-study. In SOCIOTRUST, 25% of users were not satisfied of the obtained results because they were not able to express their uncertainties about trust values using the traditional probability. SUBJECTIVETRUST allows users to express their uncertainty because it is based on subjective logic. In a future work, we aim to confront SUBJECTIVETRUST approach to real users through a real case-study.

References

1. Agudo, I., Fernandez-Gago, C., Lopez, J.: A Model for Trust Metrics Analysis. In: Furnell, S.M., Katsikas, S.K., Lioy, A. (eds.) TrustBus 2008. LNCS, vol. 5185, pp. 28–37. Springer, Heidelberg (2008)
2. Alhadad, N., Busnel, Y., Serrano-Alvarado, P., Lamarre, P.: Graph-Based Trust Model for Evaluating Trust Using Subjective Logic. Technical Report hal-00871138, LINA – CNRS: UMR6241 (October 2013)
3. Alhadad, N., Lamarre, P., Busnel, Y., Serrano-Alvarado, P., Biazzini, M., Sibertin-Blanc, C.: SocioPath: Bridging the Gap between Digital and Social Worlds. In: Liddle, S.W., Schewe, K.-D., Tjoa, A.M., Zhou, X. (eds.) DEXA 2012, Part II. LNCS, vol. 7447, pp. 497–505. Springer, Heidelberg (2012)
4. Alhadad, N., Serrano-Alvarado, P., Busnel, Y., Lamarre, P.: Trust Evaluation of a System for an Activity. In: Furnell, S., Lambrinoudakis, C., Lopez, J. (eds.) TrustBus 2013. LNCS, vol. 8058, pp. 24–36. Springer, Heidelberg (2013)
5. Cook, K.: Trust in Society. Russell Sage Foundation, New York (2001)
6. Gambetta, D.: Can we Trust Trust. Trust: Making and Breaking Cooperative Relations, 213–237 (2000)
7. Golbeck, J.: Computing and Applying Trust in Web-based Social Networks. PhD thesis, Department of Computer Science, University of Maryland (2005)
8. Golbeck, J., Hendler, J.A.: Inferring Binary Trust Relationships in Web-Based Social Networks. ACM Transactions on Internet Technology 6(4), 497–529 (2006)
9. Hang, C.-W., Wang, Y., Singh, M.P.: Operators for Propagating Trust and their Evaluation in Social Networks. In: Proceedings of the 8th International Conference on Autonomous Agents and Multiagent Systems (AAMAS), pp. 1025–1032 (2009)
10. Jøsang, A.: A Logic for Uncertain Probabilities. International Journal of Uncertainty, Fuzziness and Knowledge-Based Systems 9(3), 279–311 (2001)
11. Jøsang, A., Bhuiyan, T.: Optimal Trust Network Analysis with Subjective Logic. In: Proceeding of the 2nd International Conference on Emerging Security Information, Systems and Technologies (SECURWARE), pp. 179–184 (2008)
12. Jøsang, A., Hayward, R., Pope, S.: Trust Network Analysis with Subjective Logic. In: Proceedings of the 29th Australasian Computer Science Conference (ACSC), pp. 85–94 (2006)
13. Jøsang, A., Ismail, R., Boyd, C.: A Survey of Trust and Reputation Systems for Online Service Provision. Decision Support Systems 43(2), 618–644 (2007)
14. Li, L., Wang, Y.: A Subjective Probability Based Deductive Approach to Global Trust Evaluation in Composite Services. In: Proceedings of the 9th IEEE International Conference on Web Services (ICWS), pp. 604–611 (2011)
15. Liu, G., Wang, Y., Orgun, M., Lim, E.: Finding the Optimal Social Trust Path for the Selection of Trustworthy Service Providers in Complex Social Networks. IEEE Transactions on Services Computing PP(99), 1 (2011)
16. Richardson, M., Agrawal, R., Domingos, P.: Trust Management for the Semantic Web. In: Fensel, D., Sycara, K., Mylopoulos, J. (eds.) ISWC 2003. LNCS, vol. 2870, pp. 351–368. Springer, Heidelberg (2003)
17. Uslaner, E.M.: The Moral Foundations of Trust. Cambridge University Press, Cambridge (2002)
18. Zhang, P., Durresi, A., Barolli, L.: Survey of trust management on various networks. In: Proceedings of the 5th International Conference on Complex, Intelligent and Software Intensive Systems (CISIS), pp. 219–226 (2011)

A Hash-Based Index Method for Securing Biometric Fuzzy Vaults

Thi Thuy Linh Vo[1], Tran Khanh Dang[1], and Josef Küng[2]

[1] Faculty of Computer Science and Engineering
HCMC University of Technology, VNUHCM, Vietnam
khanh@cse.hcmut.edu.vn
[2] FAW Institute, Johannes Kepler University Linz, Austria
jkueng@faw.jku.at

Abstract. Traditional cryptography helps to protect information and establish secure interactions by using a cryptographic key to encode/decode user secret data. The problem related to managing such keys has gained much attention from the research as well as commercial communities, but there exists many security concerns that are still open. Such limitations can be solved by *Biometric Cryptosystems (BCSs)*. We propose a method to help increasing the security level of one of the most popular key-binding BCSs: Fuzzy Vault. We remove x-coordinates out of the vault while indexing y-coordinates by evaluation of corresponding x-coordinate values based on a suitable hash function. We carry out experiments on a Fuzzy Vault scheme based on iriscode. Our method has increased the min-entropy to 52 bits (it was 40 bits in the original scheme) and reduced the size of the vault dramatically. The proposed method also helps to prevent attacks via record multiplicity and stolen key attacks.

Keywords: Biometric Cryptosystems, Fuzzy Vault, Iriscode, Noisy Data, Privacy.

1   Introduction

Cryptography is the traditional branch of science that systematically investigates and develops tools for protecting information and establishing secure interactions. It not only protects data from theft or alteration, but can also be used for user authentication. There are, in general, three types of cryptographic schemes typically used to accomplish these goals: secret key (or symmetric) cryptography, public-key (or asymmetric) cryptography, and hash functions. In all cases, the initial unencrypted data is referred to as plaintext. It is encrypted into ciphertext, which will in turn (usually) be decrypted into usable plaintext. The encryption and decryption processes depend on a secret called key. The key must, however, be long enough so that an attacker cannot try all possible combinations. Thus, it is so hard for user to remember the key, so a user-defined password is usually used to protect the key. This requires user protecting their password just like it is the key. The security of the cryptographic key is now as

C. Eckert et al. (Eds.): TrustBus 2014, LNCS 8647, pp. 60–71, 2014.

good as the password. On the other hand, using password does not ensure that the legitimate user is the only person who could encrypt/decrypt data. By any chance, if an attacker knew the password, he could access a cryptographic system as well as the legitimate user. This happens because of lacking of direct connection between the password and its legitimate user. Those limitations of password can be alleviated by using biometric.

Biometric is about measuring unique personal features, such as a subject's voice, fingerprint, or iris. It provides the potential to identify individuals with a high degree of assurance, thus providing a foundation for trust. Biometric has been used to replace the password in protecting cryptographic key in recent researches, which leads to the creation of Biometric Cryptosystems: "Biometric Cryptosystems (BCSs) are designed to securely bind a digital key to a biometric or generate a digital key from a biometric" (A. Cavoukian and A. Stoianov [1]). The use of biometric in cryptography has overcome disadvantages of using password: 1) User no longer has to remember the password anymore; 2) Link a user with a secret at a high level of assurance. The difficulty in biometric cryptosystems comes from the fact that biometric data is variable and noisy: the same biometric may change between consecutive acquisitions (due to injury, ageing, even mood etc.) and noise can be introduced to a biometric signal by an acquisition device or the environment. Meanwhile, cryptography demands correctness in keys.

The majority of BCSs requires the storage of biometric dependent public information, applied to retrieve or generate keys, which are referred to as helper data. Based on how helper data are derived, BCSs are classified as key-binding or key-generation systems. In key generation, helper data is derived only from the biometric template. Cryptographic keys are directly generated from the helper data and a given sample [2, 3, 4]. In key binding, helper data is obtained by binding a chosen key to a biometric template [5].

In this paper, we work on one of the most popular BCSs - Fuzzy Vault, which is also a key-binding system. Fuzzy Vault is originally proposed by A. Juels and M. Sudan [6] and is used widely with fingerprint minutiae points. We modified the data which is stored in the vault to overcome known weakness of Fuzzy Vault while increasing the security level of the vault.

2   Background

Fuzzy Vault is one of the most popular BCSs, originally proposed by A. Juels and M. Sudan and was used mostly with fingerprint. The scheme is designed to secure biometric features that are represented as an unordered set. Supposing user secret is K and user biometric is represented as unordered set A, in enrollment scheme, a polynomial P in a single variable x is generated by embedding of K in its coefficients. Treating the elements of A as distinct x-coordinate values, we compute evaluation of P on the elements of A to get corresponding y-coordinate values. We may think that the elements of A are projected onto points lying on the polynomial P, called genuine points. Then a number of random points, called chaff points, are generated and added to genuine point set. Now, the points lying on P are hidden among a large number of random chaff points that do not lie on P and the union of genuine point set and chaff point set constitutes the helper data or vault V, which will be stored in database. Without the original biometric data, it's computationally hard to identify genuine points in V. Thus, the template is secured.

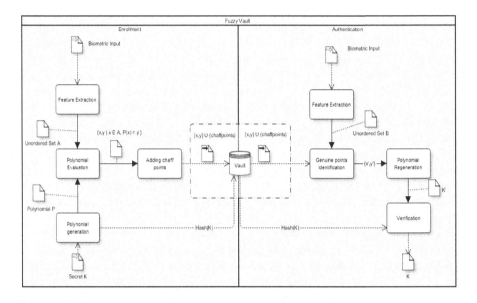

Fig. 1. Original Fuzzy Vault Scheme

During the authentication scheme, again, user provides biometric representation B – also an unordered set. If A and B come from the same biometric of the same user, their elements would almost be the same and user could identify many points in V that lie on P. Suppose that P is a polynomial degree d, if A and B overlap at least $d + 1$ elements, it means user could identify at least $d + 1$ points that lie on P. In this case, we could reconstruct P successfully (by using Reed-Solomon decoder, Lagrange Interpolation…) as well as reconstructing user secret K. A. Juels and M. Sudan have come up with a pair of vault locking/unlocking algorithms LOCK/UNLOCK (Figure 2) that allows reconstruction of the plaintext K when the decryption set B is close to the encryption set A. At the same time, the vault V should not reveal K.

Although A. Juels and M. Sudan proved that the fuzzy vault scheme satisfies some security properties, it is still vulnerable to some attacks. Many approaches which are used to attack a fuzzy vault system have been analyzed: for decoding a vault, we need to find enough points that lie on secret polynomial P in V, E-C Chang et al. [7] have proposed the technique to identify the original point set among chaff points. Meanwhile, P.M. Ãllescu [8] worked to reconstruct the polynomial, which is identified as a brute-force attack. To increase the complexity of brute-force attacks, multi-biometric is used (J. Merkle et al. [9], K. Nandakumar and A. K. Jain [10]). Increasing the key entropy has also proposed as a solution for defending brute-force attack (D. Moon et al. [11], M.S. AlTarawneh et al. [12]).

LOCK	UNLOCK
Public parameters: a field F, a Reed-Solomon decoding algorithm RSDecode	**Public parameters**: a field F, a Reed-Solomon decoding algorithm RSDecode
Input: Parameters k,t and r such that $k \leq t \leq r \leq q$. A secret $\in F^k$.	**Input**: a fuzzy vault V_A comprising a parameter triple (k,t,r) such that $k \leq t \leq r \leq q$ and a set R of points $\{(x_i,y_i)\}_{i=1}^r$
$\quad$ A set $A = \{a_i\}_{i=1}^t$, where $a_i \in F$	such that $x_i, y_i \in F$.
Output: A set R of points $\{(x_i,y_i)\}_{i=1}^r$ such that $x_i, y_i \in F$	$\quad$ A set $B = \{b_i\}_{i=1}^t$, where $b_i \in F$
Let $\in_U$ denote uniformly random selection from a set.	
$X,R \leftarrow \emptyset$;	**Output**: A value $K' \in F \cup \{'null'\}$
$p \leftarrow K$;	
$\quad$ *for i = 1 to t do*	$Q \leftarrow \emptyset$;
$\qquad (x_i,y_i) \leftarrow (a_i, p(a_i))$;	$\quad$ *for i = 1 to t do*
$\qquad X \leftarrow X \cup x_i$;	$\qquad (x_i,y_i) \xleftarrow{(b_i,0)} R$;
$\qquad R \leftarrow R \cup (x_i,y_i)$;	$\qquad Q \leftarrow Q \cup (x_i,y_i)$;
$\quad$ *for i = t +1 to r do*	$\quad K' \leftarrow RSDecode(k,Q)$;
$\qquad x_i \in_U F - X$;	$\quad$ *Output K'*
$\qquad y_i \in_U F - \{p(x_i)\}$;	
$\qquad R \leftarrow R \cup (x_i,y_i)$	
$\quad$ *Output R*;	

Fig. 2. Fuzzy Vault LOCK and UNLOCK algorithms

W.J. Scheirer and T.E. Boult [13] have classified non brute-force attacks on fuzzy vaults into three groups:

- *Attacks via record multiplicity*: Assuming the attacker has accessed to multiple vaults locked by the same biometric from a specific user; we found that the attacker could reduce the number of candidate polynomials by exploiting the following properties: 1) Keys used to lock the vaults are the same; 2) Chaff points are generated randomly and are independent of the key; 3) Chaff points vary from vault to vault. The goal of the attacker is to identify and remove chaff points, thus, reducing the number of spurious polynomials. (A. Kholmatov and B. Yanikoglu [14], H.T. Poona and A. Miria [15])
- *Stolen key-inversion attack*: if an attacker could get access to a secret key released from a successful authentication, then, using this key, the attacker could reconstruct the biometric representation (unordered set A). The direct link between x and y coordinates in the vault is one of significant points used to attack the system by "Attacks via record multiplicity" and "Stolen key-inversion attack" as

well as traditional brute-force attack. A. Nagar et al. [16] have separated these values into 2 sets $\{x\}$ and $\{y\}$; then used the minutiae descriptor of each x value to encode respective y before storing both in the vault. Although this method prevents attacker from successfully authenticating even if he knows the genuine points, it did not prevent the exposing of our biometric representation (genuine x-coordinates) from cross-matching template.

- *Blended substitution attack*: consider the situation where a malicious attacker injects his own genuine points into someone's vault such that both attacker and legitimate user will be able to successfully authenticate against the same enrollment record. Thus, legitimate user does not know that his vault has been touched. To prevent this kind of attack, usually, the secret key is hashed by an one-way hash function and stored in database at enrollment phase. This value will be used to validate the generated key during authentication.

Hence, many works have been done for both attacking and defending a fuzzy vault scheme. Almost implementations of fuzzy vault perform on fingerprint minutiae points. So, some solutions for defending and preventing malicious accesses also utilize the characteristic of fingerprint minutiae points and hard to be used for other biometrics. In this paper, we propose a method for storing the vault which helps to increase the complexity of significant attacks on fuzzy vault as well as could be used for many types of biometric. We do the implementation of our proposed method on a fuzzy vault scheme based on iriscode.

3   Proposed Modification in Fuzzy Vault Scheme

3.1   A Hashing Method for Protecting Vault

The explicit representation of user's biometrics, x-coordinates, and direct links between x and y coordinates in the vault are significant for attackers. We try to remove x-coordinates out of the vault while keeping an implicit link between each x and y coordinate: after Polynomial Evaluation step in Figure 1, we collect 2 separated lists $\{x_i | x_i \in A\}_{i=1}^{n}$ and $\{y_i | y_i = P(x_i)\}_{i=1}^{n}$. Then each x_i will be hashed by a one-way hash function H to obtain $\{H(x_i) | x_i \in A\}_{i=1}^{n}$. Meanwhile, we encrypt each y_i value by executing the XOR operator on binary form of each y_i and x_i to collect $\{y'_i | y'_i = E(x_i, y_i)\}_{i=1}^{n}$ (function E is described in Figure 4). Those y'_i will be embeded into an array V, length v; and $V[H(x_i)] = y'_i$. The rest of the array are filled by random values and stored as vault V (Figure 3a). At authentication phase, feature set $\{x_i | x_i \in B\}_{i=1}^{n}$ from user biometric (Figure 1) are used to select those y'_i in V as well as re-produce their original y_i. Firstly, the hash function H is also applied on each $\{x_i | x_i \in B\}_{i=1}^{n}$ to obtain $\{H(x_i) | x_i \in B\}_{i=1}^{n}$. Those values are used to querying list y'_i from V: $\{y'_i | y'_i = V[H(x_i)], x_i \in B\}_{i=1}^{n}$. Decrypting each y'_i by the XOR operator between the binary form of that y'_i and correspoding x_i to get $\{y_i | y_i = E(x_i, y'_i)\}_{i=1}^{n}$. Pairing those x_i and y_i, we have $\{(x_i, y_i) | x_i \in B, y_i = E(x_i, y'_i)\}_{i=1}^{n}$; then processing the Polynomial Regeneration step to continue the authentication phase.(Figure 3b).

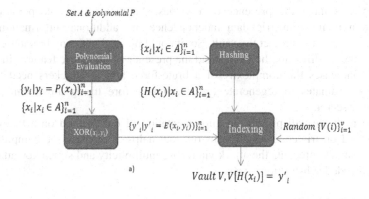

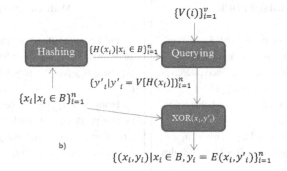

Fig. 3. A) Using hash function for indexing the Vault; b) Genuine points regeneration

---

Function E

Input: $x, y \in F$

Output: $z \in F$

        $bin(x) \leftarrow binary\ form\ of\ x;$

        $bin(y) \leftarrow binary\ form\ of\ y;$

        $bin(z) \leftarrow bin(x)\textbf{XOR}\ bin(y);$

        $z \leftarrow decimal\ value\ of\ bin(z);$

        $Output\ z;$

Fig. 4. Encrypt/Decrypt Function E

Following this idea, LOCK and UNLOCK algorithms are also modified (cf. Fig. 5).

Using this modification, our proposed vault will only contain encrypted values of y among chaff values. In this case, a matching between multiple vaults locked by the same biometric of a specific user just gives us a set of encrypted y values, without any information about their corresponding x. From those encrypted y values, it is impossible to regenerate the polynomial as well as the secret key. Attacks via record multiplicity is prevented. Moreover, consider a stolen key-inversion attack, even if the attacker already knows the secret key, he still not have enough information to retrieve genuine y'_i, without the presence of x values. Another remarkable point of this modification is its biometric data independence: no additional information from biometric is needed to protect the vault. So, it could be used with any biometric types. Moreover, the modification helps to avoid the presence of biometric features in public data, thus increases the complexity of a brute-force attack: attackers need to find proper x-coordinates to regenerate (x, y) points before trying any techniques to retrieve user secret.

In next part, we will present an implementation of our method on a fuzzy vault scheme based on iris code which turns out that helps to increase the complexity of brute-force attack, prevents the attack via record multiplicity and stolen key attacks as well as a blended substitution attack.

Modified LOCK	Modified UNLOCK
Public parameters: a field F, a Reed-Solomon decoding algorithm $RSDecode$, <u>a one-way hash function H</u> ; encrypt/decrypt function E	**Public parameters**: a field F, a Reed-Solomon decoding algorithm RSDecode, <u>a one-way hash function H;</u> encrypt/decrypt function E
Input: Parameters k,t and r such that $k \le t \le r \le q$. A secret $\in Fk$. A set $A = \{a_i\}_{i=1}^t$, where $a_i \in F$ **Output**: An array $R = \{(y_i)\}_{i=1}^r$ such that $y_i \in F$	**Input**: a fuzzy vault V_A comprising a parameter triple (k,t,r) such that $k \le t \le r \le q$ and an array $R = \{(y_i)\}_{i=1}^r$ such that $y_i \in F$. A set $B = \{b_i\}_{i=1}^t$, where $b_i \in F$ **Output**: A value $K' \in F \cup \{null\}$

$R \leftarrow \{f_i\}_{i=1}^r, f_i \in F$
 $p \leftarrow K$;
    for $i = 1$ to t do
      $(x_i, y_i) \leftarrow (a_i, p(a_i))$;
      $index_i = H(x_i)$;
      $R[index_i] \leftarrow E(x_i, y_i)$
    Output R;
	$Q \leftarrow \emptyset$;
	    for $i = 1$ to t do
	      $index_i = H(b_i)$;
	      $(x_i, y'_i) \leftarrow (b_i, R[index_i])$;
	      $(x_i, y_i) \leftarrow (x_i, E(x_i, y'_i))$;
	      $Q \leftarrow Q \cup (x_i, y_i)$;
	 $K' \leftarrow RSDecode(k, Q)$;
	    Output K'

Fig. 5. Modified LOCK and UNLOCK algorithms

3.2   An Implementation of Fuzzy Vault Scheme Based on Iriscode

Iriscode is the most common representation scheme used for matching iris image [17]. It is well known that iriscodes obtained from different iris images of the same user contain variabilities which are referred to as errors. There are two types of errors in iriscodes: (1) background errors caused by the camera noise, image capture effects, etc., and (2) burst errors which are a result of specular reflections, occlusions, etc. (F. Hao et al. [18]).

Because iriscode is a fixed length binary vector, we could not directly protect it by fuzzy vault framework. Here, we use the same technique described by Karthik Nandakumar and Anil K. Jain [10] for constructing the iris cryptosystem: applying a salting (invertible) transform to the iriscode template based on a randomly generated transformation key, then representing the transformation key as an unordered set and secure it using the fuzzy vault scheme. The transformation iriscode template and the vault that embeds the transformation key constitute the helper data. Both the salting and fuzzy vault steps can account for intra-user variations in the iriscode template.

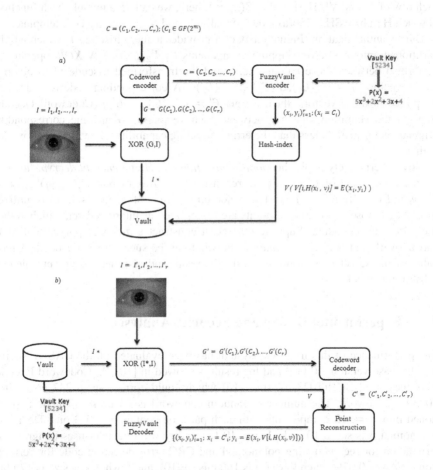

Fig. 6. Schematic diagram of the Fuzzy Vault scheme based on Iriscode: a) Enrollment; b) Authentication

Karthik Nandakumar and Anil K. Jain directly used BCH-encoding which helps to correct bit-errors in iriscode at salting step: firstly, an array $C = (C_1, C_2, ..., C_r); (C_i \in GF(2^m)$ is randomly generated. Then BCH encoder is applied individually to binary form of each element to obtain an array G of r binary codewords $G(C_1), G(C_2), ..., G(C_r)$, each of length M_k bits (Codeword Encoder step, Figure 6a).

Meanwhile, the iriscode is also partitioned into r non-overlapping components $I_1, I_2, ..., I_r$ such that each component contains exactly M_k bits. Then, an XOR operation is performed between those components and C to obtain the components of the transformed iriscode I*. After this step, we collect r numbers C and I*. C could be directly represented as an unordered set and secured using the fuzzy vault.

Enrollment scheme continues with fuzzy vault encoder step and releases an array $(x_i, y_i)_{i=1}^r; (x_i = C_i)$. Now, we encrypt y_i by x_i and embed $E(x_i, y_i)$ values into a 2-dimensional array V, size r x v so that each $E(x_i, y_i)$ value will be stored on each row of V and V[i,H(xi , v)] = $E(x_i, y_i)$; here, we call H a modulo hash function, in which H (a,b) = SHA-256(a) mod b. Finally, I* and V are stored as our template.

During authentication (Figure 6.b)), user provides a query iriscode I' which will be partitioned into r non-overlapping components $I'_1, I'_2, ..., I'_r$. A XOR operator is performed between those r components and the transformed iriscode $I*$ to obtain r binary vectors $G' = G'(C_1), G'(C_2), ..., G'(C_r)$. A corresponding codeword decoder is applied to those vectors, then, we get $C' = (C'_1, C'_2, ..., C'_r)$ (Codeword Decoder step). If the Hamming distance between each vector in G' and the corresponding original vector in G is less than the error correcting capability, C' will almost overlap with C.

Now, alternatively apply the *modulo hash-function H* and *encrypt/decrypt function E* on each element of C' in order to reconstruct an array of points $\{(x_i, y_i)_{i=1}^r; x_i = C'_i; y_i = E(x_i, V[i, H(x_i, v)])\}$. The order information of elements in C is utilized here. Next, those reconstructed points are represented as unordered set, which is then used for vault decoding. Suppose our secret construct a *d*-degree polynomial, if C' and C overlap at least *d+1 elements*, the vault can be successfully decoded. A hash value of the secret K is stored to verify the result and also help to prevent blended substitution attack.

4   Experimental Design and Security Analysis

The performance of this iris cryptosystem has been evaluated on the CASIA iris image database version 1.0 [19] and the result is showed in [10]. At Codeword Encoder step, they used BCH(1023,16) (m = 16) which could correct up to 247 errors in a 1023-bit codeword. The number of random codeword is set to 48; iriscode is partitioned into r = 48 components with each partition containing 1023 bits. Degree of polynomial was set to 10 and 11 (n = 10,11). Fuzzy vault decoder uses Langrage interpolation for reconstructing polynomial and CRC-error detecting code for verification. FAR is 0.02% when key size is 160 bits (n=10), and 0 when key size is 176 bits (n=11). GAR in both situations is 88%.

We have changed the way the vault is stored, which only affects the security level of the vault without changing its performance: as discussed in section 3.2, after Fuzzy encoder step, we collect r points (x, y), embed encrypted values of y-coordinates into a 2-dimensional array V, size $r \, x \, v$ so that each value will be stored on each row of V and $V[i, H(x_i , v)] = E(x_i, y_i)$. Similarly, this process is inverted during authentication for reconstructing r points (x, y). We stored hash value of the key for further verification. We tested our modification on CASIA version 1 and CASIA version 4, using OSIRIS [20] for extracting iriscode from image. We set r = 32 and n = 11; and also used BCH(1023;16) which could correct up to 247 bit-errors in 1023-bit code word. FAR of our experimental is 0.02% on CASIA version 1 (equal to the old scheme) meanwhile it is 2.97% on subset of CASIA version 4 iris-interval and is 0.3% on subset of CAISA version 4 iris-lamp.

The security of fuzzy vault framework is analyzed by measuring the average min-entropy of the biometric template given the vault. This iris cryptosystem consists of two components: the transformed iriscode template $I*$ and the vault V that secures the transformation key C used to obtain $I*$. Min-entropy of template iriscode $I*$ has been analyzed in [10] is approximately 52 bits. With our modification, min-entropy of the vault must be changed.

Recall that a vault V is a two-dimensional array of size $r_x v$, each row of V has exactly one y'-value of a genuine point. Suppose that random key $K \in GF(2^m)$ and the secret polynomial has degree d, the vault can be decoded only if we could reconstruct a candidate set L consisting of $(d + 1)$ points (x, y') by choosing $(d + 1)$ distinct x values from $GF(2^m)$ and their respective y' values from each of $(d + 1)$ rows of V. Actually, when we already have x-values, finding the corresponding y'-values is not a complicated matter.

Because $x \in GF(2^m)$, to choose $(d + 1)$ distinct x values from $GF(2^m)$, we have $\begin{bmatrix} 2^m \\ d+1 \end{bmatrix}$ ways, each of them can be ordered in $(d + 1)!$ ways. Total number of candidate set L is $\begin{bmatrix} 2^m \\ d+1 \end{bmatrix}(d + 1)!$.

The min-entropy of a template M^T given V is calculated as follows:

$$H_\infty(M^T|V) = -\log\left(1 / \left(\begin{bmatrix} 2^m \\ d+1 \end{bmatrix}(d + 1)!\right)\right) = -\log\left(\frac{(2^m-(d+1))!}{2^m!}\right) \quad (1)$$

Here, when m = 16, d=10, $H_\infty(M^T|V) = 176$ bits and when d = 11, $H_\infty(M^T|V) = 192$ bits.

Therefore, entropy of the vault is much greater than min entropy of template iriscode $I*$. Min-entropy of the whole scheme will be 52 bits compare to 40 bits in [10]. Furthermore, the complexity of this scheme does not depend on v (1): V could just be a r-dimensional vectors and we could reduce the effort to generate chaff values as well as the size of our vault.

In case of attacker know which are right y' values in the vault by a cross-matching template of the same user, he still need to try all possible x values from $GF(2^m)$ for each of y' because the position of y' in V left no information for retrieving x. Thus, the complexity of an attack via record multiplicity is as hard as a brute-force attack. The same thing will happen to a stolen key-inversion attack: even when attacker know the key, he still need to try all possible value of x to obtain its corresponding y' as well as list of genuine (x, y).

5   Conclusion

In this paper, we proposed a method for storing the biometric fuzzy vault which targets to break the direct link between each x and y-coordinates in the original fuzzy vault scheme and avoiding the explicit presence of x-coordinates (is usually the representation of biometric features) in the vault. The proposed method helps to deal with known weaknesses of fuzzy vault schemes: prevent attacks via record multiplicity and stolen key attacks while decreasing possibility of blended substitution attack. Additionally, the complexity of a brute-force attack has also been increased.

We also constructed an implementation of the proposed method on a fuzzy vault scheme based on iriscode. With our implementation, the size of the vault has dramatically decreased while min-entropy of whole scheme has been increased to 52 bits (comparing to 40 bits in the previously introduced scheme) and the entropy of the vault is from 176 bits.

Utilizing the characteristic that iriscode is a fixed-length binary vector, we construct a simple and effective hash-based function for indexing the new vault with collision-free. This type of hash function could only be used with ordered biometrics data (e.g., iriscode, face, etc.). To employ the newly proposed method for unordered biometrics data (e.g., fingerprint minutiae points, iris minutiae points, etc.) we must further investigate and carry out intensive experiments to see how collision would affect performance of the system and find the way to effectively deal with collision. This issue is also of our interest in the future research activities. Besides, integrate the proposed method with biosmetric-based (co-)authentication systems on smartphones [21] will also be of great interest.

Acknowledgement. This research is funded by Vietnam National University Ho Chi Minh City (VNU-HCM) under grant number B2013-20-02. Besides, we also want to show our great appreciation to all members of D-STAR Lab (www.dstar.edu.vn) for their enthusiastic supports and helpful advices during the time we have carried out this research.

References

1. Cavoukian, A., Stoianov, A.: Biometric Encryption. In: Encyclopedia of Biometrics, pp. 260–269. Springer (2009)
2. Dodis, Y., Reyzin, L., Smith, A.: Fuzzy Extractor: How to Generate Strong Keys from Biometrics and Other Noisy Data. In: Cachin, C., Camenisch, J.L. (eds.) EUROCRYPT 2004. LNCS, vol. 3027, pp. 523–540. Springer, Heidelberg (2004)
3. Huynh Van, Q.P., Thai, T.T.T., Dang, T.K., Wagner, R.: A Combination of ANN and Secure Sketch for Generating Strong Biometric Key. Journal of Science and Technology, Vietnamese Academy of Science and Technology 51(4B), 203–212 (2013)
4. Dang, T.T., Truong, Q.C., Dang, T.K.: Practical Constructions of Face-based Authentication Systems with Template Protection Using Secure Sketch. In: Mustofa, K., Neuhold, E.J., Tjoa, A.M., Weippl, E., You, I. (eds.) ICT-EurAsia 2013. LNCS, vol. 7804, pp. 121–130. Springer, Heidelberg (2013)

5. Truong, Q.C., Le, T.B.T., Nguyen, T.A.T., Dang, T.K.: A Hybrid Scheme of Fuzzy Vault and Feature Transformation for Biometric Template Protection. Journal of Science and Technology, Vietnamese Academy of Science and Technology 51(4B), 30–39 (2013) ISSN 0866-708X
6. Juels, A., Sudan, M.: A Fuzzy Vault Scheme. In: Proc. of IEEE, International Symposium on Information Theory, p. 408 (2002)
7. Chang, E.-C., Shen, R., Teo, F.W.: Finding the Original Point Set Hidden among Chaff. In: Proceedings of the ACM Symposium on Information, Computer and Communications Security, pp. 182–188 (2006)
8. Ällescu, P.M.: The Fuzzy Vault Fingerprints is Vulnerable to Brute Force Attack. In: Proceedigs of the International Conference of Biometrics Special Interest Group (BIOSIG), pp. 43–54 (2009)
9. Merkle, J., Niesing, M., Schwaiger, M., Lhmor, H.: Performance of the Fuzzy Vault for Multiple Fingerprints. In: Proceedings of the International Conferece of Biometrics Special Interest Group (BIOSIG), pp. 57–72 (2010)
10. Nandakumar, K., Jain, A.K.: Multibiometric Template Security Using Fuzzy Vault. In: Proceedings of the IEEE Second International Conference on Biometrics: Theory, Application and Systems (BTAS), Arlington, VA, USA, pp. 1–6 (2008)
11. Moon, D., Choi, W.-Y., Moon, K., Chung, Y.: Fuzzy Fingerprint Vault using Multiple Polynomials. In: Proceedings of the 13th IEEE International Symposium on Consumer Electronics, Kyoto, Japan, pp. 290–293 (2009)
12. AlTarawneh, M.S., Woo, W.L., Dlay, S.S.: Fuzzy Vault Crypto Biometric Key Based on Fingerprint Vector Features. In: Proceedings of the 6th International Symposium on Communication Systems, Networks and Digital Signal Processing, Graz, pp. 452–456 (2008)
13. Scheirer, W.J., Boult, T.E.: Cracking Fuzzy Vaults and Biometric Enscryption. In: Proceedings of Biometrics Symposium, Baltimore, MD, pp. 1–6 (2007)
14. Kholmatov, A., Yanikoglu, B.: Realization of Correlation Attack Against the Fuzzy Vault Scheme. In: Proceedings of the SPIE 6819, Security, Forensics, Steganography, and Watermarking of Multimedia Contents X (2008)
15. Poona, H.T., Miria, A.: A Collusion Attack on the Fuzzy Vault Scheme. The ISC International Journal of Information Security, 27–34 (2009)
16. Nagar, A., et al.: Securing Fingerprint Template: Fuzzy Vault with Minutiae Descriptors. In: Proceedings of the 19th International Conference on Pattern Recognition (ICPR), pp. 1–4 (2008)
17. Daugman, J.: How Iris Recognition Works? IEEE Transactions on Circuits and Systems for Video Technology 14(1), 21–30 (2004)
18. Hao, F., Anderson, R., Daugman, J.: Combining Crypto with Biometrics Effectively. IEEE Transactions on Computers 55(9), 1081–1088 (2006)
19. CASIA Iris Image Database: http://biometrics.idealtest.org/
20. Krichen, E., Dorizzi, B., Sun, Z., Garcia-Salicetti, S., Tan, T.: Iris Recognition. In: Petrovska-Delacrétaz, D., Chollet, G., Dorizzi, B. (eds.) Guide to Biometric Reference Systems and Performance Evaluation, pp. 25–50. Springer (2009)
21. Van Nguyen, N., Nguyen, V.Q., Nguyen, M.N.B., Dang, T.K.: Fuzzy Logic Weight Estimation in Biometric-Enabled Co-authentication Systems. In: Linawati, Mahendra, M.S., Neuhold, E.J., Tjoa, A.M., You, I. (eds.) ICT-EurAsia 2014. LNCS, vol. 8407, pp. 365–374. Springer, Heidelberg (2014)

A Private Walk in the Clouds: Using End-to-End Encryption between Cloud Applications in a Personal Domain

Youngbae Song[1], Hyoungshick Kim[1], and Aziz Mohaisen[2]

[1] Department of Computer Science and Engineering,
Sungkyunkwan University, Republic of Korea
{youngbae,hyoung}@skku.edu
[2] Verisign Labs, USA
amohaisen@verisign.com

Abstract. This paper presents Encrypted Cloud (EnCloud), a system designed for providing end-to-end encryption between cloud applications to facilitate their operation and enable users trust in providers. EnCloud relieves end-users' privacy concerns about the data stored in cloud services so that the private data are securely stored on the cloud server in an encrypted form while the data owner's EnCloud applications are only allowed to decrypt the encrypted data. To show the feasibility of EnCloud, we implemented a prototype for Dropbox. The experimental results of the prototype demonstrate that the additional time delay incurred by EnCloud operations is acceptable (within 11.5% of the total execution-time).

Keywords: Cloud, Domain Management, Privacy, End-to-End Encryption.

1 Introduction

Cloud computing services offer many benefits (e.g., data storage and computing infrastructure). However, they also raise serious privacy concerns [14]. These concerns are not only limited to the prying eyes of providers but also include government programs violating their citizens' basic rights.

The Snowden's leaks exposed that US and UK government agencies have collected online users' activities from cloud service providers. Reportedly, these agencies can directly access data on central servers of several companies (e.g., Microsoft, Apple, Facebook, Yahoo, Google, PalTalk, and AOL) for their surveillance efforts [6]. Also, providers like Google regularly get requests from governments and courts around the world to hand over users' data. In 2012, Google received 21,389 requests for information affecting 33,634 user accounts, where Google provided at least some data in response (about 66% of the time) [11]. Even worse, such cooperation is legal – the US Patriot Act, which was designed to give the US government access to information that may help prevent terrorist attacks, provides the legal platform for US law enforcement agencies to access corporate and users data when necessary. To that end, users are starting to distrust cloud providers, and many users would prefer to store their data on their own devices at home, when possible [5,7].

C. Eckert et al. (Eds.): TrustBus 2014, LNCS 8647, pp. 72–82, 2014.

To contain such a powerful adversary, we propose *EnCloud,* a new security application that prevents an attacker from accessing cloud-based data without the owner's knowledge or consent. EnCloud is designed to provide end-to-end encryption between multiple cloud applications in the data owner's personal domain. The proposed system is quite different from existing commercial products in the key management (cf. §6): All encryption and decryption keys in EnCloud are located at the client side rather than the server side. From a privacy perspective, users can then truly control the use of keys and manage their personal data. To this end, our key contributions can be summarized as follows:

- We introduce EnCloud, a framework to address end-users' privacy concerns in cloud storage settings. We propose a secure domain management framework so that the user's data can only be accessed by cloud applications registered for her personal domain (cf. §3).
- We show that EnCloud can achieve data confidentiality against powerful adversaries who can access not only the data stored in the cloud storage but also any network communication at home by analyzing the security properties of the EnCloud system (cf. §4).
- We demonstrate the deployability of EnCloud by implementing a prototype to support end-to-end encryption between cloud applications for Dropbox. With this prototype, we analyze the overhead of EnCloud and demonstrate that the additional time overhead incurred by the encryption and decryption operations is rather marginal (within 11.5% of the total execution-time) compared with the overall execution-time (cf. §5).

The rest of this paper is organized as follows. In §2 we introduce the threat model. In §3 we outline the design of EnCloud. In §4 we discuss a security analysis of EnCloud. A prototype implementation and results are introduced in §5. The related work is reviewed in §6, followed by concluding remarks in §7.

2 Threat Model

We consider a powerful adversary who acts as a government agency. The adversary can access the data stored in the cloud storage and can monitor the traffic between the end-user and cloud provider. We assume a computationally bounded adversary running in a polynomial time, and is not capable of breaking the encryption algorithm without knowing the key(s) used for encryption; this assumption is reasonable since breaking advanced encryption algorithms (e.g., AES [3]) is computationally infeasible for the most powerful supercomputers.

We assume end-hosts are trusted and not under the control of the adversary. However, the adversary is able to guess a user-chosen password using a low-cost offline password attack – in offline password attacks, an adversary holds any password-related messages or data, and then iteratively guesses the user's password and verifies whether his guess is correct or not in an offline manner.

Our goal is to protect the user's private data stored in the cloud so that the adversary only knows the presence of the encrypted data and their characteristics (e.g., creation time, size, etc.) but not the contents or intended use.

Table 1. The notations used in the EnCloud system

Notation	Description	Notation	Description
U	User of EnCloud	S	Cloud Server
DM	Domain Manager	DC_i	Domain Client with the name of i
d	Data being stored in the cloud	k	Domain key
dek	Data encryption key	id_d	Unique identifier of data d
c_i	PIN code for DC_i	sk_i	Session key for DC_i
puk_i	Public key for DC_i	prk_i	Private key for DC_i

3   EnCloud System

To achieve the security goal described in §2, a user U's data should always be stored on the cloud server in an encrypted form. If U uses a single machine, end-to-end encryption is simple enough to be implemented – the encryption and decryption keys can easily be managed by an application on that machine.

However, nowadays a cloud service is not anymore accessed by a client application on one single machine. Users can use the cloud service for their PCs, Smartphones, tablets, smart TVs or any device equipped with the client applications. Thus a major challenge is how to share keys securely between these devices. EnCloud is designed to do this by creating a personal domain of authorized applications (or devices) that can decrypt the data on the cloud storage, in turn, ensuring that no unauthorized application can decrypt the data.

EnCloud has two functional components: Domain Manager (DM) and Domain Client (DC). To use a cloud server S in a private manner, the user U installs a DM application on one of her devices (e.g., PC or smartphone) – in principle DM should always be available for the communication with DC's; U also installs a DC application on her other devices to create her personal domain. We briefly explain the roles of DM and DC as follows (shown in Figure 1):

- **Domain Manager** (DM) is an application which is responsible for managing its domain members (i.e., Domain Clients) by registering and revoking them. The user U has to install this application on a network-enabled device (e.g., PC or Smartphone). This device would have processing, storage and display capabilities. The DM application creates a domain key and distributes the key to the domain clients in a secure manner. Here we assume that DM should always be available for the communication with its domain members although DC's can often be turned off and turned back on.
- **Domain Client** (DC) is an application which is responsible for encrypting user data when the data are exported from originating domain and decrypting the encrypted data when encrypted data are imported into the domain. An existing cloud application interacts with DC to encrypt user data before uploading the data to the cloud server directly. A user U has to install the DC application on all the user's devices which will use the cloud server S.

With these two components, EnCloud securely protects U's private data within her personal domain devices through (1) end-to-end encryption and (2) domain management.

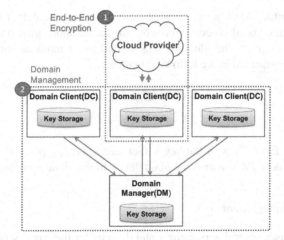

Fig. 1. The proposed EnCloud framework. Domain Manager (DM) is responsible for managing its domain members (i.e., Domain Clients) by registering and revoking them; a Domain Client (DC) can securely access the data created by one of DC's in the same domain.

In the following subsections, we will present how EnCloud works for protecting user data on the cloud server S. The notations used in outlining the operation of EnCloud are summarized in Table 1.

3.1   End-to-End Encryption

In EnCloud, encryption and decryption operations are processed at each DC application for end-to-end encryption between cloud applications. When uploading the data to the cloud server S, the data should be encrypted while the encrypted data should be decrypted only after downloading the data so that the user's data can be accessed by authorized applications only in her personal domain. Here we assume that each DC application holds the domain key k. In §3.2, we will discuss how to manage k for DC applications.

Uploading Data. When a user U uploads her personal data d from a cloud application to the cloud server S, the cloud application asks for the encryption of the data d by interacting with DC_i. DC_i creates a *data encryption key dek* to encrypt the data d. After encrypting the data d with dek, dek is also encrypted to be securely stored in the cloud storage. A unique identification string id_d is used to associate dek with d. For example, the *file name* of d can be used to implement id_d. After creating these objects, DC_i returns them to the cloud application and then the cloud application sequentially uploads them instead of the original data d. This process can be represented in the following manner:

$$U \longrightarrow S : (E_{dek}(d), id_d)$$
$$U \longrightarrow S : (E_k(dek), id_d)$$

Downloading Data. When a user U wishes to download the data d from the cloud server S via its associated cloud application, the cloud application returns $(E_{dek}(d), id_d)$ and $(E_k(dek), id_d)$. The identifier id_d is used as an index to obtain them. This process can be represented in the following manner:

$$S \longrightarrow U : (E_{dek}(d), id_d)$$
$$S \longrightarrow U : (E_k(dek), id_d)$$

DC_i decrypts $E_k(dek)$ with the key k then decrypts $E_{dek}(d)$ with dek. After decrypting both objects, DC_i returns the plain data d to the cloud application.

3.2 Domain Management

When a user U uses several applications and devices for the cloud server S, it is necessary to securely share keys between them for an application to freely exchange the encrypted data with other applications installed on other devices.

Creating Domain. After choosing a device which is proper for DM, U installs the DM application on the device. The DM application runs with default configuration settings and generates a random key k as domain key. The domain key k is securely stored.

Registering Device. When U registers a device with the name of i into her domain, U installs the DC application on the device. The DC application (i.e., DC_i) then searches DM via a network interface (e.g., WiFi). When the proper DM application is found, U requests the DM application to join DC_i into the domain managed by the DM application by sending the JOIN request message. This process can be represented in the following manner:

$$DC_i \longrightarrow DM : \text{JOIN}, DC_i, DM$$

When DM receives the JOIN request message, the unique identifier i for DC_i and a randomly generated PIN code c_i are displayed on DM. The displayed information is used to prevent man-in-the-middle attacks. U has to input the code c_i on DC_i for establishing a secure communication channel between DM and DC_i. When U successfully types the code c_i on DC_i, both DM and DC_i generate a session key sk_i derived from the common secret code c_i (i.e., $sk_i \leftarrow \mathcal{G}(c_i)$ where $\mathcal{G}$ is a randomized algorithm that takes c_i as input and returns sk_i).

In addition, DC_i generates its own public/private key pair puk_i and prk_i to securely exchange messages with the DM application. To register puk_i to DM, DC_i first encrypts (puk_i, DC_i, DM) with sk_i and sends it to DM. After receiving this message, DM decrypts it with sk_i and checks whether DC_i and DM are correctly obtained. If they are valid, DM stores the information about DC_i including its public key puk_i and sends the domain key k to DC_i encrypted with puk_i. This process can be represented in the following manner:

$$DC_i \longrightarrow DM : E_{sk_i}(puk_i, DC_i, DM)$$
$$DM \longrightarrow DC_i : E_{puk_i}(k, DC_i, DM)$$

After receiving the above message, DC_i decrypts $E_{puk_i}(k, DC_i, DM)$ with its private key prk_i and then securely stores k for later end-to-end encryption. In this step, DC_i also checks whether DC_i and DM are correctly obtained by the decryption to prevent modification of $E_{puk_i}(k, DC_i, DM)$ by an adversary.

Removing Device. When U removes a device i from her domain, U uninstalls the DC application (i.e., DC_i) from the device. While DC_i is uninstalled, it securely deletes the domain key k, its own public/private key pair and then sends the LEAVE request message. This process can be represented as follows:

$$DC_i \longrightarrow DM : \text{LEAVE}, DC_i, DM$$

After receiving the LEAVE request message, DM displays DC_i's identifier i and asks U to remove DC_i from her domain. When U agrees to remove DC_i, DM deletes all the data related to DC_i (i.e., puk_i and i for DC_i).

Updating Domain Key. When a domain device is stolen or lost, U needs to update the domain key k since she does not want to allow the stolen (or lost) device to still access her personal data. To accomplish this task, U manually selects to remove the stolen (or lost) device from the domain members – DM deletes all the data related to the DC application to be removed.

When U tries to update the domain key, DM generates a new domain key $\hat{k}$ and then searches actively running DC applications via a network interface. If there exist multiple running DC applications, DM (randomly) chooses an application as key updater; DM sends the new domain key $\hat{k}$ with the UPDATE message to the chosen DC application (without loss of generality, we assume that DC_i is chosen). This process can be represented in the following manner:

$$DM \longrightarrow DC_i : \text{UPDATE}, DC_i, DM, E_{puk_i}(\hat{k})$$

After receiving the above message, DC_i displays the DM application's identifier and asks U to update the domain key. When U agrees to replace the old domain key k with $\hat{k}$, DC_i decrypts $E_{puk_i}(\hat{k})$ with prk_i to obtain the new domain key $\hat{k}$ and starts downloading all encrypted *data encryption keys* from the cloud server S. After downloading all *data encryption keys* encrypted with the old domain key k, DC_i decrypts them with k, and re-encrypts the *data encryption keys* with the new domain key $\hat{k}$. Finally, DC_i uploads all the *data encryption keys* encrypted with $\hat{k}$ to S and then sends the UPDATED message to DM. This process can be represented in the following manner:

$$S \longrightarrow DC_i : (E_k(dek), id)$$
$$DC_i \longrightarrow S : (E_{\hat{k}}(dek), id)$$
$$DC_i \longrightarrow DM : \text{UPDATED}, DC_i, DM$$

After receiving the UPDATED message, DM periodically sends the new domain key $\hat{k}$ to the remaining domain members over secure and authenticated channels created using their public keys until no more DC applications with the old domain key k are found.

Replacing Domain Manger. We also need to consider replacing the domain manager DM with a new one. This task can be implemented by a sequential combination of 'creating domain', 'registering device' followed by 'updating domain key'. After creating a new domain and registering all the current DC applications to the new domain, domain key should be updated with the new domain manager. To support this feature, each DC application keeps the last domain key when it was registered again.

4   Security Analysis

In EnCloud, encryption provides confidentiality of user data – the encrypted data are protected with the data encryption key dek which is randomly generated by an individual DC application; the dek is encrypted again with the domain key k so that only a DC application with the domain key k can obtain the data encryption key dek.

With the information about the user data stored in the cloud storage, an adversary cannot obtain any information about the data encryption key dek and the domain key k except for their associated identifiers if the adversary cannot break the encryption algorithms used for $E_k(dek)$.

Furthermore, even if the adversary can monitor all the communications between the DM and DC applications, the message including the domain key k is encrypted with the DC_i's public key puk_i. Thus, it is infeasible to obtain k for the adversary since the DC_i's private key prk_i securely stays in DC_i.

A major challenge which we address in EnCloud is to prevent an adversary who performs an offline brute force attack on the PIN code c_i. With the captured messages between DM and DC applications, an adversary might still try to guess c_i and check his guesses by attempting decryption of $E_{sk_i}(puk_i, DC_i, DM)$. However, the session key sk_i is only used to provide the integrity of puk_i. With puk_i alone, an adversary cannot obtain any information about k.

EnCloud engages users in actions by showing on-screen messages with the requested device's identifier to continue performing tasks like registration into a domain, removal of a domain, and update of a domain key. These interactions can help rule out unauthorized commands and man-in-the-middle attacks.

5   Prototype Implementation

In this section, we demonstrate a prototype implementation of EnCloud for Dropbox. The purpose of this implementation shows that the EnCloud system can practically be implemented without incurring significant overhead. We implemented an app on the Android platform for Dropbox. Dropbox APIs (sdk-1.6) were used to upload and download files. We simplified the implementation of EnCloud by assuming that the

Table 2. The execution-time measurements (SD: Standard Deviation) for encryption/decryption operations and the total processing with varying file sizes. The time units are in milliseconds.

File Size		Encryption	Decryption	Total
	Mean	1545.73 (1.38%)	4710.73(4.19%)	112366.16
20MB	Max	1919.00 (0.74%)	7459.00 (2.88%)	259086.00
	SD	207.96 (0.63%)	914.07 (2.77%)	32981.14
	Mean	2796.26 (1.53%)	8032.70 (4.40%)	182738.23
40MB	Max	3537.00 (1.40%)	9798.00 (3.88%)	252612.00
	SD	294.50 (0.76%)	984.22 (2.54%)	38808.89
	Mean	4394.83 (1.44%)	13855.57 (4.54%)	304931.63
60MB	Max	5327.00 (1.19%)	19079.00 (4.25%)	448645.00
	SD	599.61 (0.70%)	2585.83 (3.02%)	85367.29
	Mean	7251.43 (1.40%)	32864.33 (6.33%)	519346.70
80MB	Max	92648.00 (7.22%)	57218.00 (4.46%)	1281747.00
	SD	674.48 (0.29%)	8799.67 (3.85%)	228689.78
	Mean	8389.26 (1.22%)	69905.77 (10.16%)	687818.37
100MB	Max	9779.00 (0.39%)	79668.00 (3.16%)	2523523.00
	SD	1257.80 (0.31%)	5598.06 (1.36%)	410183.42

domain client application already holds a domain key. We particularly focused on the feasibility of end-to-end encryption rather than domain management. For encryption, we used AES-256 (with CBC and PKCS5Padding) in the `javax.crypto` package. When a user uploads a file d, this app internally creates two files where one is for d and the other one is for its *data encryption key dek*. The file d is encrypted with dek; dek is encrypted with a domain key k internally stored in the EnCloud app.

When a file is uploaded and downloaded, we measured the execution-time incurred by encryption and decryption operations compared with the total execution-time. To decrease the bias associated with the performance realized from the testing samples, we repeated the test procedure 30 times with varying file sizes from 20MB to 100MB. We used a Samsung Galaxy Note 2 (with a 1.6 GHz Quad-core CPU, 533MHz GPU and 2GB RAM) running the Android 4.3 version, and equipped with a non-congested 100 Mbit/s WiFi connection to a LAN that was connected to the Internet via a Gigabit-speed link; the execution-time overhead was measured using the method `System.currentTimeMillis()`. The experimental results are shown in Table 2.

The test results show that the execution-time overhead incurred by encryption and decryption operations is marginal compared to the overall overhead. For example, when the file size was 20MB, the total execution-time was 112,366 milliseconds on average while the execution-time measurements for two encryption and two decryption operations were only about 1,545 and 4,710 milliseconds, respectively, on average (for the 30 trials; about 1.37% and 4.19% of the total execution-time). Although the average encryption and decryption time was greatly affected by the file size, the additional overheads of encryption and decryption operations were still manageable: the average additional delay incurred by encryption and decryption was less than 11.5% of the total execution time in the worst case. This is because file transfer may overwhelm other operations such as encryption and decryption. Interestingly, we can see the significant difference in execution time between encryption and decryption. We surmise that the underlying physical characteristics of NAND flash memory used in the prototype implementation may explain this characteristic – read and write operations are needed only once for encryption whereas one read and two write operations are needed, respectively, for decryption. If we consider the fact that read is typically at least twice faster than write for flash memory, the performance difference between encryption and decryption seems natural.

We now discuss the execution-time for updating domain key. When a domain device is stolen or lost, the domain key should be updated. We tested the key update procedure 30 times with a 100MB file under the same conditions to measure the execution-time to process this task. The average execution-time was 2,258 milliseconds, concluding that the proposed key update procedure is efficient compared with, for instance, the case of the time it takes to download (or upload), encrypt, and decrypt the same file with a domain key k, which yields the total average execution-time of 364,393 milliseconds.

The space overhead can generally be computed with the number of stored files as follows: For a file d to be stored in the cloud storage, the EnCloud system stores the following files: $encrypted\ data = (E_{dek}(d), id_d)$ and $data\ encryption\ key = (E_k(dek), id_d)$ where dek is a randomly generated key and id_d is a unique identification string for d. If we use a m-bits block cipher for the encryption E, $|E_{dek}(d)| \leq |d| + m$ since the maximum length of the padding is less than m. To store $E_k(dek)$ and two id_d strings, the additional overhead of m bits and $2 \cdot |id_d|$ is also needed, respectively. Therefore the worst case space overhead is $n \cdot (2 \cdot m + 2 \cdot |id_d|)$ where n is the number of files to be securely stored in the cloud storage. For example, if 30,000 private files are stored and the EnCloud system uses AES-256 for encryption E with 256 bits for id_d, the total storage overhead is about 3.66MB ($\approx$ 30,000kb). In the EnCloud system, the space overhead is proportional to the number of files to be stored and is rather marginal.

6   Related Work

The cloud computing [12] promises many opportunities while posing a unique security and privacy challenges. Takabi et al [14] argued that privacy is a core issue in all the challenges facing cloud computing – many organizations and users are not comfortable storing their data on off-premise data centers or machines.

End-users do not trust cloud services to store their personal data, and would prefer to store the data on their devices at home. Ion et al. [7] showed that many users believe that the data stored in cloud services can be exposed or stolen. Similarly, a survey by the Fujitsu Research Institute showed that about 88% of cloud customers were concerned with unauthorized access to their data [5].

In practice, the user data in cloud services are often exposed to the risk of unauthorized access. For example, Dropbox recently suffered an authentication bug that made it possible to log into some users' accounts without a password for about 4 hours [10]. In addition, the Snowden's leaks [1] explain why privacy concerns on the cloud are not far fetched – some intelligence agencies (e.g., NSA and GCHQ) have collected online users' data, even from cloud providers. These cases show how cloud computing services could be vulnerable in real-world situations, not only by external but also internal adversaries.

Kamara and Lauter [8] proposed several architectures for cryptographic cloud storage based on cryptographic primitives such as *searchable encryption* and *attribute-based encryption* to mitigate privacy risks in cloud services. They are particularly interested in sharing a secure cloud storage between users. We extend their work for a different scenario where a user wants to share her personal data between her cloud applications. Our focus is to design a simple, efficient, and general framework that provides end-to-end encryption between cloud applications in the data owner's personal domain.

Slamanig [13] demonstrated how to use side channels (CPU time or storage space) in cloud to infer the behavior of co-located users. Khan and Hamlen [9] proposed a framework called AnonymousCloud based on Tor [4] (which is designed to resist traffic analysis) in order to conceal ownership of cloud data.

There are several solutions providing end-to-end encryption for off-premise user data. To that end, Voltage Security (www.voltage.com) introduced a commercial security product based on identity-based encryption (IBE) [2] to protect files and documents used by individuals and groups. While usable in many applications, like email, an obvious shortcoming of the technique is that the provider can also decrypt its users' data for having access to users' private keys. In other words, in order for the system to work, users have to trust the provider, a requirement we set to avoid in this work. Encryption services such as Boxcryptor (https://www.boxcryptor.com) and Cloudfogger (http://www.cloudfogger.com) encrypt user data locally and then the encrypted data sync with the user's cloud storage. However, the security of their solutions relies on the difficulty of guessing passwords since the decryption keys in their services are protected with a password typed by the user at login. Unlike these products, EnCloud is designed to provide end-to-end encryption to defeat offline dictionary attacks; all encryption and decryption keys in EnCloud are located at the client side rather than the server side.

7 Conclusions

We proposed a system named EnCloud against powerful adversaries (e.g., an intelligence agency) who can access cloud-based data. EnCloud is designed to provide end-to-end encryption between cloud applications in the data owner's personal domain so that the private data are securely stored on the cloud server in an encrypted form while the data owner's EnCloud applications are only allowed to decrypt the encrypted data.

We also demonstrated EnCloud's feasibility by analyzing the security and performance on a prototype implementation for Dropbox. We highlighted that the additional execution-time overhead incurred by EnCloud is not significant compared with the overall execution-time. This shows that EnCloud can be implemented without a significant overhead while providing an effective end-to-end encryption between cloud applications. However, in this prototype, the adversary can learn some meta attributes about files (e.g., creation time, size, etc.). In future work, we will consider how to hide such information.

Acknowledgements. This research was supported by the MSIP (Ministry of Science, ICT & Future Planning), Korea, under the ITRC (Information Technology Research Center) support program (NIPA-2014-H0301-14-1010) supervised by the NIPA (National IT Industry Promotion Agency).

References

1. Ball, J., Borger, J., Greenwald, G.: Revealed: How US and UK spy agencies defeat internet privacy and security (2013)
2. Boneh, D., Franklin, M.: Identity-based encryption from the Weil pairing. SIAM J. of Computing 32(3), 586–615 (2003); extended abstract in Crypto 2001
3. Daemen, J., Rijmen, V.: The Design of Rijndael. Springer-Verlag New York, Inc. (2002)
4. Dingledine, R., Mathewson, N., Syverson, P.: Tor: The second-generation onion router. In: Proceedings of the 13th Conference on USENIX Security Symposium (2004)
5. Fujitsu Research Institute: Personal data in the cloud: A global survey of customer attitudes (2010)
6. Gellman, B., Poitras, L.: U.S., British intelligence mining data from nine U.S. Internet companies in broad secret program (2013)
7. Ion, I., Sachdeva, N., Kumaraguru, P., Čapkun, S.: Home is safer than the cloud!: Privacy concerns for consumer cloud storage. In: Proceedings of the Seventh Symposium on Usable Privacy and Security, pp. 13:1–13:20. ACM (2011)
8. Kamara, S., Lauter, K.: Cryptographic Cloud Storage. In: Proceedings of the 14th International Conference on Financial Cryptograpy and Data Security, pp. 136–149 (2010)
9. Khan, S., Hamlen, K.: Anonymouscloud: A data ownership privacy provider framework in cloud computing. In: Proceedings of the 11th International Conference on Trust, Security and Privacy in Computing and Communications, pp. 170–176 (2012)
10. Kincaid, J.: Dropbox security bug made passwords optional for four hours (2012)
11. Mearian, L.: No, your data isn't secure in the cloud (2013)
12. Mell, P., Grance, T.: The NIST definition of cloud computing (2011),
    http://csrc.nist.gov/publications/nistpubs/
    800-145/SP800-145.pdf
13. Slamanig, D.: More privacy for cloud users: Privacy-preserving resource usage in the cloud. In: 4th Hot Topics in Privacy Enhancing Technologies, HotPETs (2011)
14. Takabi, H., Joshi, J.B.D., Ahn, G.J.: Security and privacy challenges in cloud computing environments. IEEE Security and Privacy 8(6), 24–31 (2010)

Towards an Understanding of the Formation and Retention of Trust in Cloud Computing: A Research Agenda, Proposed Research Methods and Preliminary Results

Marc Walterbusch and Frank Teuteberg

Osnabrück University, Osnabrück, Germany
{marc.walterbusch,frank.teuteberg}@uni-osnabrueck.de

Abstract. This research offers a constitutive, mixed-method approach in order to identify trust-influencing and -influenced factors in cloud computing, which should lead to a fundamental understanding of the formation and retention of trust in cloud computing. In cloud computing, sensitive data and whole processes are transferred and outsourced to the cloud provider, without necessitating face-to-face communication with a sales assistant. We find the research methods literature review, laboratory experimental research, semi-structured expert interviews, surveys, vignettes, and (retrospective) think aloud complemented by neuroscientific methods to be suitable to reach the target set. Since vignettes, think aloud and neuroscientific methods are underrepresented or rather new to the information systems domain, in this contribution we pay special attention on these. Our mixed-method approach has the ability to verify, reaffirm, and refine theories affected by cloud computing or even to create new ones. Based on the findings of this research, recommendations for actions as well as implications for users and providers alike can be deduced. Since we rely on triangulation of the data set, the limitations of the whole approach reflect the limitations of each applied research method. Preliminary results indicate that 76% of cloud users focus primarily on data security, whereas 58% name the price of a certain cloud computing service to be relevant to provider selection.

Keywords: cloud computing, trust, laboratory experiment, behavioral science, online trust, empirical research, mixed-method analysis

1 Introduction

In cloud computing, users transfer (sensitive) data to the cloud computing vendor. Due to the unilateral dependency on the cloud computing vendor and the lack of a face-to-face interaction, which creates perceived and behavioral uncertainty, trust – both in the vendor and the applied cloud computing technology – plays a fundamental role in building relationships [1, 2]. However, specific requirements, e.g., with regard to security, privacy, accountability, and auditability, also need to be met in order to fulfill the expectations of the business partners, gain their trust and build long-term

C. Eckert et al. (Eds.): TrustBus 2014, LNCS 8647, pp. 83–93, 2014.
© Springer International Publishing Switzerland 2014

business relationships. Indeed, the recent news on the PRISM program has brought these aspects to the forefront of public interest. In the context of the evolutionary paradigm of cloud computing, researchers try once more to provide a commonly accepted, uniform definition of trust. Unfortunately, these definitions are not holistic as they only concentrate on one segment of reality. For example, some definitions solely concentrate on the social relationship between client and provider and lack other trust relationships, e.g., the customer's confidence in the technology itself [1]. The difficulties in finding a holistic definition, covering the dynamic and multifaceted subtleties of the term trust, arise because of *(a) the many different forms of trust* [3] and because of *(b) the difficult conceptualization* [4]. The predominant service and deployment models in cloud computing environments [5] make a conceptualization of trust even more complex. A deep analysis at different levels is necessary [6] in order to identify all *influencing* as well as *influenced* facets of the term trust. Our aim is to analyze trust in the realm of cloud computing, to identify influencing as well as influenced factors and therefore to provide a fundamental understanding of the concept. Corresponding research questions are (i) *What factors influence trust (in the area of cloud computing)?* and (ii) *In which way do these factors influence trust, is there a hierarchal or even dependent order?*. Based on this essential, fundamental understanding of the formation and retention of trust in cloud computing, recommendations for actions as well as implications for users and providers can be deduced. Further objectives and deliverables comprise corresponding IT artifacts capable of establishing and promoting trust in cloud computing, e.g., a meta-model for the conceptualization of trust. This research not only verifies existing theory on the subject, but also indicates the possibility for new approaches. In order to answer our research questions, we will use a mixed-method approach consisting of the research methods *literature review, laboratory experimental research, semi-structured expert interviews, surveys, vignettes* and *(retrospective) think aloud* complemented by *neuroscientific methods* within the information systems (IS) domain (*NeuroIS*). After exploring the research methods *vignettes, think aloud* and *NeuroIS* in section 2, we will introduce our mixed-method approach in section 3. Subsequently, in section 4, first results will· be presented. We close by discussing limitations as well as future research directions in section 5.

2   Potential of the Mixed-Method Approach

We consider the research methods *literature review, expert interview, surveys* and *experimental observation* to be common in the IS domain; consequently, we will focus on the potentials of the remaining research methods in our mixed-method approach: *vignette, (retrospective) think aloud* and *NeuroIS*. In order to identify scientific publications on the aforementioned research methods, we conducted a systematic literature review following a synthesis of the guidelines by Webster and Watson (2002) and Vom Brocke et al. (2009) [7, 8]. We limited the search to the top 20 (out of 125) journals included in the AIS ranking in order to achieve high-quality results. In a next step we searched the conference proceedings of the leading international IS conferences AMCIS, ECIS, ICIS and PACIS. Based on these results, we carried out a forward (review of reference lists) and backward search (author-centric review). Our findings indicate that the research methods *think aloud* and *vignette* are underrepresented in the IS domain. In the high-ranked journals and well-known conferences, we only identified 203 publications that either focus on the research method *think aloud* or use this method during the research process. The research method *vignette* is used in 55 publications.[1] While the application of both *vignette* and *think aloud* research methods is widespread in other disciplines (e.g., psychology), in the IS domain it is still uncommon.

2.1   Vignette

Since the research method *vignette* is underrepresented in the IS domain, we have synthesized the definition to the following: *Vignettes are focused descriptions or short stories about hypothetical characters, approximate real-life situations, a series of events and structures – normally limited to a brief time span, to one or a few key actors, to a bounded space, or all three –, which can make reference to important points in the study of perceptions, beliefs and attitudes, to which a subject – assuming a role of a fictitious character – is invited to respond to in a variety of formats (e.g., making a decision, rating on a scale, evaluating a behavior of the actor in the vignette or giving free text answers)* [9–22]. In order to avoid problems such as experimenter approval or social desirability [23, 24], vignettes ask the test person to act as a fictional person. Whereas vignettes with a rating-scale (e.g., Likert-scale) limit the expected answers to a predefined set of ratings and seek for empirical evidence, free text answers seek its validity on "plausibility and cogency of logical reasoning in describing the results in drawing conclusions from them" [25, 26]. One limitation, however, is that it can be assumed that test persons might respond in a different manner when they are presented a vignette rather than a real setting [11, 22]. By making use of a vignette in the context of cloud computing, situations such as the user's intentional action to a hypothetical incident can be analyzed.

2.2   Think Aloud

Through experimental observation, much information can be gathered [27], but the cognitive processes involved, such as decision making and social processes, usually remain unobserved. Quantitative data, e.g., *time until provider selection,* do not provide a comprehensive picture of a decision. Different factors (e.g., previous experiences with a cloud computing provider) can affect such quantitative data. The majority of decision making processes are obscured, as they take place in the human mind. Before the rise of NeuroIS, the closest equivalent to a verbal description of a thought process were verbal protocols [28]. In order to trace the related cognitive processes, the test persons can be asked to think aloud while or after fulfilling a

---

[1]   Publications in which the search terms have been used in another context (e.g., appearance in the references list) have not been regarded. The detailed literature reviews can be found online: http://www.uwi.uni-osnabrueck.de/Appendix_TrustBus.pdf.

certain task. Think aloud protocols require the test person to orally paraphrase thought processes. Based on transcripts of these verbalizations the experimenter can understand the cognitive processes and the resulting behavior [27]. However, think aloud protocols are limited by the test persons' ability to articulate their thoughts [27]. Since it is hard to simultaneously perform a certain task and think aloud, we will fall back on retrospective think aloud. In the context of cloud computing, e.g., participants' reasoning for choosing a certain provider can be captured. These can include answers not caught by standardized questionnaires.

2.3   NeuroIS

The aforementioned neuroscientific methods within the area of Information Systems are meant to complement, not substitute other research methods and are particularly helpful in situations where test persons may be especially susceptible to biases such as subjectivity bias, desirability bias or demand effects [29]. Moreover, by collecting continuous real-time data, neurophysiological tools are able to capture the temporal order of activated brain areas. NeuroIS promises a better understanding of the interplay between IT and human behavior by means of detailed insights into the functioning of the brain. This enhanced understanding can lead to better IS theories [30]. Riedl et al. (2010) define NeuroIS as follows [30]: *"NeuroIS is a subfield in the IS literature that relies on neuroscience and neurophysiological theories and tools to better understand the development, use, and impact of information technologies (IT). NeuroIS seeks to contribute to (i) the development of new theories that make possible accurate predictions of IT-related behaviors, and (ii) the design of IT artifacts that positively affect economic and non-economic variables (e.g., productivity, satisfaction, adoption, well being [sic])."* As included in this definition, NeuroIS enables significant progress to be made concerning fundamental existing and new IS theories on the prediction of user behavior. By identifying neural correlates we are in a position to gain a deeper understanding of the nature and the dimensionality of the adoption and utilization of systems. Related, hidden processes during system adoption can also be identified [29]. These processes are, but not limited to, decision-making processes (e.g., risk, loss, intentions or uncertainty), cognitive processes (e.g., information processing), emotional processes (e.g., happiness, sadness or fear) and social processes (e.g., trust or distrust) [31]. In our work, NeuroIS subsumes the following non-invasive methods: (i) *measuring vital signs*: the heart frequency, respiratory rate and depth and (ii) *measuring further neuropsychological parameters*: galvanic skin response, eye movement and the size of the pupils as well as brain activity.

3   Research Design and Data Collection

The whole research design, divided into five steps in accordance with Walterbusch et al. (2013a) and Wilde (2008), is described in the following and depicted in *Fig. 1*:

1. Observation & Induction. A theory is developed, whereby existing theory may be referred to. This step will be achieved by using the research methods *literature review*, *vignette* and *expert interview*. Existing literature and studies have to be identified in order to consolidate factors concerning trust in cloud computing. Furthermore, expert interviews with cloud computing mediators, providers and consultants will be conducted (cf. *Preliminary Results*). Moreover, vignettes will be used to identify relevant factors from a user's perspective (cf. *Preliminary Results*). During the expert interviews and vignettes, not only the mutual trust relationship between user and provider, but also the perception of the respective market participant towards the cloud technology itself has to be taken into account. In a next step, all findings have to be summarized and consolidated.

2. Formulation of Hypotheses. In accordance with logical inductions, hypotheses derived from the previously developed theories (cf. *Step* 1) are formulated. In more detail, the target dimension has to be operationalized (trust in cloud computing regarding the whole market and every trust relationship), key indicators (cf. *Preliminary Results*) have to be identified (a conceptual explanatory model arises) and reduced to systemically relevant model constructs with causal connections (leading to a logic model of hypotheses).

3. Data Collection. Since we strive for a preferably holistic picture of trust in cloud computing, the subsequent logical model of hypotheses might be complex and consist of many hypotheses. Therefore we are going to split up the logical model of hypotheses into several sub-models, which will be verified or falsified in different experiments. We are planning to conduct one basic experiment in form of a serious game. In this serious game, the whole cloud computing market will be adapted and test persons will act as market participants. In a pilot study [1], we also referred to a serious game, but we solely focused on the unidirectional trust relationship from a user towards a provider or mediator (cf. *Preliminary Results*). Based on the initial findings in the basic experiment, we will carry out several follow-up experiments, namely an emotional, an eye-tracking and an electroencephalography (EEG) experiment. The *emotional experiment* focuses on the emotions accompanied with cloud computing. These emotions include, inter alia, fear (e.g., of a security risk) and anger (e.g., in case of an unplanned downtime). In order to recognize and monitor the predominant emotions caused during an incident, we rely on objective data in the form of pupil diameter and eye movements recorded during the experiment and also on retrospective think aloud data combined with video recordings for the analysis of facial expressions, gestures and action-related interpretations of verbal statements. Then, we can gain further insights by conducting interviews about feelings/emotions using a standardized survey method and map the statements against vital and other body parameters. The *eye-tracking experiment* concentrates on factors influencing trust of real providers. Therefore, we will make websites of various cloud providers available offline. These websites will be shown to randomized groups of test persons. In a first step, their task is to look for certain information not related to trust. After the task, whether the respondents in the different groups noticed the factors influencing trust (recall questionnaire) or if they did not recognize them at all (eye-tracking) will be evaluated. In a second step, all test groups have to browse the webpages with special regard to *trust*. During the task we will employ web analytics (e.g., click path analysis). It can be analyzed if a test persons moves from webpage to webpage in a fast manner and revisits single webpages several times or if he/she stays on certain pages (e.g., description of certificates) comparatively longer. Subsequently, members of all groups will be asked to respond to a questionnaire regarding the trustworthiness of the providers. Again, by using eye-tracking during and a recall questionnaire after the experiment (stimulus-posttest-design), it will be evaluated if the respondents in the different groups noticed the factors influencing trust (recall questionnaire) or if they did not recognize them at all (eye-tracking). The last follow-up experiment is the EEG experiment. Since Plöchl et al. (2012) concluded "[…] to complement EEG measurements with eye-tracker information in order to address the problems and pitfalls that are connected to recording EEG in the presence of eye movements […]"[33] we again want to follow a mixed-method approach. With this EEG experiment, we want to translate modern methods developed in the neurosciences to information systems research. Specifically, we will be able to conclude whether the EEG methodology is suitable to evaluate IT artifacts in combination with other methods and which requirements have to be fulfilled. Furthermore, by investigating pupil responses in conjunction with cortical activity, we will be able to characterize the arousal state of an individual, for example, during an (perceived) incident. By way of example, this applies when a stakeholder group is more interested in detailed written Service Level Agreements (SLA) than just illustrated certificates and reference customers.

4. Verification & Adaption: The hypotheses will be verified by the utilization of adequate (inference-) statistical methods. If a hypothesis is not verified, it will either be adapted and retested or rejected.

5. Design and Evaluation: Based on the fundamental findings, various IT artifacts will be designed: (a) a system dynamics model (capable of depicting and simulating trust processes in the field of cloud computing), (b) a meta-model for the conceptualization of trust (a notation/description for the assessment of trust), (c) implications for science and the realm of practice (foundation stone for business models enhancing trust; catalogue of measures and requirements for the development of relationships enhancing trust; best practices catalogue; maturity model), (d) diffusion and improvement of applied research methods, (e) translation and validation of neuroscientific

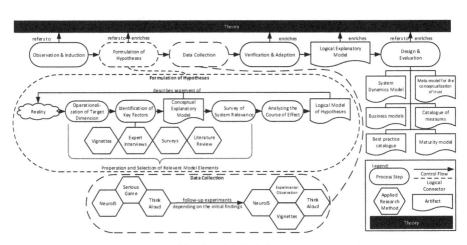

Fig. 1.   Methodology

methods and (f) verification, reaffirmation, refinement of existing or creation of new theories. The utility, quality and efficacy of our IT artifacts will be rigorously demonstrated via well-executed evaluation methods.

4   Preliminary Results

In the period from November 2010 through October 2013, we conducted 34 interviews with representatives working in international companies providing cloud computing services, reselling them with added features or obtaining them. After coding these interviews we found that a provider's information-policy and reputation are of paramount importance for the trust building-process [1]. Moreover, the trust relationship between user and provider is significantly affected by incidents (e.g., data loss). We integrated these and more trust-influencing factors into a pilot study in form of a serious game, in which the test persons act as users in the cloud computing market.

The user has to decide between obtaining a cloud computing service directly from one of three possible providers or indirectly from a mediator. Each provider is positively or negatively affected by events capable of influencing the trust of the test person towards him. We found statistical evidence that a user's trust in a provider is influenced by his risk aversion ($\tau = -.184, p < .01$), the available information on the provider ($\tau = .366, p < .001$), his personal affectedness ($\tau = -.193, p < .01$), the provider's (negative/average/positive) reputation ($\tau = .398/.133/.279, p < .001/.01/.001$) and the costs of a cloud computing service (paired-sampled t-test with $p < .001$). Based on our pilot study and an analysis of IS theories [41], we identified a first set of model constructs to be integrated in the conceptual explanatory model, listed in *Table 1*. Furthermore, we already started carrying out a vignette study with 222 undergraduate students. We asked the students to respond to a fictional setting in which a friend was asked which factors to consider when it comes to choosing a cloud computing provider. The vignette was 165 characters in length and ended with a few open questions (e.g., "What are the points Louisa should focus on during her provider selection?" and "Do you have any concerns you tell Louisa immediately?").[2] The students' average response length was approximately 1058 characters. For reading the vignette and stating their answers, the students needed 10.43 minutes on average. 76% of the students recommended focusing on data security (e.g., "[…] the customer has no overview on how one's data are handled, where they are stored and who has access to them.") and 58% suggested considering the price for the cloud computing service (e.g., "[…] the cost/performance-ratio should be appropriate."). Whereas 43% named the availability as a main aspect to evaluate potential cloud computing providers (e.g., "[…] a provider, […], where you can access your data any time."), 41% would rely on anonymous recommendations (e.g., "[…] get information on the internet on experiences or read test reports, as these are (more) objective and they convey strengths and weaknesses at one glance.").

---

[2]   The vignette as well as all results can be found online:
  http://www.uwi.uni-osnabrueck.de/Appendix_TrustBus.pdf.

Table 1. Theories and model constructs to be integrated in the conceptual explanatory model

Theory / Model Construct		Description / References (examples)
Transaction Cost Theory (TCT)	Uncertainty	Uncertainty refers to the cost associated with an unexpected outcome. Since user and/or provider spent more time and money in monitoring, a higher level of uncertainty generally implies a higher transaction cost. [34]
	Asset Specificity	Asset specificity refers to "durable investments that are undertaken in support of particular transactions, the opportunity cost of which investment is much lower in best alternative uses or by alternative users". [34]
	Transaction Cost	Transaction Costs cover any costs associated with obtaining a Cloud Computing Service, e.g., monetary weighted time for provider evaluation and selection as well as energy surcharges and costs for monitoring. [35]
	Acceptance	Acceptance is the result of the evaluation between uncertainty, asset specificity and transaction costs. It can either result in positive (the cloud computing service will be obtained) or negative acceptance (the cloud computing service will not be obtained). [34]
Technology Acceptance Model (TAM)	Perceived Usefulness	Perceived usefulness is the degree to which a user believes that using a specific cloud computing service enhances his performance. [36]
	Perceived Ease of Use	The belief that using a cloud computing service is free of effort. [36]
	Behavioral Intention to Use	A user's intention to use a cloud computing service. [36]
	Actual System Use	The actual adoption of a cloud computing service. The differentiation between the behavioral intention to use a cloud computing service and the actual use of it arise due to constraints like time or organizational limits. [36]
Commitment-Trust Theory (CTT)	(perceived) Benefits	Competition requires that providers continually offer cloud computing services, processes and technologies that add value to the user (e.g., product profitability, customer satisfaction or product performance). Users will choose providers that deliver (perceived) superior benefits. [37]
	Termination Costs	Termination Costs cover costs for backsourcing or discarding of a cloud computing service. In this context, the topic vendor-lock-in is often discussed. [37]
	Communication	Communication can be defined the as the synthesis of formal and informal sharing of meaningful information between two stakeholders. [37]
Expectation Confirmation Theory (ECT)	(perceived) Performance	Consumers use expectations to evaluate perceptions of the actual performance of a cloud computing service, leading to a judgment about disconfirmation. The perception(s) of how well a product or service functions is of subjective nature. [38]
	Expectation	Expectations indicate predictive attributes of a cloud computing service. They are reflected by anticipated behavior. [38]
	Disconfirmation	Disconfirmation is hypothesized to affect satisfaction, with positive disconfirmation leading to satisfaction and negative disconfirmation leading to dissatisfaction. It is the gap between expectation and (perceived) performance(s) of a cloud computing service. Disconfirmation can be either positive or negative. [38]
	Satisfaction	If a cloud computing services surpasses expectations, it will result in end-user satisfaction (positive disconfirmation). If a cloud computing service stays behind expectations the end-user will be dissatisfied (negative disconfirmation). Satisfaction is the evaluation between expectation and (perceived) performance. [38]
Agency Theory (AT)	Information Asymmetry	The user is not able, due to difficulty or expensiveness, to verify how the provider behaves. [39]
	Risk Sharing	The user and provider might have different attitudes to risk, consequently, both parties may prefer different actions. [39]
	Credibility	Since the provider may have different goals than the user and due to Information Asymmetry, the user is not able to estimate the provider's credibility (a priori). [39]
	Successful Contracting	These problems (Information Asymmetry, Risk Sharing and unknown Credibility) may be counteracted by appropriate incentive schemes or contracts (Service Level Agreements). [40]

5   Limitations, Implications and Future Research

In this paper, we present a mixed-method approach in order to identify factors able to influence or be influenced by trust in cloud computing environments. Since we rely on a triangulation of the data, the limitations of the whole approach reflect the limitations of each applied research method. The limitations indicated in the section

Potential of the Mixed-Method Approach, justify why we are following a mixed-method approach. In this way, we do not have to rely on a single source of data, but are able to consolidate data from various sources. A further limitation to be addressed is the fact that we primarily used students as subjects for our vignettes and the pilot study. Since a great majority of these students are cloud computing users, our findings are entirely representative. Even so, limitations are always present when results are achieved in an artificial, laboratory setting. From the pilot study's descriptive statistics, proactive recommendations for cloud providers can be derived. These results are also interesting for cloud users as they provide insight into the providers' behavior and users are able to get a "feel" for which factors are important in a provider selection. In the following we will first name the recommendation followed by a short description of the pilot studies' results in brackets: (a) meeting the expectations (the decision for a particular provider is maintained until the test person is disappointed), (b) trust-enhancing effect by signaling (pure information do not necessarily constitute a reason to switch providers; providers should overcome information asymmetry in the beginning in order to gain the user's trust), (c) allow the direct purchase of cloud services (the test persons prefer a provider over a mediator), (d) cost leadership strategy (during a selection the costs stand in the foreground), (e) offer flexible pricing models and security levels (if the potential monetary damage in case of risk occurrence increases, also the test persons' safety requirements increase) and (f) take the dependence between mediators and providers into account (a user's positive trust into a provider has a positive effect on the trust in the mediator).Future research directions mainly encompass the application of our mixed-method approach. Moreover, the identified model constructs and related theories have to be refined. Finally, further research potentials will arise while undertaking our mixed-method approach as well as during the design of the various IT artifacts.

Acknowledgements. This work is part of the project IT-for-Green (Next Generation CEMIS for Environmental, Energy and Resource Management). The IT-for-Green project is funded by the European regional development fund (grant number W/A III 80119242). The authors would like to thank the vignette participants, the other project members, specifically Mr. Gräuler, Ms. Imhorst and Mr. Richter, who provided valuable insights, help and substantive feedback during the research process, as well as the reviewers for their constructive feedback.

References

1. Walterbusch, M., Martens, B., Teuteberg, F.: Exploring Trust in Cloud Computing: A Multi-Method Approach. In: Proceedings of the 21st European Conference on Information Systems (ECIS 2013). Utrecht (2013)
2. Benlian, A., Hess, T.: The Signaling Role of IT Features in Influencing Trust and Participation in Online Communities. International Journal of Electronic Commerce 15, 7–56 (2011)
3. Josang, A., Ismail, R., Boyd, C.: A survey of trust and reputation systems for online service provision. Decision Support Systems 43, 618–644 (2007)

 4. Gefen, D., Straub, D.W.: Managing User Trust in B2C e-Services. Florida Libraries 2, 7–24 (2003)
 5. Mell, P., Grance, T.: The NIST Definition of Cloud Computing - Recommendations of the National Institute of Standards and Technology (2011)
 6. Pearson, S., Benameur, A.: Privacy, Security and Trust Issues Arising from Cloud Computing. In: 2010 IEEE Second International Conference on Cloud Computing Technology and Science, pp. 693–702 (2010)
 7. Webster, J., Watson, R.T.: Analyzing the past to prepare for the future: Writing a Literature Review. MIS Quarterly 26, 13–23 (2002)
 8. Vom Brocke, J., Simons, A., Niehaves, B., Riemer, K., Plattfaut, R., Cleven, A.: Reconstructing the Giant: On the Importance of Rigour in Documenting the Literature Search Process. In: Proceedings of the European Conference on Information Systems. Verona, Italy (2009)
 9. Goyal, S., Limayem, M., Davis, F.: Unfulfilled Obligations in Recommendation Agent Use. In: Proceedings of the International Conference on Information Systems 2012, pp. 1–15 (2013)
10. Gould, D.: Using vignettes to collect data for nursing research studies: How valid are the findings? Journal of Clinical Nursing 5, 207–212 (1996)
11. Dennis, A., Robert, L.: Trust Is in the Eye of the Beholder: A Vignette Study of Postevent Behavioral Controls' Effects on Individual Trust in Virtual Teams. Information Systems Research 23, 546–558 (2012)
12. Robert, L.P., Denis, A.R., Hung, Y.-T.C.: Individual Swift Trust and Knowledge-Based Trust in Face-to-Face and Virtual Team Members. Journal of Management Information Systems 26, 241–279 (2009)
13. Miles, M.B., Huberman, A.M.: Qualitative data analysis: An expanded sourcebook. Sage Publications, Thousand Oaks (1994)
14. Hughes, R.: Considering the Vignette Technique and its Application to a Study of Drug Injecting and HIV Risk and Safer Behaviour. Sociology of Health and Illness 20, 381–400 (1998)
15. Finch, J.H.: The vignette technique in survey research. Sociology 21, 105–114 (1987)
16. Zafar, H., Clark, J., Ko, M.: Security Risk Management Can Be Investigated! Presenting the Relation Between Research Rigor and an Effective Study. In: Proceedings of Americas Conference on Information Systems, Seattle, Washington (2012)
17. Staples, D., Jarvenpaa, S.: Using electronic media for information sharing activities: A replication and extension. In: Proceedings of the International Conference on Information Systems 2000 (2000)
18. Barnett, T., Bass, K., Brown, G.: Ethical ideology and ethical judgment regarding ethical issues in business. Journal of Business Ethics 13, 469–480 (1994)
19. Aronson, E., Carlsmith, J.M.: Experimentation in social psychology. In: Handbook of Social Psychology, pp. 1–79. Addison Wesley, Reading, MA (1968)
20. Trevino, L.K.: Experimental Approaches to Studying Ethical-Unethical Behavior in Organizations. Business Ethics Quarterly 2, 121–136 (1992)
21. Chae, B., Paradice, D., Courtney, J.F., Cagle, C.J.: Incorporating an ethical perspective into problem formulation: Implications for decision support systems design. Decision Support Systems 40, 197–212 (2005)
22. Greenberg, J., Eskew, D.E.: The Role of Role Playing in Organizational Research. Journal of Management 19, 221–241 (1993)

23. Siponen, M., Vance, A., Willison, R.: New insights into the problem of software piracy: The effects of neutralization, shame, and moral beliefs. Information & Management 49, 334–341 (2012)
24. Havlena, W.J., Holbrook, B.M.: The Varieties of Consumption Experience: Comparing Two Typologies of Emotion in Consumer Behavior. Journal of Consumer Research 13, 394–404 (1986)
25. Oja, M., Galliers, R.: Affect and Materiality in Enterprise Systems Usage: Setting the Stage for User Experience. In: Proceedings of the European Conference on Information Systems 2011 (2011)
26. Walsham, G.: Interpreting Information Systems in Organizations. John Wiley and Sons, Inc., New York (1993)
27. Seaman, C.B.: Qualitative Methods in Empirical Studies of Software Engineering. IEEE Transactions on Software Engineering 25, 557–572 (1999)
28. Yager, R.R.: On a Generalization of Variable Precision Logic. IEEE Transactions on Systems, Man, and Cybernetics 20, 248–252 (1990)
29. Dimoka, A., Banker, R.D., Benbasat, I., Davis, F.D., Dennis, A.R., Gefen, D., Gupta, A., Ischebeck, A., Kenning, P., Pavlou, P.A., Müller-Pütz, G., Riedl, R., vom Brocke, J., Weber, B.: On the Use of Neurophysiological Tools in IS Research: Developing a Research Agenda for NeuroIS. Management Information Systems Quarterly 36, 679–702 (2012)
30. Riedl, R., Banker, R.D., Benbasat, I., Davis, F.D., Dennis, A.R., Dimoka, A., Gefen, D., Gupta, A., Ischebeck, A., Kenning, P., Müller-Putz, G., Pavlou, P.A., Straub, D.W., Vom Brocke, J., Weber, B.: On the Foundations of NeuroIS: Reflections on the Gmunden Retreat 2009. Communications of the AIS 27, 243–264 (2010)
31. Dimoka, A.: What does the brain tell us about trust and distrust? Evidence from a functional neuroimaging study. MIS Quarterly 34, 373–396 (2010)
32. Wilde, T.: Experimentelle Forschung in der Wirtschaftsinformatik (english: Research Methods in Information Systems. An empirical Study). Verlag Dr. Kovač, Hamburg (2008)
33. Plöchl, M., Ossandón, J.P., König, P.: Combining EEG and eye tracking: identification, characterization, and correction of eye movement artifacts in electroencephalographic data. Front. Hum. Neurosci. 6 (2012)
34. Williamson, O.E.: The Economic Institutions of Capitalism. Free Press, New York (1985)
35. Walterbusch, M., Martens, B., Teuteberg, F.: Evaluating Cloud Computing Services from a Total Cost of Ownership Perspective. Management Research Review 36 (2013)
36. Davis, F.D.: A technology acceptance model for empirically testing new end-user information systems: Theory and results (Doctoral dissertation, Sloan School of Management, Massachusetts Institute of Technology) (1986)
37. Morgan, R.M., Hunt, S.D.: The Commitment-Trust Theory of Relationship Marketing. Journal of Marketing 58, 20–38 (1994)
38. Churchill, G.A.J., Surprenant, C.: An Investigation Into the Determinants of Customer Satisfaction. Journal of Marketing Research 19, 491–504 (1982)
39. Coleman, J.: Foundations of Social Theory. Harvard Univ. Pr. (1994)
40. Bhattacherjee, A.: Managerial Influences on Intraorganizational Information Technology Use: A Principal- Agent Model. Decision Sciences 29, 139–162 (1998)
41. Schneberger, S., Wade, M., Allen, G., Vance, A., Eargle, D.: Theories Used in IS Research Wiki, http://istheory.byu.edu/

Privacy-Aware Cloud Deployment Scenario Selection[*]

Kristian Beckers[1], Stephan Faßbender[1], Stefanos Gritzalis[2], Maritta Heisel[1], Christos Kalloniatis[3], and Rene Meis[1]

[1] paluno - The Ruhr Institute for Software Technology – University of Duisburg-Essen
{firstname.lastname}@paluno.uni-due.de

[2] Department of Information and Communications Systems Engineering,
University of the Aegean, Greece sgritz@aegean.gr

[3] Department of Cultural Technology and Communication, University of the Aegean, Greece
chkallon@aegean.gr

Abstract. Nowadays, IT-resources are often out-sourced to clouds to reduce administration and hardware costs of the own IT infrastructure. There are different deployment scenarios for clouds that heavily differ in the costs for deployment and maintenance, but also in the number of stakeholders involved in the cloud and the control over the data in the cloud. These additional stakeholders can introduce new privacy threats into a system. Hence, there is a trade-off between the reduction of costs and addressing privacy concerns introduced by clouds. Our contribution is a structured method that assists decision makers in selecting an appropriate cloud deployment scenario. Our method is based on the privacy requirements of the system-to-be. These are analyzed on basis of the functional requirements using the problem-based privacy threat analysis (ProPAn). The concept of clouds is integrated into the requirements model, which is used by ProPAn to automatically generate privacy threat graphs.

1 Introduction

Cloud computing is a relatively new technology that allows one to build scalable IT-infrastructures that multiple users can access over the network. There is an increasing trend to use clouds to outsource IT-infrastructures and services, but privacy concerns are a major show stopper for the usage of clouds[1][2][3]. The type and number of users that use a

---

[*] This work was supported in part by the EU project Network of Excellence on Engineering Secure Future Internet Software Services and Systems (NESSoS, ICT-2009.1.4 Trustworthy ICT, Grant No. 256980) and the Ministry of Innovation, Science, Research and Technology of the German State of North Rhine-Westphalia and EFRE (Grant No. 300266902 and Grant No. 300267002).

[1] http://download.microsoft.com/download/F/7/6/
F76BCFD7-2E42-4BFB-BD20-A6A1F889435C/Microsoft_Ponemon_Cloud_
Privacy_Study_US.pdf

[2] http://www.itu.int/dms_pub/itu-t/oth/23/01/
T23010000160001PDFE.pdf

[3] http://www.virtustream.com/company/buzz/press-releases/
neovise-research-report

C. Eckert et al. (Eds.): TrustBus 2014, LNCS 8647, pp. 94–105, 2014.
© Springer International Publishing Switzerland 2014

cloud and how they can access it heavily differs. The National Institute of Standards and Technology (NIST) defines four deployment models for the cloud: *private*, *community*, *public*, and *hybrid clouds* [1]. A private cloud is exclusively used by a single organization, and therefore the costs for deployment are high, but the number of additional stakeholders is small, and they are most likely trustworthy, because they belong to the company or are bound to specific contracts. Community clouds are exclusively used "by a specific community of consumers from organizations that have shared concerns." [1]. The costs for this deployment scenario are lower than the costs for the private cloud, because a community of multiple companies shares the costs of the cloud infrastructure. The number of privacy-relevant stakeholders for a community cloud increases in comparison with the private cloud, because additionally there are stakeholders of the other companies of the community that also use the cloud. A public cloud "is provisioned for open use by the general public" [1]. Hence, the number of different stakeholders using a public cloud is larger than the number of those in the community cloud scenario, and, furthermore, it is harder to predict which stakeholders have access to the data in the cloud. But the deployment and maintenance costs for the public cloud are low, because cloud providers can sell their service to a larger number of customers. Hybrid clouds are "compositions of two or more distinct cloud infrastructures" [1].

For companies it is hard to choose the cloud deployment scenario that best fits their needs, when they want to outsource IT-resources. The motivation for outsourcing IT-resources into the cloud is surely the reduction of costs to build and maintain the IT-infrastructure. A barrier for the usage of cloud technology is the number of privacy threats inferred by the usage of cloud technology. As already sketched above, the different cloud scenarios have different properties concerning the costs for deployment and maintenance and the number of additional stakeholders.

In this paper, we present a method that guides requirements engineers and decision makers to decide which cloud deployment scenario best fits the needs of the customer concerning the privacy requirements that exist on the system-to-be. Our method is built upon the problem-based privacy threat analysis (ProPAn) [2] that visualizes possible privacy threats in the system-to-be based on the requirements that the system-to-be shall satisfy, and the facts and assumptions about the environment. The contribution of this paper is an extension of the ProPAn method that embeds the concept of clouds in an modular way into existing requirement models. The ProPAn-tool[4] was extended with wizards that guide the tool-user through the definition of the deployment scenarios and the resources that shall be outsourced into the cloud. From these definitions, diagrams are created, are stored in a UML model, and are used to visualize possible privacy threats that stem from the respective deployment scenario using ProPAn's privacy threat graphs. We applied the method proposed in this paper to a real case study. This case study is concerned with the Greek National Gazette (GNG) that wants to migrate some of its services into the cloud to reduce costs.

The remainder of this work is structured as follows. Section 2 introduces previous work, and Section 3 shows the contribution of this paper. Section 4 discusses related work, and Section 5 concludes.

---

[4] available at http://www.uni-due.de/swe/propan.shtml

2   Previous Work

Problem frames are a requirements engineering approach proposed by Jackson [3]. We developed the UML4PF-framework [4] to create problem frame models as UML class diagrams, using a UML profile. All diagrams are stored in *one* global UML model. Hence, we can perform analyses and consistency checks over multiple diagrams and artifacts of the software development process.

The first step of the problem frames approach is to create a *context diagram*. A context diagram represents the environment (e.g., stakeholders, other software) in which the machine (i.e., software) shall be built. The context diagram consists of domains and connections between them. Jackson distinguishes the domain types causal domains that comply with some physical laws, lexical domains that are data representations, and biddable domains that are usually people. Connections between domains describe the phenomena they share. Then the problem of building the machine is decomposed until subproblems are reached which fit to problem frames. Problem frames are patterns for frequently occurring problems. An instantiated problem frame is represented as a problem diagram, which, in addition to a context diagram, also contains a requirement. A requirement can refer to and constrain phenomena of domains. Both relations are expressed by dependencies from the requirement to the respective domain annotated with the referred to or constrained phenomena.

ProPAn extends the UML4PF-framework with a UML profile for privacy requirements and a reasoning technique. A privacy requirement in ProPAn consists of two domains of the system, namely a *stakeholder* and a *counterstakeholder*. It states that the counterstakeholder shall not be able to obtain personal information of the stakeholder using the system-to-be. The reasoning technique identifies to which domains personal information of the *stakeholder* can flow and which domains *counterstakeholders* can access. For each privacy requirement, we visualize the information flows starting from a stakeholder s and the access capabilities of the counterstakeholder c in the privacy threat graph $\mathcal{P}_{s,c}$. A privacy threat $\mathcal{P}_{s,c} \subseteq \mathsf{Domain} \times \mathsf{Statement} \times \mathsf{Domain}$ is a directed graph with domains as nodes and edges annotated with statements that refer to and constrain domains of the environment of the machine. In the UML4PF-framework, we distinguish the statement types requirements that are optative properties of the environment after the machine is integrated, facts that are indicative truths about the environment, and assumptions that are indicative properties of the environment that we rely on, but may not hold. As sketched above, we distinguish two kinds of edges in the privacy threat graph $\mathcal{P}_{s,c}$. Edges $(c, st, d) \in \mathcal{P}_{s,c}$ starting from the counterstakeholder c represent that the counterstakeholder has possibly access due to statement st to information about the stakeholder s available at domain d. All other edges $(d_1, st, d_2) \in \mathcal{P}_{s,c}$ have the semantics that due to statement st there is possibly an information flow from domain d_1 to d_2. We are able to derive both types of edges automatically from the UML model using the ProPAn-tool. An access edge (c, st, d) is generated if the statement st refers to or constrains the counterstakeholder c and the domain d. An information flow edge (d_1, st, d_2) is generated if the statement st refers to the domain d_1 and constrains the domain d_2. Details about the graph generation based on requirements can be found in [2] and an extension of ProPAn for the consideration of indirect stakeholders in [5].

3 Method

Our method is presented in Fig. 1 as a UML 2.0 activity diagram [6]. The starting point for our method is a requirements model of the software in problem frames notion (Context Diagram and Problem Diagrams) as a UML model. In the first step, we define the clouds, based on the given Deployment Scenario. The defined clouds are stored in Domain Knowledge Diagrams in the UML model. Based on the given context diagram and the defined clouds, we select the domains that are put into the cloud in the second step of our method. This information is again stored as domain knowledge diagrams in the UML model. To analyze the impact of the modeled cloud deployment scenario on the privacy of the system stakeholders, we apply ProPAn's graph generation algorithm on the given problem diagrams, the given Privacy Requirements, and the domain knowledge diagrams created in the previous steps. The result of this step is a set of Privacy Threat Graphs that visualize the possible privacy threats that exist in the system-to-be. Finally, these graphs are analyzed to decide whether the privacy threats that were identified for the defined cloud deployment scenario are reasonable or not in the last step of our method. The contribution of this paper is the modular integration of clouds into the requirements model in the first two steps of the method, so that these are considered by ProPAn's re-used graph generation algorithms. Additionally, we extended ProPAn's analysis step for the consideration of cloud-specific threats.

Running Example. We illustrate our approach using a real-life scenario. In 2010, the Greek National Gazette (GNG) decided to provide a service for electronic submission of the manuscripts sent for publication. To reduce the costs for an own IT-infrastructure for the GNG system, it shall be investigated whether and which cloud infrastructures can be used for the system. The privacy requirement on the GNG system is that the anonymity of the employees involved in the GNG system shall be preserved against external entities. The system is concerned with the electronic submission of manuscripts and the digitalization of sent-in hard copies of organizations. Employees digitalize the hard copies using text scanners and format the documents to issues and paper volumes. Several integrity checks are performed before the documents are published on the online portal of the GNG with the consent of the government's and GNG's general secretary. Using the GNG portal, all Internet users are able to access the published manuscripts. For more details on the GNG system see, [7].

Step 1: Define Clouds. In this step, we define the clouds of the deployment scenario we want to analyze. We distinguish three kinds of clouds: *private*, *community*, and *public* [1]. A *hybrid* cloud scenario can be analyzed by defining multiple clouds of different types. For the privacy analysis, we are interested in the number of stakeholders that are able to access the information provided to the cloud. These stakeholders vary for

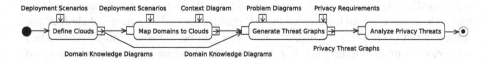

Fig. 1. Process for a privacy analysis of cloud deployment scenarios

different cloud types. Beckers et al. [8] identified for their PACTS method eight stake-holders relevant for clouds and represent their relationship to the cloud using a cloud system analysis pattern. For the method presented in this paper, we derived Table 1 from the cloud system analysis pattern. Table 1 groups the eight stakeholders into four groups. The first group consists of the stakeholders that provide and maintain the cloud. These are the *Cloud Provider* that provides the cloud, and the *Cloud Support* and *Cloud Administrator* that both work for the cloud provider and have directly or indirectly access to the cloud. The second group summarizes the stakeholders that use the cloud to build services. These are the *Cloud Customer*, who deploys his/her infrastructure and services into the cloud of the cloud provider, and the *Cloud Developer*, who works for the cloud customer. The third group consists of the stakeholders that use the services that are run in the cloud. Only the *End Customer* of the cloud customer belongs to this group. The last group is the indirect environment of the cloud. We consider the *Legislator* as a relevant stakeholder, as they are may allowed to access the data of the cloud due to laws, regulations, or bills. The relevant legislators for a cloud are given by the locations of the cloud, cloud provider, cloud customer, and end customer.

Furthermore, Table 1 gives an overview whether these generic cloud stakeholders are known and trusted in the respective deployment scenario. We consider a stakeholder as *trusted* if we can neglect the assumption that the stakeholder introduces privacy issues. When we define a cloud, we first select the deployment scenario we want to consider. For the selected cloud deployment scenario, we have to check the respective entries of Table 1. For each maybe entry a stakeholder has in our selected deployment scenario, we have to decide whether we know/trust the stakeholder in the concrete cloud deployment scenario. Additionally, we have to consider if the other predefined entries are correct for our concrete scenario. For example, if we use a private cloud, we may want to consider cloud customers as possible malicious insiders or to be vulnerable to social engineering attacks. Then we change the trusted entry for the cloud developer of the private cloud scenario from yes to no. Another example is that we know all other cloud customers of a public cloud because the cloud provider makes the list of all its customers publicly available. In this case, we would change the known entry for the cloud customer of the public cloud scenario from no to yes. Note that a yes in the known/trusted column means that all possible instances of the generic stakeholder are known/trusted. Respectively, a no means that we may know/trust some instances of the generic stakeholder, but we do not know/trust all of them. Furthermore, we assume that an unknown stakeholder possibly acts maliciously and cannot be trusted. Hence, we do not allow that a stakeholder is unknown but trusted in a deployment scenario.

Depending on the yes/no pair that we now have from the adjusted table for each stakeholder, we have to instantiate the stakeholders of the cloud. We distinguish three cases. First, a stakeholder can be known and trusted (yes-yes pair). Then we do not need to instantiate this stakeholder because we do not assume that any privacy issues are caused by him/her. Second, a stakeholder can be known but not trusted (yes-no pair). Then we create an instance of the stakeholder for each concrete stakeholder that we know but do not trust. Third, a stakeholder can be unknown (no-no pair). Then we create an unknown instance. For example, the cloud customer in a private cloud is only the organization for which the software is built, and is hence trusted. In this

Table 1. Overview of cloud stakeholders and their properties in the cloud deployment scenarios

Group	Stakeholder	Private		Community		Public	
		known	trusted	known	trusted	known	trusted
Provide and maintain cloud	Cloud Provider	yes	maybe	yes	maybe	yes	maybe
	Cloud Administrator	yes	maybe	yes	maybe	maybe	maybe
	Cloud Support	yes	maybe	yes	maybe	maybe	maybe
Use cloud to build services	Cloud Customer	yes	yes	yes	maybe	no	no
	Cloud Developer	yes	maybe	yes	maybe	no	no
Use Services	End Customer	yes	maybe	maybe	no	no	no
Indirect Environment	Legislator	yes	maybe	maybe	maybe	no	no

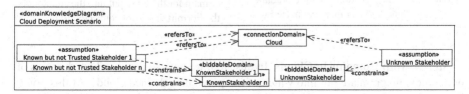

Fig. 2. Cloud definition patterns for the different deployment scenarios

case, the instantiation is not needed. A community cloud has a set of organizations with shared concerns as cloud customers. These organizations are known, but we may decide that they are not trustworthy. In that case, we have to instantiate the cloud customer with the other organizations that use the cloud. In a public cloud scenario, the other cloud customers are not known in general and hence not trustworthy. In this case, we instantiate the cloud customer with the possibly malicious unknown cloud customer. The other cloud stakeholder are treated analogously.

The instantiated stakeholders and their relation to the cloud of the specific deployment scenario are represented in a domain knowledge diagram that is added to the global UML model. The general form of this domain knowledge diagram is shown in Fig. 2. The domain knowledge diagram represents the assumptions that the instantiated cloud stakeholders (known but not trusted or unknown) are possibly able to access all information that is accessible through the cloud. This is expressed by referring to the cloud and by constraining the cloud stakeholders to be able to access the information. The generation of the domain knowledge diagrams for the concrete deployment scenario can be performed in a computer-aided way on the basis of Table 1, using wizards.

Application to GNG Example. The Greek National Gazette decided to evaluate a public and a private deployment scenario for the GNG system. To compare the two deployment scenarios, we created one model for the private and one for the public cloud scenario. In the public cloud scenario, we consider the fictive cloud provider Hulda. As Hulda is located in the USA, we have the USA as a legislator. All other cloud stakeholders are unknown and represented by possibly malicious instances. In the private cloud scenario, the GNG is itself the cloud provider, customer, and end customer. Greece as a legislator was not selected as possibly malicious legislator. Furthermore, we do not consider the cloud support for the private cloud scenario as the cloud administrators additionally shall provide the support. We only consider the cloud administrator and developer as relevant and possibly malicious cloud stakeholders.

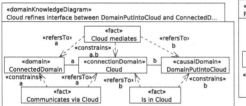

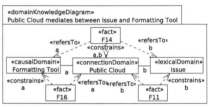

Fig. 3. Domain knowledge diagram introducing a cloud as a connection domain for a domain to be put in the cloud and a domain connected to it

Fig. 4. Domain knowledge diagram introducing the public cloud as a connection domain for the Issue put into the cloud and the Formatting Tool connected to it

Step 2: Map Domains to Clouds. In this step, we have to decide which domains of our context diagram are put into which of the previously defined clouds. At this point, it is not necessary for our method to distinguish the different cloud service levels, such as *software as a service*, *platform as a service*, or *infrastructure as a service* [1]. This is because for the information flow analysis, it does not matter whether a domain is virtualized in the cloud or if the domain represents a cloud service. In any case, the incoming and outgoing information flows have to go through the cloud. If we decide that a domain shall be put into a specific cloud, then this cloud acts as a connection domain that refines all interfaces of the domain and acts as a mediator between the domain that is put into the cloud and the domains which are connected to it. The domain knowledge diagram in Fig. 3 illustrates what this means. The domain knowledge diagram contains three facts. The first fact constrains the Cloud to mediate between the DomainPutIntoCloud and its connected domain ConnectedDomain. The other two facts constrain the ConnectedDomain and the DomainPutIntoCloud, respectively, to use the Cloud as mediator. For each domain that shall be put into a specific cloud, we create a respective domain knowledge diagram on basis of the interfaces described in the context diagram. The creation of these domain knowledge diagrams can again be performed in a computer-aided way, using wizards.

Application to GNG Example. The domains that shall be outsourced into a cloud are the lexical domains eDocument, Issue, and Paper Volume. As in both scenarios we only consider one cloud, the needed domain knowledge diagrams only vary in the name of the cloud. The domain knowledge diagram for the introduction of the Public Cloud as a connection domain between the Issue that is put into the cloud and the Formatting Tool that is connected to the Issue in the context diagram is shown in Fig. 4.

Step 3: Generate Threat Graphs. The generation of the threat graphs is performed automatically by the ProPAn-tool. But before we can generate the graphs, we have to define a privacy requirement for each biddable domain whose privacy shall be protected. Note that a privacy requirement in the ProPAn method normally consists of a stakeholder whose privacy shall be preserved and a counterstakeholder from whom the stakeholder shall be protected. We extended the graph generation algorithms such that in the case that no counterstakeholder is specified in a privacy requirement, all biddable domains of the requirements model are considered as counterstakeholders. We create the domain knowledge diagrams in the previous steps in such a way that ProPAn's

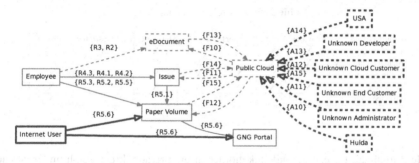

Fig. 5. Privacy threat graph for public cloud deployment

graph generation algorithms automatically consider these diagrams and add respective information flow and access edges to the privacy graphs.

Application to GNG Example. The anonymity of the employees of the GNG shall be protected. Hence, we define a privacy requirement with the stakeholder Employee and leave the counterstakeholder undefined. The privacy threat graph for the GNG system with the public cloud deployment scenario is shown in Fig. 5. We draw the domains, information flows, and access edges as dashed lines, which are newly introduced by the cloud deployment scenario. The solidly drawn part of Fig. 5 is the privacy threat graph for the GNG system before the definition of a deployment scenario. The privacy threat graph for the private cloud deployment scenario looks similar to Fig. 5, but only contains the Cloud Developer and Cloud Administrator as cloud stakeholders.

Step 4: Analyze Privacy Threats. To analyze the privacy threats that are introduced by the concrete deployment scenarios, we have to check the dashed edges of the respective privacy threat graph. These edges visualize the information flows and access relationships that are introduced by the deployment scenario and did not exist before. By comparing the different threat graphs of the deployment scenarios, we have to decide for the deployment scenario that fits best to the privacy needs of the system-to-be. We distinguish three kinds of edges in our analysis: the information flows directed to the cloud, the flows from the cloud back into the system, and the access edges pointing from the cloud stakeholders, who are considered as counterstakeholders, to the cloud.

First, we have to evaluate the information flows into the cloud with respect to our privacy requirements. We have to investigate which information relevant for the privacy requirements possibly flows into the cloud. If we can assume that there are no information flows relevant for the privacy requirements, then the cloud does not introduce additional privacy threats for the privacy requirements under consideration. Otherwise, we proceed with our method.

Second, we have to investigate whether the access capabilities of the cloud stakeholders of our concrete deployment scenario lead to a violation of our privacy requirements. For each access edge, we have to evaluate which information the stakeholder is able to access and whether this is a threat to our privacy requirements. To assist this evaluation process, we use five cloud-specific threats that are relevant for a privacy analysis. We selected these threats out of the ten that Beckers et al. [8] identified for their PACTS method. The threats and the stakeholders related to them are shown in Table 2. We use

Table 2. Privacy relevant cloud threats

Cloud Threat	Provider	Admin.	Support	Customer	Developer	End Customer	Legislator
Insecure API	X	X		X	X	X	
Shared technology	X	X		X	X	X	
Malicious insider	X	X	X	X	X	X	X
Hijacking	X	X	X	X	X	X	X
Data location							X

Table 2 to check for each cloud stakeholder in the privacy threat graph under consideration if the associated cloud threat has to be considered for our concrete deployment scenario. We structured the five threats into three groups. The first group represents threats that stem from the cloud technology. It consists of the threats *Insecure API* and *Shared technology*. The threat *Insecure API* refers to possibly insecure interfaces and APIs that are provided by the cloud provider to cloud administrators, cloud customers, cloud developers, and end customers. The provided interfaces have to ensure correct authentication, access control, encryption, and activity monitoring to protect against accidental and malicious attempts to access the cloud. The threat *Shared technology* arises because multiple services use the same hardware in a cloud infrastructure. As hardware is often not designed to offer strong isolation properties, there can be unintended information flows or possibilities to access information. Examples are shared CPU caches and hard disks. The second group represents malicious behavior of the cloud stakeholders. It consists of the threats *Malicious insider* and *Hijacking*. The threat *Malicious Insider* considers the misuse of a cloud stakeholder's capabilities to access information from the cloud or to get it from other cloud stakeholders for themselves or to provide the information to others. The threat *Hijacking* refers to attacks that try to steal or guess credentials and passwords of user accounts or cloud services. A hijacked account or service can be used to access the information provided by it and the information that it will provide in the future. We assume that each cloud stakeholder is able to perform an attack related to this threat group. The last group only consists of the threat *Data location*. The threat *Data location* refers to the location of the cloud servers. Depending on the location of the cloud servers, different legislators may have the right to access the information stored and processed on the servers.

Third, we have to consider if the introduced cloud adds an information flow feedback into the system. If multiple domains are put into a cloud, then it is possible that there are information flows between the domains in the clouds and those connected to them. These unintended information flows could stem from the *Shared technology* threat that we discussed above. From the information flow feedback, it is possible that counter-stakeholders are able to access more information than they were able to access before the cloud was introduced.

On basis of the analysis of the generated privacy threat graphs, we have now to decide if the privacy threats introduced by the concrete deployment scenarios are acceptable or if respective countermeasures have to be implemented. The costs for the realization of respective countermeasures have to be compared with the cost reduction that is expected by the usage of the cloud infrastructure. This comparison can assist decision makers to select a concrete deployment scenario.

Application to GNG Example. If we compare the privacy threat graph of the GNG system without a cloud with those graphs for the private and public cloud deployment scenario, then we observe that the complexity of these graphs is significantly increased. The graphs for the different deployment scenarios only differ in the number and kind of counterstakeholders that have access to the cloud. Hence, the analysis of the information flows going into the cloud and coming out of the cloud is the same for both scenarios, but the analysis of the access edges has to be done separately for both scenarios. The information flows into the cloud in both scenarios introduce a privacy threat to the anonymity of the employees that was previously not existent in the system-to-be. The new threat is that an employee's anonymity is possibly revealed by the collection of the information which and how documents are changed over the time. Using this meta information it is possible to reduce the set of employees who possibly performed the changes on a document. This threat stems from the logging mechanisms of clouds and the possibility to eavesdrop the connection to the cloud. For the GNG system, we do not expect relevant information flow feedback from the cloud to other domains. Such a flow would provide additional information to the Internet user which is able to access the published paper volumes using the GNG portal (see Fig. 5). We do not consider such a flow as relevant because the paper volumes are checked by an employee before they are uploaded to the GNG portal.

The public cloud deployment scenario has four unknown cloud stakeholders, namely the developer, the cloud customer, the end customer and the administrator (see Fig. 5). As all these stakeholders are potentially malicious, we have to consider all threats related to them in Table 2. These threats are *Insecure API*, *Shared technology*, *Malicious insider*, and *Hijacking*. We also assume that the fictive cloud provider Hulda possibly causes these threats. Furthermore, we know due to the *Data location* threat, that the USA is possibly able to access the data stored in the cloud. It is possible to implement countermeasures that mitigate these threats, but their implementation is expensive and the performance advantages of the cloud are reduced by their implementation. In the private cloud deployment scenario, we have only two cloud stakeholders. These are the developers and administrators of the private cloud. Due to Table 2, we have to consider whether these stakeholders will use insecure interfaces or APIs, or shared technology issues to access information they are not allowed to have. Furthermore, we have to investigate whether the administrators and developers have to be considered as malicious insiders providing sensitive information to others or use their privileges to hijack accounts or services. None of these threats can be neglected, but as the administrators and developers are employed by the GNG, it is easier to implement respective countermeasures as in the public cloud scenario.

To sum up, the privacy threats introduced by the public cloud scenario are the most critical ones. That is because it is not predictable who is able to access the information in the cloud, as there are multiple unknown and possibly malicious cloud stakeholders. For the private cloud scenario, we have only two newly introduced counterstakeholders, namely the cloud administrator and developer. As these two stakeholders are employed by the GNG, we are able to assume that these two cloud stakeholders are not malicious or we can easily implement countermeasures for the threats they introduce. Hence, the recommendation for the GNG system is to select the private cloud deployment scenario.

4   Related Work

An early analysis of privacy threats is necessary for all information systems. The introduction of clouds introduces further stakeholders and information flows that possibly lead to privacy threats depending on the selected cloud deployment scenario.

Kalloniatis et al. [7] propose a process for the evaluation of cloud deployment scenarios based on security and privacy requirements. The process identifies organizational entities and their needs and defines the security and privacy requirements for the system. Then cloud deployment scenarios are described and analyzed. On the basis of this analysis a deployment scenario is selected. The method is based on the PriS method [9] and Secure Tropos [10]. The processes described by Kalloniatis et al. is broader than the one described in this paper, as it analysis security and privacy in combination. But the process is at many points relatively abstract. We propose in this paper a more detailed method for the analysis of cloud-specific privacy threats.

The LINDDUN-framework proposed by Deng et al. [11] is an extension of Microsoft's security analysis framework STRIDE [12]. In contrast to ProPAn, the system to be analyzed is modeled as a data flow diagram (DFD), which has to be set up carefully. ProPAn is based on a problem frames model which is assumed to be already existing and which is systematically created using the problem frames approach [3].

The topic of cloud migration has already been discussed in various papers e.g., [13,14]. These works focus mainly on the financial costs of a cloud migration and identify privacy as a restricting factor for a migration. But in contrast to our work, they do not provide guidance for the identification of privacy issues that have to be considered when migrating to the could.

In contrast to the above methods, we integrate cloud deployment scenarios into a requirements model in a modular way to perform a privacy analysis and provide tool-support. The definition of deployment scenarios using separate diagrams allows us to evaluate different deployment scenario without effecting other artifacts.

5   Conclusion and Future Work

In this paper, we presented a privacy-aware decision method for cloud deployment scenarios. This method is built upon the ProPAn and PACTS method. The first step of the presented method is the definition of the clouds used in concrete deployment scenarios and their cloud stakeholders. Then we decide which domains shall be put into which defined cloud. We capture the defined clouds, cloud stakeholders, and the relation between existing domains and the defined clouds in domain knowledge diagrams. We can apply ProPAn's graph generation algorithms on these domain knowledge diagrams together with a given model of the functional requirements in problem frames notation. The resulting privacy threat graphs are then analyzed to decide which deployment scenario best fits the privacy needs in the last step of the method. To support our method, we extended the ProPAn-tool with wizards that guide the user through the definition of the deployment scenarios and that automatically generate the corresponding domain knowledge diagrams. The proposed method scales well due to the modular way in that the relevant knowledge for the cloud deployment scenarios are integrated into the requirements model and the provided tool-support. Our contributions are:

- A systematic method to analyze the privacy impact of cloud deployment scenarios on a concrete software that shall be built.
- An overview of the kinds of cloud stakeholders that have to be considered in the different deployment scenarios.
- A modular way to add the knowledge relevant for clouds into the problem frames requirements model using domain knowledge diagrams.
- A slight modification of ProPAn's graph generation that considers all biddable domains as possible counterstakeholders if no counterstakeholder is defined.
- A mapping of the cloud stakeholders to cloud-specific threats that they can cause.

The application of ProPAn and the extension presented in this paper to an industrial-size case study and an empirical evaluations are part of our future work.

References

1. National Institute of Standards and Technology: The NIST definition of cloud computing (2011)
2. Beckers, K., Faßbender, S., Heisel, M., Meis, R.: A problem-based approach for computer aided privacy threat identification. In: Preneel, B., Ikonomou, D. (eds.) APF 2012. LNCS, vol. 8319, pp. 1–16. Springer, Heidelberg (2014)
3. Jackson, M.: Problem Frames. Analyzing and structuring software development problems. Addison-Wesley (2001)
4. Côté, I., Hatebur, D., Heisel, M., Schmidt, H.: UML4PF – a tool for problem-oriented requirements analysis. In: Proceedings of RE, pp. 349–350. IEEE Computer Society (2011)
5. Meis, R.: Problem-Based Consideration of Privacy-Relevant Domain Knowledge. In: Hansen, M., Hoepman, J.-H., Leenes, R., Whitehouse, D. (eds.) Privacy and Identity 2013. IFIP AICT, vol. 421, pp. 150–164. Springer, Heidelberg (2014)
6. UML Revision Task Force: OMG Unified Modeling Language: Superstructure (May 2012)
7. Kalloniatis, C., Mouratidis, H., Islam, S.: Evaluating cloud deployment scenarios based on security and privacy requirements. Requir. Eng. 18(4), 299–319 (2013)
8. Beckers, K., Côté, I., Faßbender, S., Heisel, M., Hofbauer, S.: A pattern-based method for establishing a cloud-specific information security management system - establishing information security management systems for clouds considering security, privacy, and legal compliance. Requir. Eng. 18(4), 343–395 (2013)
9. Kalloniatis, C., Kavakli, E., Gritzalis, S.: Addressing privacy requirements in system design: The PriS method. Requir. Eng. 13, 241–255 (2008)
10. Mouratidis, H., Giorgini, P.: Secure tropos: A security-oriented extension of the tropos methodology. International Journal of Software Engineering and Knowledge Engineering 17(2), 285–309 (2007)
11. Deng, M., Wuyts, K., Scandariato, R., Preneel, B., Joosen, W.: A privacy threat analysis framework: Supporting the elicitation and fulfillment of privacy requirements. In: RE (2011)
12. Howard, M., Lipner, S.: The Security Development Lifecycle. Microsoft Press, Redmond (2006)
13. Khajeh-Hosseini, A., Sommerville, I., Bogaerts, J., Teregowda, P.: Decision support tools for cloud migration in the enterprise. In: IEEE Int. Conf. on Cloud Computing (CLOUD), pp. 541–548. IEEE Computer Society (July 2011)
14. Hajjat, M., Sun, X., Sung, Y.E., Maltz, D., Rao, S., Sripanidkulchai, K., Tawarmalani, M.: Cloudward bound: Planning for beneficial migration of enterprise applications to the cloud. In: Proc. of the ACM SIGCOMM Conf., pp. 243–254. ACM, New York (2010)

Closing the Gap between the Specification and Enforcement of Security Policies

José-Miguel Horcas, Mónica Pinto, and Lidia Fuentes

CAOSD Group, Universidad de Málaga, Andalucía Tech, Spain
{horcas,pinto,lff}@lcc.uma.es

Abstract. Security policies are enforced through the deployment of certain security functionalities within the applications. Applications can have different levels of security and thus each security policy is enforced by different security functionalities. Thus, the secure deployment of an application is not an easy task, being more complicated due to the existing gap between the specification of a security policy and the deployment, inside the application, of the security functionalities that are required to enforce that security policy. The main goal of this paper is to close this gap. This is done by using the paradigms of Software Product Lines and Aspect-Oriented Programming in order to: (1) link the security policies with the security functionalities, (2) generate a configuration of the security functionalities that fit a security policy, and (3) weave the selected security functionalities into an application. We qualitatively evaluate our approach, and discuss its benefits using a case study.

Keywords: Security enforcement, security policy, aspect-oriented programming, software product lines.

1 Introduction

A security policy is a set of rules that regulate the nature and the context of actions that can be performed within a system according to specific roles (i.e. permissions, interdictions, obligations, availability, etc) to assure and enforce security [1]. The security policies have to be specified before being enforced. This specification can be based on different models, such as OrBAC [2], RBAC [3], MAC [4], etc. and describes the security properties that an application should meet. Once specified, a security policy is enforced through the deployment of certain security functionalities within the application. For instance, the security policy "the system has the *obligation* to use a digital certificate to authenticate the users that connect using a laptop" should be enforced by deploying, within the application, "an authentication module that supports authentication based on digital certificates". This module must be executed before the user connects to the application using a laptop. In order to make explicit this relationship between the security policies and the security functionalities that are needed to enforce them, the links between both should be specified.

This relationship is needed because, normally, the same application can be deployed with different security policies. This implies that a variable number of security functionalities will be used by the application, but not all of them

C. Eckert et al. (Eds.): TrustBus 2014, LNCS 8647, pp. 106–118, 2014.

simultaneously. For example, in this paper we use an e-voting case study where the administrator can create elections of different types (e.g. national elections, coorporative elections, social event elections, etc.). These elections are deployed with different security policies. For instance, in a national election, users must be authenticated by an X.509 digital certificate provided by a trusted certification authority before they are joined to the election. Votes must be encrypted and must preserve their integrity and authenticity. However, in a corporative election users must be authenticated by using a user/password mechanism, while in a social event election users do not need to authenticate. In other words, there are different levels of security depending on the kind of election, and thus, each security policy is enforced by different security functionalities.

All this means that the secure deployment of an application is not an easy and straightforward task. Moreover, this is complicated even further due to the existing gap between the specification and the enforcement of a security policy. This gap is generated by the lack of a well-defined approach that would automatically introduce into an application, the security functionalities that are required to enforce the security policy. The main goal of this paper is to close this gap. We do this by using two advanced software engineering approaches, Software Product Lines (SPLs) [5] and Aspect-Oriented Programming (AOP) [6].

On the one hand, we use SPLs to: (1) model the commonalities and variabilities of the security properties represented in the security policies, (2) link the security properties to the modules that implement the security functionalities, and (3) automatically generate a security configuration including only the security functionalities that are required to enforce a particular security policy. On the other hand, we use AOP to: (1) design and implement the security functionalities separately from the applications (implementing them as aspects), and (2) deploy a security configuration in an application without modifying the original application. This work has been done in the context of the European project Inter-operable Trust Assurance Infrastructure (INTER-TRUST) [1] that aims to develop a framework to support trustworthy applications that are adapted at runtime to enforce changing security policies.

The rest of the paper is organized as follow. Section 2 describes the SPL and AOP approaches, introducing the main terminology. Section 3 provides an overview of our approach, while Section 4 and Section 5 describe it in an example-driven way using the e-voting case study. Section 6 evaluates our approach. The remaining sections present the related work, conclusions and future work.

2   Background Information

This section introduces the SPL and AOP approaches, and the main terminology.

2.1   Software Product Lines

In software engineering we usually need to create and maintain applications that contain: (1) a collection of similar functionalities from a shared set of software assets (i.e. *commonalities*) and (2) a collection of variant functionalities (i.e. *variabilities*). These applications require software developers to build a base on the application commonalities, and to efficiently express and manage the application variabilities, allowing the delivery of a wide variety of applications in a fast, comprehensive and consistent way. The enabling technology to do that is the Software Product Lines (SPLs) [5]. SPLs allow the specification and modeling of the commonalities and variabilities of applications in an abstract level, creating different *configurations* of those variabilities for the implemented functionalities, and generating final applications with the customized functionalities according to those configurations.

The security functionalities that need to be deployed inside an application are clearly variable. One the one hand, security is composed by many concerns, such as authentication, authorization, encryption, and privacy concerns, among others, which are regarded as configurable functionalities of security. For instance, there are many possible mechanisms to authenticate users (e.g. digital certificate, password based, biometric based), or there are a variable number of places within an application where communications need to be encrypted. On the other hand, an application will require different levels of security, based on the requirements specified in different security policies. So, different security configurations for the same application can be generated by modeling security using an SPL.

Between the methods, tools and techniques provided by SPLs to model variability with the guarantee of a formal basis, some of the most commonly used are feature models [7] in which the variability functionalities are specified in the abstract level by using tree-based diagrams that include optionals and mandatories features, multiplicity, cross-tree constraint, among other characteristics. In this paper, we will use the Common Variability Language (CVL) [8] that apart from providing the same characteristics of feature models, is a domain-independent language and allows modeling and resolving the variability over models defined in any language based on Meta-Object Facility (MOF) [9].

2.2 Aspect-Oriented Programming

In object-oriented programming and component-based software engineering, there are concerns of an application that are dispersed or replicated in multiple modules. This occurs even when the functionalities are well-encapsulated in a class or a component (e.g. an encryption component), because the rest of the modules requiring these concerns need to include implicit calls to them (e.g. all the components in the application need to call the encryption component in order to encrypt/decrypt their interactions). These kinds of properties are known as *crosscutting concerns*, and their direct incorporation into the main functionality of an application cause *scattered* (i.e. dispersion) and *tangled* (i.e. mixing) code.

Security is a well-known crosscutting concern in the aspect-oriented community [10,11]. Figure 1 shows an example of how several security functionalities crosscut the base components of our e-voting application. For instance, `Authentication` is required for voters and administrators, so this functionality is scattered within the `Voter Client` and `Admin Client` components. In addition, the code of the authentication functionality is tangled with these main components. `Integrity` and `Signature` functionalities are also tangled within the `Voting Ballot` component; while `Encryption` is also dispersed in several

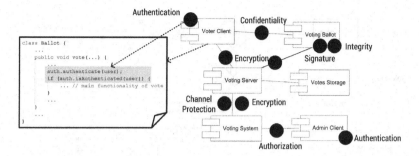

Fig. 1. Security functionalities crosscutting an e-voting application

places in the application. Modeling the variability of these security functionalities joinly with the base application is a difficult and error-prone task.

One of the most advanced techniques for dealing with crosscutting concerns is Aspect-Oriented Programming (AOP) [6]. AOP separates crosscutting concerns from the base functionality of an application by first encapsulating them in entities called *aspects*, and by then *weaving* (i.e. incorporating) these aspects into the existing code of the base application without modifying it. Aspects are described in terms of *join points*, *pointcuts* and *advices*. The points inside the code of the base application in which the crosscutting concerns come into play are known as *join points*; *pointcuts* are expressions that pick out certain join points; and *advices* is the crosscutting behaviour to be executed when a pointcut is reached. The mechanism in charge of weaving the main functionality of the application and the aspects is the *weaver*.

Separating the security functionalities from the base functionality of the application smoothes coupling between modules and increases the cohesion of each of them. As a consequence of a low coupling and a high cohesion, the maintainability of the global system improves due to the fact that changes in a module affect only that module; and thus, the modeling of the security variability and consequent deployment and enforcement of different security policies is easier. Moreover, the reusability also improves because the three elements (the base code, the security functionalities and the security policies) can be more easily reused in different systems.

3   Our Approach

As we presented in the introduction, an application can be deployed with different security policies and each security policy is enforced by different security functionalities. Top of Figure 2 shows the *problem* of the existing gap between the specification snd the enforcement of the security policies. Bottom of Figure 2 shows our *solution* to close this gap.

As previously mentioned, our approach combines the use of SPL and AOP. Firstly, as shown in Figure 2, left side under the Solution label, we model the variability of the security functionalities in an abstract level by specifying all the possible features of each security functionality in a tree-based diagram (i.e. we

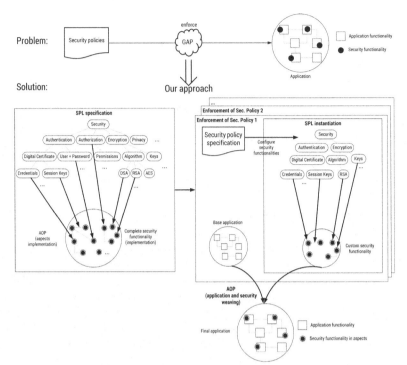

Fig. 2. Problem overview and solution proposal

specify the SPL). This variability model is linked to the complete implementation of the security functionalities, by linking each feature in the tree to the pieces of code that have to be included and configured (e.g. a class, a parameter, a value,...). Secondly, the right-hand side of Figure 2, under the `Solution` label, shows how, for each security policy, we create a configuration of the previously specified SPL by selecting those features in the tree that meet the security policy — i.e. we instantiate the SPL. This step can be done by a security expert or can also be done automatically by a reasoning engine that extracts the knowledge of the security policy and selects the appropriate features.

Using AOP, the security functionalities are implemented as aspects with the purpose of deploying them in the application without modifying the base code of the original application. Thus, the last step of our approach (see bottom half of Figure 2) is weaving the application and the aspects that implement a particular security configuration. The generated application includes the security functionalities that are needed to guarantee the enforcement of the security policy. The following sections describe our approach in more detail.

4   Variability Modeling of Security Functionalities

In this section we explain how to specify the SPL for modeling the variability of the security functionalities. We use the variability model of CVL that comprises two parts: (1) the variability specifications (VSpecs) tree (i.e. the abstract level)

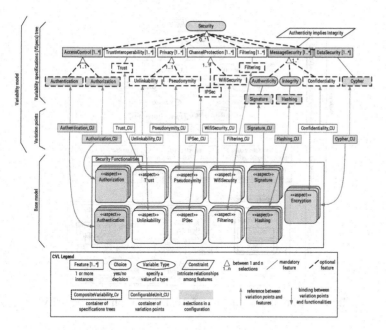

Fig. 3. Modeling security concepts in CVL

that allows us to specify the security features in a tree-structure with the relationships between them; and (2) the variation points, that allows us to link the features of the tree with the implementation of the security functionalities.

Figure 3 shows the variability model with these two parts and the implementation of the security functionality encapsulated inside the aspects. In the VSpecs, security is decomposed into more specific concepts and configurable features. For instance, the `AccessControl` concept contains the `Authentication` and `Authorization` features. The multiplicity [1..*] beside the `AccessControl` concept indicates that we can create multiple instances of it, each of them will require the configuration of different `Authentication` or `Authorization` features. For each of these instances there will be an aspect instantiated with the appropriate security functionality configured. In this case, variation points link each feature with the aspect that contains the configurable functionality.

Since security is composed by a lot of functionalities, and each of them has many configurable features, we define the variability model in two levels of detail using several related tree diagrams: (1) a high level VSpecs with all the main security functionalities represented as features (Figure 3); and (2) a VSpecs tree for each of these features in order to configure them appropriately. For instance, Figure 4 shows the part of the variability model that specifies the details to configure the `Authentication` functionality. Authentication is decomposed in a set of configurable features such as the authentication mechanism (`DigitalCertificate` or `UserPassword`) and the parameters and variables that contain the selected functionality (kind of certificate (`Credentials`), certificate authority (`TrustedCA`), ldots). These can be defined as optional features

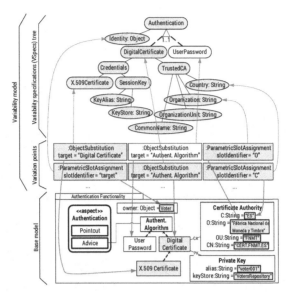

Fig. 4. Variability Modeling of Authentication functionality

(`ObjectExistence` variation point), variable features (`ObjectSubstitution` variation point), parameterizable features (`ParametricSlotAssignment` variation point), among others. In our case, we only need to use the `ObjectSubstitution` and the `ParametricSlotAssignment` variations point in order to substitute the selected authentication mechanism to be used (`Authent. Algorithm`) and to assign the values to the variables (e.g. parameters of the `TrustedCA`).

Note that the main benefit of our approach is that this SPL specification, although it is complex, only needs to be specified once by a software engineer, expert on security. Then, application developers will only have to select those security functionalities that need to be used in their applications and, as explained in the next section, our approach will generate a security configuration that enforces the required security policy, and is ready to be used by the application.

5   Enforcement of Security Policies

This section explains how to create a security configuration that enforces a security policy and how to deploy it within the application.

5.1   Configuring the security functionality

In order to select and configure the proper functionality that enforces a security policy, the security rules specified in the policy need to be analyzed and interpreted. This can be done by a security expert, an administrator, or automatically, by a reasoning engine that extracts the security knowledge from the rules, selects the security features, and assigns the appropriate values in the VSpecs — i.e. we instantiate the SPL by creating a configuration for the VSpecs.

Following our e-voting case study, Listing 1.1 shows an excerpt of a security policy defined in the OrBAC model for a national election in Spain. The first two rules specify that voters and administrators must be authenticated by a digital certificate in the spanish administration server (GOB_ES). The other rules specify permission for administrators and voters in order to create elections (rule 3) and to access the general elections (rule 4) respectively, to guarantee the authenticity and integrity of the votes (rule 5), and the encryption of all the interactions between the users and the server (rule 6).

Listing 1.1. Excerpt of an OrBAC security policy

```
1    Obligation(GOB_ES, User, Authenticate, Certificate, Authent_conditions) ∧
2    Obligation(GOB_ES, Admin, Authenticate, Certificate, Authent_conditions)
       ∧
3    Permission(GOB_ES, Admin, Create, Election, default) ∧
4    Permission(GOB_ES, User, Access, General_Election, default) ∧
5    Permission(GOB_ES, User, Sign, Votes, Signature_conditions) ∧
6    Permission(GOB_ES, User, Encrypt, Messages, Encrypt_conditions)
```

From these rules a configuration of the VSpecs is created. Some elements of the security policies are used to select the desired functionality, while other elements are used to configure the selected functionality. Features in a dark color in Figure 3 represent the security features selected for those rules. From rules 1-4 we have selected the AccessControl security concept with the Authentication (rules 1-2) and Authorization (rules 3-4) functionality, and this requires providing two different configurations for each of these functionalities — i.e. this implies two different instances of the authentication aspect and two different instances of the authorization aspect, properly configured. For rule 5 we have selected the MessageSecurity concept that includes the Signature functionality, but also the Hashing functionality since there is a constraint in the SPL specification indicating that Authenticity implies Integrity. So, in order to enforce this requirement two different aspects should be configured: Signature and Hashing. Finally, for rule 6 we have selected the DataSecurity concept with the Cipher functionality in order to encrypt the information exchange between the users and the server, and thus, an encryption aspect should be configured.

Each of these aspects contain the functionality that should be configured based on the knowledge specified in the policy. So, we have to provide a configuration for each instance of these aspects in the VSpecs. For example, features in a dark color in Figure 4 and concrete values assigned to the variables represent a configuration for the instance of the Authentication aspect corresponding to security rule 1 of the security policy[1]. For instance, the credential parameters and the trusted CA information are obtained from the context of the policy in the OrBAC model, but can also be manually assigned if the security model does not include that information.

In order to resolve the variability and automatically generate the configured security aspects, the CVL engine is executed taking as inputs the security variability model, the particular configuration created for the variability model, and the implementation of the security functionalities encapsulated into aspects.

---

[1] For reasons of space, we represent the configuration directly over the VSpecs.

5.2 Deploying the Security Aspects into the Application

Once the security aspects have been generated according the specifications of the security policy, the deployment of them inside the base application can be performed in a non-intrusive way — i.e., without modifying the existing code of the application, by using the AOP. The mechanism in charge of composing the main functionality of the application and the aspects is the weaver, and how the weaver deploys the aspects within the application depends on the AOP framework chosen to define the aspects (e.g. AspectJ, Spring AOP, JBoss AOP, etc.). For instance, Figure 5 shows an example of the `Authentication` aspect (in AspectJ) woven with the e-voting application. This aspect encapsulates the authentication functionality (`AuthenticationModule`). The pointcut picks out the execution of the method `vote` and before it runs, the user is authenticated (advice code). We can observe how the application class `Ballot` does not contain any reference to the authentication functionality or to any other functionality related to security, which are all introduced as aspects.

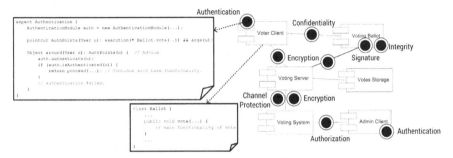

Fig. 5. Security functionality deployed within the e-voting application using AOP

6   Evaluation Results

Our approach uses consolidated software engineering technologies (SPLs and AOP), and a proposed standard language (CVL). So, in this section we qualitatively discuss our work to argue the correctness, maintainability, extendibility, separation of concerns, reusability, and scalability of our approach.

Correctness. SPLs and AOP do not improve the correctness of applications or security functionalities as such. Functionality in both cases is the same. However, modularizing security concerns in separate modules with AOP considerably facilitates the verification of the security properties of an application since a security expert does not have to check all the modules in the base application to ensure that all security requirements are correctly enforced. Instead, only the code of the aspects and the definition of the pointcuts where the aspects will be introduced need to be checked [10].

Maintainability and extendibility. On the one hand, due to the variability expressed in the SPL, changes of specifications in security policies are adapted easily by re-configuring the security functionality according to those changes.

Moreover, the variability model can be extended to cover more security concerns. On the other hand, AOP facilitates: (1) the modification of the security functionalities after being deployed due to the improved modularization, and (2) the extension of the points in which the security functionalities take place since we only need to extend the pointcuts of the aspects.

Separation of Concerns. Our approach improves the separation of concerns because we separate the specification of the security policies from the implementation of the core security functionalities, and from the deployment of the functionalities as aspects within the application.

Reusability. Following our approach, we can reuse the same security functionality with different applications and security policies. The main drawback is that we cannot reuse the same generated aspects for all the applications because the aspects are generated for a particular security policy and may also contain application dependent knowledge (e.g. pointcuts).

Scalability. Variability models have a considerable lack of scalability because the tree-diagrams become unmanageable as they grow (e.g. in feature models). However, CVL allows us to decrease the complexity of the model by dividing the VSpecs into different levels of details, using Composite Variability features and Configurable Units as we described in Section 4. Also, tree-diagrams is only syntactic sugar, but it is built onto a formal basis [7] and can also be specified using a text-based language [12].

In our follow-up work, we plan to improve our qualitative evaluation by using Delphi [13] techniques in order to evidence the benefits and usefulness of our approach from external experts.

7   Related Work

There is a growing interest in the SPL and AOP communities in resolving the gap between the security policies and the security functionalities that enforce the security policies [14,15,16]. For instance, in [14] the authors address the issue of formally validating the deployment of access control security policies. They use a theorem proving approach with a modeling language to allow the specification of the system jointly with the links between the system and the policy, and with the certain target security properties. The described algorithms, which perform the translation of the security policy inside specific devices' configurations, are based on the OrBAC model with the B-Method specifications, and thus, this approach does not close the gap completely, but only for specific OrBAC models. In addition, they do not separate the specification of the security functionality from the base functionality of the system as we do using AOP. In [17] the authors use a dynamic SPL to model runtime variability of services and propose different strategies for re-configuring a base model using CVL (e.g. model increments/decrements). They focus on the concrete variability transformations that need to be done in the base model in order to re-configured it, but they do not relate the specification of the requirements and the functionality provided as we do. Note that our approach can be extended to be applied to other requirements, not only for security.

The INTER-TRUST project [1] also aims to cover the gap, but in a different context. The INTER-TRUST framework regards the dynamic negotiation of changing security policies (specified in OrBAC) between two devices. The output of this negotiation is an agreement on interoperability policies, which must be dynamically enforced in both devices. This implies configuring applications and generating the security aspects that must be integrated into the applications [15]. The approach presented in this paper have to be seen as a possible implementation of the aspect generation module of the INTER-TRUST framework, which is the module in charge of determining the aspects that need to be deployed in order to enforce a security policy.

Several papers deal with security in an aspect-oriented way such as [11,16]. However, none of them consider security policies for the specification of the security requirements in the applications. Moreover, most approaches in the AOP community focus more on the security issues introduced by the AOP technology in the applications, such as in [10]. In [16], the authors propose a framework for specifying, deploying and testing access policies independently from the security model, but only suitable for Java applications. They follow a model-driven approach based on a generic security meta-model that is automatically transformed into security policies for the XACML platform by using the appropriate profile of the security model (e.g. OrBAC, RBAC). Then, the derived security components are integrated inside the applications using AOP. The main drawback to this framework is that the generated security components depend on the profiles of the specific security model used, and thus, the functionality cannot be reused. Moreover, re-deploying a security policy implies again generating the appropriate functionality with the consequent model transformations, which is a expensive process. The use of an SPL allows our approach the re-deployment of the security policy more easily and quickly.

In a previous work [18], we combined CVL and model transformations in order to weave security functionalities within the applications and focused on defining different weaving patterns for each security concern. Although the weaving process was inspired in AO modeling techniques, it was completely implemented in CVL without using AOP and the final application did not contain any aspects, in contrast to the approach presented in this paper where security is incorporated into the application using aspects. In [19] the authors also use CVL to specify and resolve the variability of a software design. However, their approach depends on an external Reusable Aspect Model (RAM) weaver to compose the chosen variants.

8   Conclusions and Future Work

The approach presented in this paper closes the existing gap between the specification and the enforcement of security policies by using consolidate software engineers technologies, such as SPLs and AOP. These techonologies bring significant benefits to our approach, including a better modularization, maintainability, extendibility, and reusability. Also the use of CVL as the variability modeling language improves the scalability of our approach and makes it suitable for any MOF-based model. Moreover, separating the specification of the security policies from the implementation of the security functionalities, and from the deployment of them within the application, our approach is suitable for any security model and facilitates the verification of the security policies enforcement.

As part of our future work, we plan to adapt our approach to dynamically adapt the security functionalities to changes in the security policies at runtime. This implies using Dynamic SPLs [20] and generating the code of the aspects so as weaving them at runtime.

Acknowledgment. Work supported by the European INTER-TRUST FP7-317731 and the Spanish TIN2012-34840, FamiWare P09-TIC-5231, and MAGIC P12-TIC1814 projects.

References

1. INTER-TRUST Project: Interoperable Trust Assurance Infrastructure, http://www.inter-trust.eu/
2. Kalam, A., Baida, R., Balbiani, P., Benferhat, S., Cuppens, F., Deswarte, Y., Miege, A., Saurel, C., Trouessin, G.: Organization based access control. In: POLICY, pp. 120–131 (2003)
3. Ferraiolo, D.F., Sandhu, R., Gavrila, S., Kuhn, D.R., Chandramouli, R.: Proposed NIST standard for role-based access control. ACM Trans. Inf. Syst. Secur. 4(3), 224–274 (2001)
4. Sandhu, R.: Lattice-based access control models. Computer 26(11), 9–19 (1993)
5. Pohl, K., Böckle, G., van der Linden, F.J.: Software Product Line Engineering: Foundations, Principles and Techniques. Springer-Verlag New York, Inc. (2005)
6. Kiczales, G., Lamping, J., Mendhekar, A., Maeda, C., Lopes, C., Loingtier, J.M., Irwin, J.: Aspect-Oriented Programming. In: Akşit, M., Matsuoka, S. (eds.) ECOOP 1997. LNCS, vol. 1241, pp. 220–242. Springer, Heidelberg (1997)
7. Kang, K., Cohen, S., Hess, J., Novak, W., Peterson, A.: Feature-Oriented Domain Analysis (FODA) feasibility study. Technical Report CMU/SEI-90-TR-021, Soft. Eng. Institute, Carnegie Mellon University, Pittsburgh, Pennsylvania (1990)
8. Haugen, O., Wąsowski, A., Czarnecki, K.: CVL: Common Variability Language. In: SPLC, vol. 2, pp. 266–267. ACM (2012)
9. OMG: Meta Object Facility (MOF) Core Specification Version 2.0 (2006)
10. Win, B.D., Piessens, F., Joosen, W.: How secure is AOP and what can we do about it? In: SESS, pp. 27–34. ACM (2006)
11. Mouheb, D., Talhi, C., Nouh, M., Lima, V., Debbabi, M., Wang, L., Pourzandi, M.: Aspect-oriented modeling for representing and integrating security concerns in UML. In: Lee, R., Ormandjieva, O., Abran, A., Constantinides, C. (eds.) SERA 2010. SCI, vol. 296, pp. 197–213. Springer, Heidelberg (2010)
12. Classen, A., Boucher, Q., Heymans, P.: A text-based approach to feature modelling: Syntax and semantics of TVL. Science of Computer Programming 76(12), 1130–1143 (2011); Special Issue on Software Evolution, Adaptability and Variability
13. Gordon, T.J.: The delphi method. Futures Research Methodology 2 (1994)
14. Preda, S., Cuppens-Boulahia, N., Cuppens, F., Garcia-Alfaro, J., Toutain, L.: Model-driven security policy deployment: Property oriented approach. In: Massacci, F., Wallach, D., Zannone, N. (eds.) ESSoS 2010. LNCS, vol. 5965, pp. 123–139. Springer, Heidelberg (2010)

15. Ayed, S., Idrees, M.S., Cuppens-Boulahia, N., Cuppens, F., Pinto, M., Fuentes, L.: Security aspects: A framework for enforcement of security policies using aop. In: SITIS, pp. 301–308 (2013)
16. Mouelhi, T., Fleurey, F., Baudry, B., Le Traon, Y.: A model-based framework for security policy specification, deployment and testing. In: Czarnecki, K., Ober, I., Bruel, J.-M., Uhl, A., Völter, M. (eds.) MODELS 2008. LNCS, vol. 5301, pp. 537–552. Springer, Heidelberg (2008)
17. Cetina, C., Haugen, O., Zhang, X., Fleurey, F., Pelechano, V.: Strategies for variability transformation at run-time. In: SPLC, pp. 61–70 (2009)
18. Horcas, J.M., Pinto, M., Fuentes, L.: An aspect-oriented model transformation to weave security using CVL. In: MODELSWARD, pp. 138–147 (2014)
19. Combemale, B., Barais, O., Alam, O., Kienzle, J.: Using cvl to operationalize product line development with reusable aspect models. In: VARY, pp. 9–14 (2012)
20. Hallsteinsen, S., Hinchey, M., Park, S., Schmid, K.: Dynamic Software Product Lines. Computer 41(4), 93–95 (2008)

Business Process Modeling for Insider Threat Monitoring and Handling

Vasilis Stavrou, Miltiadis Kandias, Georgios Karoulas, and Dimitris Gritzalis

Information Security & Critical Infrastructure Protection Laboratory
Dept. of Informatics, Athens University of Economics & Business
76 Patission Ave., GR-10434, Athens, Greece
{stavrouv,kandiasm,gi.karoulas,dgrit}@aueb.gr

Abstract. Business process modeling has facilitated modern enterprises to cope with the constant need to increase their productivity, reduce costs and offer competitive products and services. Despite modeling's and process management's widespread success, one may argue that it lacks of built-in security mechanisms able to detect and deter threats that may manifest throughout the process. To this end, a variety of different solutions have been proposed by researchers which focus on different threat types. In this paper we examine the insider threat through business processes. Depending on their motives, insiders participating in an organization's business process may manifest delinquently in a way that causes severe impact to the organization. We examine existing security approaches to tackle down the aforementioned threat in enterprise business processes and propose a preliminary model for a monitoring approach that aims at mitigating the insider threat. This approach enhances business process monitoring tools with information evaluated from Social Media by examining the online behavior of users and pinpoints potential insiders with critical roles in the organization's processes. Also, this approach highlights the threat introduced in the processes operated by such users. We conclude with some observations on the monitoring results (i.e. psychometric evaluations from the social media analysis) concerning privacy violations and argue that deployment of such systems should be allowed solely on exceptional cases, such as protecting critical infrastructures or monitoring decision making personnel.

Keywords: Business Process; Business Process Management; Insider Threat; Monitoring; Privacy; Social Media.

1 Introduction

Modern enterprises and organizations operate in a dynamic environment that is constantly evolving. This dynamic environment includes the competition for high quality products and services, reduced costs, and fast development. Factors such as globalization of business activities and the rapid growth of ICT offer new opportunities and give birth to threats for the organizations, while technological novelties have created a need for new operational structures for the enterprises and organizations. Therefore, each organization needs to develop business processes that meet the above mentioned requirements, while ensuring the fulfillment of the goals set.

C. Eckert et al. (Eds.): TrustBus 2014, LNCS 8647, pp. 119–131, 2014.

A business process is defined as "*a collection of activities that takes one or more kinds of input and creates an output that is of value to the customer*" [1]. It consists of a set of activities and tasks that, together, fulfill an organizational goal. Modeling the business processes of an organization improves the understanding of the corporate milieu and augments its flexibility and competitiveness in business environments. Modelling often includes Business Process Management (BPM) [2], a holistic approach to harmonize an organization's business processes with the needs of their clients [3]. Business processes are designed to be operated by one or more business functional units. Tasks in business processes can be performed either by means of business data processing systems (e.g. Enterprise resource planning (ERP) systems), or manually. Specifically, in an enterprise environment, some process tasks may be performed manually, while others may be automated or even batch scheduled in a variety of ways: data and information being handled throughout the business process may pass through manual or computer tasks in any given order.

Business process modeling, mainly during its first stages, lacks built-in security mechanisms so as to prevent a malevolent functional unit from causing harm to the organization through the operated process. Our research focuses on mitigating the insider threat via a combination of business process security and a series of psychosocial parameters that interfere with them. Although role-based access control [5] is used in various approaches to tackle the insider threat [6], it usually fails to be mitigated, thus leading us to consider that new approaches need to be taken into account. Furthermore, regarding role-based access control (RBAC) schemes, the insider is a legitimate user of the infrastructure, who utilizes his access rights in a disrespectful manner towards the organization's security policy [6]. Thus, such schemes tend to fail against the threat.

Other, more intrusive, approaches involve monitoring techniques varying from system call activity [7] and linguistic analysis of electronic communications [8] to tracking business processes [9] and provide logging information about them. The information acquired can provide conclusions over the functional unit (i.e. the employee) who operates it and also detect possible anomaly deviations in her usage behavior that require further examination. Along with technical countermeasures, research has proved that it is possible to detect personality characteristics shared among insiders themselves through social media [10] [11], as users tend to transfer their offline behavior to the online world [12].

In this paper we revise and extend the business process monitoring model presented in previous publication of ours [4]. The proposed model is still preliminary, as it has not been developed yet. Comparing current paper to our previous work, we considerably revise and add further commentary and desired functionality over the components of the model presented. Additionally, we also examine the limitations, as well as the requirements of this approach, in order to develop a functional mechanism. Thus, aim of this paper is to propose a model based on two of CERT's patterns [28] that suggest the use of external sources of information to monitor employees and the combination of technical and behavioral monitoring to deter the insider threat. This mechanism is able to monitor user's performance at runtime level, along with its psychometric evaluations from social media, and issue alerts when a processes may involve a threat by a potential malevolent unit.

The model's input is comprised of: (a) psychometric evaluations, extracted from social media user profiles of the organization's employees, (b) the business processes each user is involved, and (c) the performance at workspace. Its output consists of: (a) alerts, when a user manifest a potential insider behavior is detected in online monitoring component and (b) the business processes that the user is involved with.

Online monitoring can facilitate insider threat mitigation since, unlike other technical approaches, it also takes the human factor into account. However, unconsented user monitoring, either at organization level or through online profiling, interferes with the user's personality and privacy rights, something that need to be taken into consideration. Therefore, a monitoring process can be ethically and legally acceptable only in cases involving high societal risk (as in critical infrastructures where national security, economic prosperity or national well-being are at stake). In most cases, the user's explicit consent must have been given in retrospect.

The paper is organized as follows: In section 2 we briefly review the existing literature. In section 3 we discuss the security approaches to mitigate the insider threat in business process. In section 4 we present a business process monitoring model. In section 5 we discuss the requirements and limitations of the approach proposed. In section 6 we examine the ethical and legal issues over online and organizational user monitoring. Finally, in section 7 we conclude and refer to plans for future work.

2   Related Work

None of the approaches introduced in the insider threat detection literature appear to combine both business process and psychometric monitoring, so as to proactively detect the current threat in the organization. To this end, we examine approaches and methodologies used to enhance business process security, under the prism of insider threat mitigation via: (a) psychosocial approaches that may predict malevolent behavior, and (b) monitoring techniques that have been used against the insider threat.

Security in business processes involves methodologies that target at satisfying requirements in their development phase [13]. A developer is advised to be aware of the security goals the implementation should achieve, since the construction of models during requirement analysis and system design can improve the quality of the resulting systems, thus providing early analysis and fault detection along with maximization of the security lifecycle of the solution.

Security and system design models are often disjoint, as they are expressed in different ways (security models as structured text vs. graphical design models in notation languages). To this end, modeling languages, such as secure UML [14], have been developed in order to bridge the gap between security requirements and model design. In particular, secure UML is designed for specifying access control policies by substantially extending Role-Based Access Control (RBAC). RBAC has bee also extended in order to address task delegation in workflow systems. In their work, Gaaloul, et al. [15], use a role-based security model in order to show how formalized delegation constrains can be injected to specify privileges into delegation policies within an access control framework.

As modern enterprise systems are becoming more business-process driven, an approach describing secure BPMN [16] has been developed, in an effort to create models with embedded security requirements that generate robust system architectures, including access control infrastructures. The proposed tool supports model-driven development of processes that integrate security and compliance requirements across all phases of the system life-cycle. Together with [17] a formal methodology for the automatic synthesis of a secure orchestrator, a set of BPMN processes is described to guarantee non-disclosure of messages exchanged in processes. Finally, model checking techniques are used for evaluating security aspects of business processes in dynamic environments [20]. Another approach [18] in business process security involves the modeling and analyzing of the participants' objectives; so as to extract security requirements from them use them to annotate business processes. To deal with organizational analysis and the integration of security and systems engineering, the goal-oriented requirements engineering domain includes approaches such as Secure Tropos [19]. Secure Tropos forms a methodology for security-aware software systems and combines requirements engineering with security engineering concepts to support the analysis and development of secure systems.

Regarding insider threat prediction, various approaches have been proposed [21]. Researchers have examined the psychosocial traits that indicate predisposition of delinquent behavior [22], while modern approaches indicate that such characteristics can be extracted through social media. To this extend, conclusions over traits, such as narcissism [10], or predisposition towards law enforcement [11], have been successfully extracted via **Twitter** and **YouTube**, respectively, thus leading towards the capability of online monitoring of users' behavior to detect potentially malevolent users.

Monitoring techniques are also used to detect potential insiders. At system level, LUARM [23] can be used to accurately specify insider threats by logging user actions in a relational model, as a forensic mechanism. Furthermore, linguistic analysis of electronic communications has been also used as a monitoring technique, so as to proactively detect potential insider threat risks in the organization [8].

3   Insider Threat Mitigation

Insider threat has been identified as a major issue not only in corporate security but also in cloud computing [25]. To mitigate the insider threat, security research has proposed various approaches, countermeasures and techniques, together with security policies, procedures and technical controls. Each organization should examine its design functionality, in order to tackle the threat at its business process level. The mitigating stages at process level are the following:

• **Design secure business processes** by extending the annotation of existing modeling languages, in order to encapsulate security requirements. For example, existing modeling languages, such as BPMN, can be extended to support features regarding integrity, confidentiality and access control [26].

• **Risk assessment** [27] at business process level in order to evaluate the risk involved in each process, with regard to security needs and the environment in which each process is deployed. Applying proper risk management ensures the balance of operational and economic costs of protective measures and security policies.

• **Monitoring each business process** of the organization and extracting conclusions. Monitoring may facilitate the location and redesign of problematic procedures and reduce the risk of an insider threat incident.

These above approaches may deter the insider threat to some extent but they do not aggregate the human factor in the result. Therefore, they try to solve the problem by using solely technical countermeasures and security policies, instead of trying to integrate the prediction front into the applied approaches.

The human factor is discussed in approaches regarding either insider threat prediction, or monitoring and screening, in order to extend employee monitoring outside an organization boundaries. A research involving employee's monitoring has been introduced by CERT. It focuses on analyzing insider threat cases in order to identify weaknesses in parts of the organization that facilitate the manifestation of such incidents. Part of this research outcome has led to 26 enterprise architecture patterns, developed as a means of protection from malevolent insiders [28].

Among the patterns developed by CERT, we focus on the following: (a) **Monitoring the organization**, which suggests the institution runs a monitoring program that collects information on the status of insider threats and incidents within the organization. This way, the organization can obtain an estimation of the risk involved by malicious insider activity. (b) **Monitoring employees**, which suggests the establishment of a legal, affordable and effective monitoring system that is acceptable to all stakeholders. Monitoring results should be secured and used solely for the purpose of optimizing resources and not for discrimination. (c) **Use optimized monitoring for early detection**, which indicates that organizations should configure their infrastructures in a way that insider attacks are detected in a short time period. (d) **Combine technical and behavioral monitoring**, which suggests that technical and behavioral monitoring can increase the effectiveness of insider threat detection by alert sharing, so as to investigate and detect malicious actions. (e) **Use external sources of information**, which suggests the use of external information sources, such as social networks, in order to expand employees monitoring.

We focus on proposing a model approach which enhances business process management systems (BPMS) with psychological evaluation approaches, along with monitoring techniques, so as to mitigate the insider threat.

4   Proposed Model

We propose a monitoring approach that combines enterprise level monitoring with social media-extracted monitoring intelligence (Fig. 1), in order to mitigate the insider threat along with managing the risk introduced due to the human factor. In order to tackle this problem, we decided to develop an integrative model that builds upon our previous work [4] on user and usage profiling via data obtained from social media. Existing business monitoring tools can be further expanded to receive input regarding the aforementioned psychometric evaluations. Such tools can monitor the organizational processes while recording the users involved in each process.

The paper mainly focuses on two of the above CERT's patterns: (a) "Use external sources of information" and (b) "Combine technical and behavioral monitoring". The remaining patterns can be utilized via existing and conventional monitoring tools. As a result, we aim at further enhancing existing monitoring tools by combining external sources of information (i.e. social media) with technical and behavioral patterns.

To this end, we build upon our previous research and propose a new architecture (Fig. 1). The architecture receives the following types of input: (a) data from business monitoring regarding employees' performance, (b) online monitoring, which involves data acquired from social media, and (c) the processes that the user under examination is involved with. The output comes in the form of: (a) potential incident alerts and (b) the risk that refers to the specific processes of the organization.

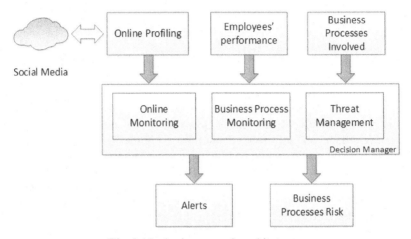

Fig. 1. Monitoring system's architecture

The model's inputs are processed by the *decision manager* module that consists of three core modules. Namely, it comprises the online monitoring, the business process monitoring, and the threat management. Each of the modules cooperates with the rest in the boundaries of the decision manager so as to achieve the desired functionality.

The contribution of this model lies on the fact that the human factor has been rarely examined in monitoring systems that focus solely on technical countermeasures. However, monitoring users at workspace usually gives rise to ethical and legal issues.

4.1   Module: Online Monitoring

The *online monitoring* module facilitates the process of behavioral analysis carried out on information system users, as manifested in the digital world. The ability to detect patterns of characteristics commonly shared among insiders enhances a monitoring system, as it integrates the prediction front of insider threat in the monitoring process. Online monitoring can be applied on social media profiles and extract conclusions over insider threat characteristics such as *narcissism* [10], *predisposition towards law enforcement* [11], and *divided loyalty* [30]. The above traits have been examined and detected through social media and can facilitate the insider threat prediction in the digital world. Thus, they have been the topic of interest in Shaw's research [22]. These traits have been also examined by the FBI [31].

One may extract the aforementioned three traits examined to detect a potential insider by examining her online behavior, by using open source intelligence (OSINT) techniques. OSINT [32] facilitates the improvement of the online monitoring efficiency. It refers to intelligence collected from publicly available sources, such as websites, web-based communities (i.e. social networks, forums, or blogs), and (openly) publicly available data.

An interesting observation is that direct access to the user social media data is not required, at least not through the network per se. Users data content in social media is usually publicly available, as most of them neglect to use the available privacy mechanisms. Therefore, anyone interested in collecting such data is free to gather information and analyze it for conclusions, targeting any user of interest.

OSINT processes often rely on vast amounts of reliable information. Due to that fact, the following key points should be taken into account:

• **Uncovering data location**: It is required to have knowledge of the locations from where the appropriate data can be gathered.

• **Sources discrimination**: The discrimination of the useful and the irrelevant sources of information is important, so to avoid collecting outdates or useless data.

• **Results refining**: After having generated conclusions over the subject of interest, one could further process the results in order to focus on the required knowledge.

The mechanisms developed in [10], [11] and [30] rely on the above mentioned key points. Also, they can be used as a means of conclusion extraction over the insider traits of narcissism, predisposition towards law enforcement, and divided loyalty, by the online monitoring module. Each of the mechanisms can indicate whether a user shares the trait examined by having as input her username and being able to access her online user-generated content.

Consequently, the decision manager can issue alerts whether manifestation of insider characteristics is detected in the online world. Additionally, it highlights the business processes where a potentially malevolent user is involved into. Then, the operator of the system can further examine the alerts of the online monitoring module and may draw conclusions over the user performance through the *business process monitoring* module.

4.2   Module: Business Process Monitoring

This module monitors an employee's performance in workspace. Process monitoring refers to real-time observations of activities, combined to accomplish a specific organizational goal. Business process monitoring involves mainly business activity monitoring, thus helping senior management gain insight into processes deployed within the organization. It also enables organizations to measure and analyze their performance, and identify critical problems proactively, thus improving speed, quality and efficiency of their processes. Additionally, being able to monitor employee's performance at workspace, one may detect deviations in the execution of the activities the user is involved into (Fig. 2.). Therefore, the decision manager can use the online monitoring module, to examine any potential change in user's online behavior. Whether a deviation in employee's performance is detected, it could have occurred due to manifestation of insider characteristics. To this end, the security officer should further examine the source of this deviation.

Fig. 2. Employee's performance monitoring

The growing need of organizational processes monitoring has led to the development of many platforms, which provide tools for the development of services and composite applications, allowing greater visibility, controls and analysis in the whole process lifecycle. Our model approach can utilize an existing business process monitoring platform and extend it, so as to include the functionality introduced by the online monitoring module. Process monitoring platforms that could be used and further be extended, in order to meet our needs, are the IBM Business Monitor[1], the Oracle Business Activity Monitoring[2] and the WSO2[3].

4.3   Module: Threat Management

Potential insiders introduce risk to the systems they operate, as they can manifest in a malevolent way that will cause severe impact to the organization. The threat management module handles this risk faced by potential insiders who operate organizational business processes.

To develop a more holistic perspective regarding the risks that business processes face due to their operators, the model can be enhanced with the ability to categorize the organization's business processes. To this end, an approach that takes into account both the risk faced by the assets involved in a process and the psychosocial traits of the operator, is required.

Based on the above, an approach should examine the processes under two perspectives: (a) the risk that a business process has due to the assets involved in it and (b) the risk occurred based on the psychosocial traits of the employee that operates it. The *risk that characterizes a process*, regarding the assets that are involved in it, refers to the impact to the organization due to a possible loss of confidentiality, integrity or availability. Therefore, the more important the asset, the severer the impact. Complementary, the *risk involved by the human factor* corresponds to the predisposition of delinquent behavior that characterizes user's online behavior. This discrimination contributes to the protection of critical processes since both risk factors are taken into account.

The risk faced by the psychosocial traits of the potential insider, should be able to be quantified. The existing mechanisms, used by the online monitoring module,

---

[1]   http://www-03.ibm.com/software/products/en/business-monitor
[2]   http://www.oracle.com/us/products/middleware/soa/
      business-activity-monitoring/overview/index.html
[3]   http://wso2.com

are able to answer whether, or not, a user manifests such behavior in social media. Thus, it is required that they quantify the amount of certainty, or the extent a user expresses the aforementioned traits in the online world. One may notice that by being able to measure the psychometrics, an underlying model could use them to express the amount of risk that a process is exposed due to its operator.

At a primary stage, this module may issue alerts anytime the online monitoring system detects a potential insider. Following the alert, it could highlight the business processes in which the malevolent user is involved and help the security officer decide on proper actions to be taken.

5   Requirements and Limitations

We now discuss the requirements and limitations of the approach introduced. In order to monitor user's online behavior it is required that the user has created a profile at least in one of the social media for which we have developed evaluation mechanisms (i.e. YouTube and Twitter). If the profile is public, then our mechanisms are able to collect and process the available data so as to draw conclusions over the user's behavior. Depending on legal parameters, a user consent is usually required in order to process such data. An additional requirement for the online monitoring module is the conversion of the collected data from an SQL schema into flat data representation. Such a conversion facilitates the partitioning and distributed processing of the data, thus leading to faster processing [11].

Regarding the log storage functionality, especially for the online monitoring behavior, the system should take into account that the size of such data is expected to grow rapidly, thus indicating that big data processing techniques should be used.

The decision manager combines the functionality of the online monitoring module, the business monitoring module, and the threat management one. In order to develop the decision manager it is required that an existing Business Process Management System (BPMS) is extended so as to integrate the desired overall functionality.

A limitation of this approach is that an intelligent insider could possibly manifest a different online behavior, knowing that her profile is monitored, and thus deceive the system. In this case a more microscopic examination of a user online behavior could indicate fragments where contradictions are presented.

It appears that, for the time being, there are no other approaches that take into account the risk introduced by the psychometric evaluations. At first, the quantification of the psychosocial traits it is required and then a sophisticated risk analysis approach should be developed in order to take into consideration the risk introduced by the psychosocial indications.

6   Ethical and Legal Issues

The proposed approach introduces a mechanism for monitoring at organizational level, along with online profiling, that aims at deterring the insider threat. However, employees' monitoring interferes with their personality and privacy rights.

The rapid evolvement of Web 2.0, together with the advent of social media, has offered to workspace monitoring an opportunity to expand by screening an employee online behavior. Employees' monitoring can no longer be performed in the workspace per se, but alternatively in the online world. Monitoring the online behavior and social communication relationships of employees augments the chances of employers to influence behavior and promote the "well-adjusted employee" [33]. Moreover, information gathering about employee performances outside the traditionally conceived work sphere has a chilling effect on individuals' personality and freedom of speech. Employees may sacrifice "Internet participation to segregate their multiple life performance" [34] and thus refrain from expressing themselves.

To improve productivity and prevent potential threats, employees are often asked to sacrifice privacy rights in favor of managerial interests. Given the fact that workplace belongs to the "private sphere", employees who are hired to attend company business cannot have a (subjective) "reasonable expectation of privacy" that society (objectively) accepts and legitimizes. American Courts are reluctant to recognize a workplace privacy right. In any case, reasonable expectation of privacy of employees should be assessed under all circumstances and should be reasonable both in inception and scope. In the employment context, privacy (if any) seems to be exchanged for something of commensurate value, like taking or keeping a job [35].

Diametrically opposite in many respects, the European approach claims that privacy is not conceived as a right to seclusion and intimacy but as a phenomenon, a protectable situation that regards the relationships between a person and its environment. The European Court of Human Rights has rejected the distinction between private life and professional life (Niemietz vs. Germany). According to the Court, European employees have "a right to dignity and a private life that does not stop at the employer's doorstep".

Profiling aims to gain probabilistic knowledge from past data, propose predictions, and identify risks for the future. This goal may infringe civilian privacy, i.e. the right for everyone to be a multiple personality and also may have a serious impact on the employee regarding social selection and unjustified discrimination.

Finally, excessive monitoring has been demonstrated to affect the employer-employee relationship. Research [35] [36] has showed that employees whose communications were monitored suffered by higher levels of depression, anxiety and fatigue than those who were not. The effect of being constantly monitored, even concerning activities that fall out of the workplace frame, has negative impacts on the employer-employee relationship, which should be based on mutual trust and confidence.

7   Conclusions

In this paper we dealt with the insider threat mitigation issue and suggested a way to improve the protection against potential insider at business process level. To this end, we proposed a structural approach that combines monitoring at process level with psychosocial monitoring through social media. We mainly focused on two of CERT's insider threat patterns; namely, on the use of external sources of information (i.e. social media), as well as the combination of technical and behavioral monitoring, to mitigate the current threat.

Our approach consists of three modules, i.e. the online monitoring, the business process monitoring and the threat management. These modules cooperate in the boundaries of the model's decision manager in order to form a unified monitoring system that helps security officers to better carry out their duties.

Our ultimate goal is to integrate the human factor into the business process security. Malevolent insiders have been found to share common characteristics. Research has indicated the feasibility of extracting such traits through social media. Thus, corporate security could better deal with the insider threat by using a mechanism which can integrate psychosocial evaluation into a business activity monitoring system.

As expected, the model approach described faces a few limitations that have to be overcome, in order to achieve full functional. Such limitations include the ability of an intelligent insider to manifest a misleading behavior to deceive the system, without being detected, and the need that a user to be monitored into the online world should have at least one profile in a social medium.

Regarding the requirements, an existing business process monitoring platform should be used in order to be extended and implement the required functionality of the monitoring system. Another requirement refers to the improvement of the existing processing mechanisms, as the vast amount of information requires demanding computing power.

One could argue over the applicability of the proposed model, as screening employees (in both business level and online behavior through social media) may violate human rights and raise serious ethical issues. To this end, we exploit the principle of proportionality by considering that the use of such a method should be solely confined in a critical infrastructure, given a prior user consent [37] [38] [39].

For future work we plan to implement the model in a test environment, so as to evaluate and detect possible performance issues and also provide a more detailed step by step description of the model's functionality as a case study. In addition, we plan on improving our data collection mechanisms from social media, so as they perform more efficiently in complexity and time execution, and also present a more holistic approach of the evaluation mechanism from social media for a better understanding of the approach proposed. Following we plan on examining how to resolve the limitations described in section 5.

Last, but not least, the development of a business process risk analysis methodology that takes into consideration the insider threat characteristics a user may have is planned. Note that by being able to quantify the personality traits of the insider extracted from social media, we could use them to represent the risk faced by the user that operates a business process.

References

1. Hammer, M., Champy, J.: Reengineering the corporation: A manifesto for business revolution. Harper Collins (2009)
2. Weske, M.: Business process management: concepts, languages, architectures. Springer (2012)

3. Karagiannis, D.: Business process management: A holistic management approach. In: Mayr, H.C., Kop, C., Liddle, S., Ginige, A. (eds.) UNISON 2012. LNBIP, vol. 137, pp. 1–12. Springer, Heidelberg (2013)

4. Gritzalis, D., Stavrou, V., Kandias, M., Stergiopoulos, G.: Insider Threat: Enhancing BPM through Social Media. In: 6th IFIP International Conference on New Technologies, Mobility and Security. IEEE (2014)

5. Basin, D., Doser, J., Lodderstedt, T.: Model driven security: From UML models to access control infrastructures. ACM Transactions on Software Engineering and Methodology 15(1), 39–91 (2006)

6. Theoharidou, M., Kokolakis, S., Karyda, M., Kiountouzis, E.: The insider threat to information systems and the effectiveness of ISO17799. Computers & Security 24(6), 472–484 (2005)

7. Nguyen, N., Reiher, P., Kuenning, G.H.: Detecting insider threats by monitoring system call activity. In: IEEE Systems, Man and Cybernetics Society, pp. 45–52. IEEE (2003)

8. Brown, C., Watkins, A., Greitzer, F.: Predicting insider threat risks through linguistic analysis of electronic communication. In: 46th Hawaii International Conference on System Sciences, pp. 1849–1858. IEEE (2013)

9. Grigori, D., Casati, F., Castellanos, M., Dayal, U., Sayal, M., Shan, M.: Business process intelligence. Computers in Industry 53(3), 321–343 (2004)

10. Kandias, M., Galbogini, K., Mitrou, L., Gritzalis, D.: Insiders trapped in the mirror reveal themselves in social media. In: Lopez, J., Huang, X., Sandhu, R. (eds.) NSS 2013. LNCS, vol. 7873, pp. 220–235. Springer, Heidelberg (2013)

11. Kandias, M., Stavrou, V., Bozovic, N., Mitrou, L., Gritzalis, D.: Can we trust this user? Predicting insider's attitude via YouTube usage profiling. In: 10th International Conference on Autonomic and Trusted Computing, pp. 347–354. IEEE (2013)

12. Amichai-Hamburger, Y., Vinitzky, G.: Social network use and personality. In: Computers in Human Behavior, vol. 26, pp. 1289–1295 (2010)

13. Backes, M., Pfitzmann, B., Waidner, M.: Security in business process engineering. In: van der Aalst, W.M.P., ter Hofstede, A.H.M., Weske, M. (eds.) BPM 2003. LNCS, vol. 2678, pp. 168–183. Springer, Heidelberg (2003)

14. Jürjens, J.: Secure systems development with UML. Springer (2005)

15. Gaaloul, K., Proper, E., Charoy, F.: An Extended RBAC Model for Task Delegation in Workflow Systems. In: Niedrite, L., Strazdina, R., Wangler, B. (eds.) BIR Workshops 2011. LNBIP, vol. 106, pp. 51–63. Springer, Heidelberg (2012)

16. Brucker, A., Hang, I., Lückemeyer, G., Ruparel, R.: SecureBPMN: Modeling and enforcing access control requirements in business processes. In: 17th ACM Symposium on Access Control Models and Technologies, pp. 123–126. ACM (2012)

17. Ciancia, V., Martinelli, F., Matteuci, I., Petrocchi, M., Martin, J., Pimentel, E.: Automated synthesis and ranking of secure BPMN orchestrators. In: International Conference on Availability, Reliability and Security (2013)

18. Paja, E., Giorgini, P., Paul, S., Meland, P.H.: Security requirements engineering for secure business processes. In: Niedrite, L., Strazdina, R., Wangler, B. (eds.) BIR Workshops 2011. LNBIP, vol. 106, pp. 77–89. Springer, Heidelberg (2012)

19. Mouratidis, H., Jurjens, J.: From goal-driven security requirements engineering to secure design. International Journal of Intelligent Systems 25(8), 813–840 (2010)

20. Arsac, W., Compagna, L., Pellegrino, G., Ponta, S.E.: Security validation of business processes via model-checking. In: Erlingsson, Ú., Wieringa, R., Zannone, N. (eds.) ESSoS 2011. LNCS, vol. 6542, pp. 29–42. Springer, Heidelberg (2011)

21. Kandias, M., Mylonas, A., Virvilis, N., Theoharidou, M., Gritzalis, D.: An insider threat prediction model. In: Katsikas, S., Lopez, J., Soriano, M. (eds.) TrustBus 2010. LNCS, vol. 6264, pp. 26–37. Springer, Heidelberg (2010)
22. Shaw, E., Ruby, K., Post, J.: The insider threat to information systems: The psychology of the dangerous insider. Security Awareness Bulletin 2(98), 1–10 (1998)
23. Magklaras, G., Furnell, S., Papadaki, M.: LUARM: An audit engine for insider misuse detection. International Journal of Digital Crime and Forensics (IJDCF) 3(3), 37–49 (2011)
24. Mulle, J., Stackelberg, S., Bohm, K.: Modelling and transforming security constraints in privacy-aware business processes. In: IEEE International Conference on Service-Oriented Computing and Applications, pp. 1–4. IEEE (2011)
25. Kandias, M., Virvilis, N., Gritzalis, D.: The insider threat in Cloud computing. In: Bologna, S., Hämmerli, B., Gritzalis, D., Wolthusen, S. (eds.) CRITIS 2011. LNCS, vol. 6983, pp. 93–103. Springer, Heidelberg (2013)
26. Rodríguez, A., Fernández-Medina, E., Piattini, M.: A BPMN extension for the modeling of security requirements in business processes. IEICE Transactions on Information & Systems 90(4), 745–752 (2007)
27. Altuhhova, O., Matulevičius, R., Ahmed, N.: An extension of business process model and notation for security risk management
28. Mundie, D., Moore, A., McIntire, D.: Building a multidimensional pattern language for insider threats. In: 19th Pattern Languages of Programs Conference, vol. 12 (2012)
29. Kandias, M., Stavrou, V., Bosovic, N., Gritzalis, D.: Proactive insider threat detection through social media: The YouTube case. In: 12th ACM Workshop on Workshop on Privacy in the Electronic Society, pp. 261–266. ACM (2013)
30. Kandias, M., Mitrou, L., Stavrou, V., Gritzalis, D.: Which side are you on? A new Panopticon vs. Privacy. In: 10th International Conference on Security and Cryptography, pp. 98–110 (2013)
31. Federal Bureau of Investigation: The insider threat: An introduction to detecting and deterring an insider spy (2012), http://www.fbi.gov/about-us/investigate/counterintelligence/the-insider-threat
32. Steele, R.: Open source intelligence. In: Handbook of Intelligence Studies, p. 129 (2007)
33. Simitis, S.: Reconsidering the premises of labour law: Prolegomena to an EU regulation on the protection of employees' personal data. European Law Journal 5, 45–62 (1999)
34. Broughton, A., Higgins, T., Hicks, B., Cox, A.: Workplaces and Social Networking - The Implications for Employment Relations. Institute for Employment Studies, UK (2009)
35. Lasprogata, G., King, N., Pillay, S.: Regulation of electronic employee monitoring: Identifying fundamental principles of employee privacy through a comparative study of data privacy legislation in the EU, US and Canada. Stanford Technology Law Review 4 (2004)
36. Fazekas, C.: 1984 is Still Fiction: Electronic Monitoring in the Workplace and US Privacy Law. Duke Law & Technology Review, 15 (2004)
37. Kotzanikolaou, P., Theoharidou, M., Gritzalis, D.: Accessing n-order dependencies between critical infrastructures. International Journal of Critical Infrastructure Protection 9(1-2), 93–110 (2013)
38. Theoharidou, M., Kotzanikolaou, P., Gritzalis, D.: A multi-layer criticality assessment methodology based on interdependencies. Computers & Security 29(6), 643–658 (2010)
39. Theoharidou, M., Kotzanikolaou, P., Gritzalis, D.: Risk-based criticality analysis. In: Palmer, C., Shenoi, S. (eds.) Critical Infrastructure Protection III. IFIP AICT, vol. 311, pp. 35–49. Springer, Heidelberg (2009)

A Quantitative Analysis of Common Criteria Certification Practice

Samuel Paul Kaluvuri[1,2,3], Michele Bezzi[1], and Yves Roudier[2]

[1] SAP Labs France
[2] Eurecom Institute
[3] Eindhoven University of Technology

Abstract. The Common Criteria (CC) certification framework defines a widely recognized, multi-domain certification scheme that aims to provide security assurances about IT products to consumers. However, the CC scheme does not prescribe a monitoring scheme for the CC practice, raising concerns about the quality of the security assurance provided by the certification and questions on its usefulness. In this paper, we present a critical analysis of the CC practice that concretely exposes the limitations of current approaches. We also provide directions to improve the CC practice.

1 Introduction

With an increasing number of cyber attacks and security issues, governmental organizations and private companies are striving to get security assurance for Information Technology (IT) products. In many cases, these organizations may not have the required knowledge or resources to assess whether a certain product has the appropriate security features nor can they rely only on the statements of vendors. This is due to the trust deficit that exists between consumers and product vendors. One way to bridge this trust deficit is through the security certification of software. Security certification provides a practical solution to address the lack of security assurance when assessing and purchasing IT solutions. Certification Authorities (*CA*) perform rigorous security assessments that a particular software system has certain security features, conforms to specified requirements, and behaves as expected [7]. A customer buying a certified product can rely on the "stamp of approval" of the *CA*. Clearly, the value of a certification depends on the reputation of the certification authority issuing it, as well as the quality of assessment performed. Ideally, software purchasers can then choose among different certified products which address similar security requirements.

Common Criteria for Information Technology Security Evaluation (ISO / IEC 15408) (CC) [2] is the most popular security certification standard. It is a globally recognized set of guidelines that provides a common framework for the specification and the evaluation of security features and capabilities of IT products. At the heart of the CC scheme lies a "common" set of security functional and

C. Eckert et al. (Eds.): TrustBus 2014, LNCS 8647, pp. 132–143, 2014.
© Springer International Publishing Switzerland 2014

security assurance requirements. These common requirements enable potential consumers to compare and contrast the certified products based on their security functional and assurance requirements and to determine whether a product fits their needs. The CC scheme allows the evaluation of the products at varying levels of evaluation rigor, called *Evaluation Assurance Levels* (EAL), in a range of 1 to 7 (7 being the highest assurance level).

Despite the wide use and economic success of the Common Criteria scheme [16,9](mostly driven by government regulations and government procurement) its current practice has been receiving significant criticisms.

1. *Comparability.* One of the main objectives of CC is to allow consumers to compare certified products on the market in an objective way from a security point of view. However, certification documents are filled with legalese and technical jargon that restricts that scope of certification, while making it hard for consumers to understand these restrictions. As a result, comparison of products that have been certified under different requirements and restrictions becomes extremely complex.

2. *"Point in time"* certification. CC certifies a particular version of the product in certain configurations. Any change to the configuration or any updates to the product that affects the *Target of Evaluation (TOE)*, which is the part of the product that is evaluated, invalidates the certification. This is not desirable, given that products evolve and are updated at a frantic pace and the certification must not be "frozen" to a specific version of the product.

3. *Long and expensive.* CC evaluation life cycle is lengthy and expensive [14,18,17]. In fact, due to the complexity of the process and the high cost, vendors have to spend a large effort on preparation for the evaluation, which adds to the cost and time of the evaluation itself. High assurance level (as EAL4) certification can take $1 - 2$ years, and, often, by the time the process is completed a new version of product is already delivered.

4. *Concerns for Mutual Recognition.* Though the CC scheme is a widely recognized international standard, there are several concerns regarding the consistency of the assessments by the evaluating laboratories located in different countries, since the *Common Criteria Recognition Arrangement* (CCRA) does not prescribe any monitoring and auditing capability. In addition, the relevance of CC certification for governmental institutions, specific national interests can impact the impartiality of the assessment [10,5].

A lot of the criticisms of the CC practice are based on anecdotal evidence however, to the authors' knowledge there is no quantitative study of this practice has been produced so far.

The major contribution of this paper is filling this gap by providing an exhaustive analysis of CC certificates. By systematically analyzing the certificates (in Section 5), we can quantitatively assess the relevance of the points 1 and 2 above. We show how these issues are well grounded and affect a large part of existing certificates. We will also present possible directions (in Section 6) to enhance the current situation, considering current evolution of CC scheme and practice under discussion, and recent research results addressing security certification for web services. The points 3 and 4 are out of scope for the paper, because: an analysis on cost and duration of CC certifications has been discussed in [14,17] (addressing Point 3), and the mutual recognition issue (point 4) cannot be analyzed looking at certificates.

2   Common Criteria Certification Scheme

The CC scheme allows product vendors to describe the Security Functional Requirements (SFRs) for the product and to prove that the set of SFRs are able to counter the threats identified for a Target of Evaluation (TOE), which identifies the specific aspects of the product that will be evaluated. In addition, the CC scheme allows product vendors to choose particular configurations of the product that will be evaluated and these "golden" configurations are also part of the TOE. This information is captured in a document called "Security Target" (CC-ST) which can be seen as the *descriptive* part of the CC certification [3]. The product vendor then defines the set of Security Assurance Requirements (SARs) that specify actions to be performed by the evaluating laboratories that will determine the *Evaluation Assurance Level* of the certification.

The drawback of this approach is that the EAL can only specify how thoroughly the evaluation has been performed, but it does not answer the question of "Is the software secure?". The answer to this question can be provided by the SFRs that are implemented in the product. The CC scheme classifies the SFRs into 11 high level classes as shown here:

SFR Classes	
Security Audit (FAU)	Communication (FCO)
Cryptographic Support (FCS)	User Data Protection (FDP)
Identification and Authentication (FIA)	Protection of TOE Security Functionality (FPT)
Privacy (FPR)	Security Management (FMT)
Resource Utilization (FRU)	TOE Access (FTA)
Trusted Path/Channels (FTP)	

An example of an SFR in the *Security Audit* class and an SAR in the *Security Vulnerability* class can be seen below:

"***SFR: FAU_GEN.2.1*** *For audit events resulting from actions of identified users, the TSF shall be able to associate each auditable event with the identity of the user that caused the event.*"

"***SAR: AVA_VAN.1.3E*** *The evaluator shall conduct penetration testing, based on the identified potential vulnerabilities, to determine that the TOE is resistant to attacks performed by an attacker possessing Basic attack potential.*"

The CC scheme is generic and does not impose specific requirements for different types of IT products. Hence product vendors can implement certain specific security functionalities (SFRs) and get specific parts of their system evaluated in a certain way (SARs) and consequently certified, which may not address the requirements of consumers. To address this issue, CC allows consumers to use Protection Profiles (CC-PP) that contain a combination of SFRs and SARs for a particular type of application, such as Operating System or Databases. When products conform to a specific protection profile, it is easier for the consumer to select and compare the best fit for their needs. But conformance to CC-PP is not mandatory, and there is a criticism that product vendors exploit this flexibility of the CC scheme, and choose not to conform to any protection profiles that could be applied for their products [15,5].

3   Analysis Objectives

The fundamental aim of our analysis is to verify whether the *CC practice* fulfills the intentions of the *CC scheme*. The main goals of the CC scheme are: *a)* Enabling the comparison of the security characteristics among (certified) "similar" products; *b)* Providing meaningful and useful security assurance to the consumer.

   We defined the possible checks to assess whether these objectives are reached by the current CC practice (Checks are indicated in **bold** in the following). For comparing products of the same category, for example databases, from the security assurance point of view, we need to evaluate them against a common set of security requirements (SFRs). To support that, CC proposed the Protection Profiles, that allow for describing a predefined set of requirement for a class of products. Accordingly, to assess if this objective is reached in the actual practice, we need to check:

- **C1**: Are Protection Profiles available for the different categories ? (**Protection Profile Availability in each category**)
- **C2**: Are Protection Profiles actually used? (**Protection Profile conformance by products per category**)
- **C3**: Do similar products (same category) address the same set of SFRs? (**Differences in the number of SFRs for a given category**)
- **C4**: Does the usage of a specific Protection Profile results in a actual common set of SFRs? (**Differences in the number of SFRs for a given class in PP conforming products**)

   To provide meaningful assurance to the consumer, the certification issued should be valid along the product lifecycle. Considering the need to perform changes in the software (e.g., security patches to address new vulnerabilities) or its environment, CC scheme introduces the Common Criteria Maintenance Agreement (CCMA). Under this scheme, a specific version of the product can be initially certified and any changes made to it in future will be localized to the aspects that have been changed instead of the whole product being reevaluated. So, our next objectives are to evaluate:

- **C5**: Is the CCMA actually used in practice? (**How many products are maintained under the CCMA?**)
- **C6**: Are CCMA certified products secure? (**How many CCMA certified products have disclosed vulnerabilities?**)

4   Research Methodology

We use data from two main sources: the Common Criteria website [6], that provides details about certified products; and the National Vulnerability Database (*NVD*) [1], that contains the list of disclosed vulnerabilities in products. In particular we considered the following data sources: *a)* List of Certified Products [6] *b)* List of Protection Profiles [6]; *c)* Security Targets of certified products [6]; *d)* CC Part 2: Security Functional Requirements Document [2]; e) NVD database [1].

The data collected from these sources require additional processing, in order to perform advanced reasoning. This additional processing consisted in the following steps: *1)* The *certified products* and the *protection profile* CSV files were converted to SQL tables and stored into the database; *2)* The Security Target files (in PDF format) were downloaded for each certified product (URLs are contained in the CSV file of certified products) *3)* We stored the standardized SFRs contained in *CC: Part* 2 document into the database; *4)* We search the CC-STs for SFRs and stored these occurrences; *5)* We cross-reference certified products against the *NVD* for disclosed vulnerabilities. Except for steps *3* and *5*, the rest of the analysis is automated.

The certified product can be classified into three categories: *a)* Certified products; *b)* Certified products under *maintenance agreement*; *c)* Archived certified products. We considered only products with valid certificates (1971 certified products) and ignored the archived certificates for our analysis. Due to technical reasons, such as malformed URL or a digitally signed PDF document that could not be parsed into text, we could not process 95 certificates. Hence the data set that we considered in our analysis was 1532 security targets of certified products and 344 security targets of products under the maintenance agreement.

5   Analysis Results

Due to space constraints we present the most important results from our analysis. The results presented here are focused on products certified at EAL4+, since most products are certified at level (close to 40 % of the certified products).

5.1   Comparability of Certified Products

Products that conform to protection profiles are expected to have homogeneity both in terms of functionality and security features. Hence, we examined the availability of protection profiles compared with the number of certified products across various product categories and the results are shown in Figure 1. It can be noted that the availability of protection profiles is rather low across all categories of products except the *ICs and Smart Card* category.

Figure 2 presents the percentage of certified products that conform to at least one protection profile across various categories. The average PP conformance rate among certified products of our data set is 14 %, with standard deviation

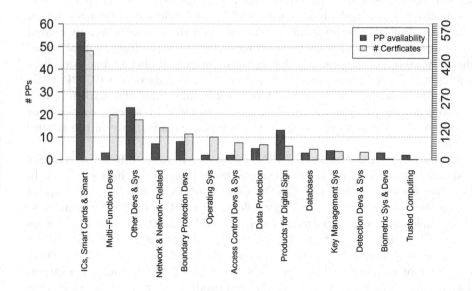

Fig. 1. Protection Profile Availability and Certified Products across categories

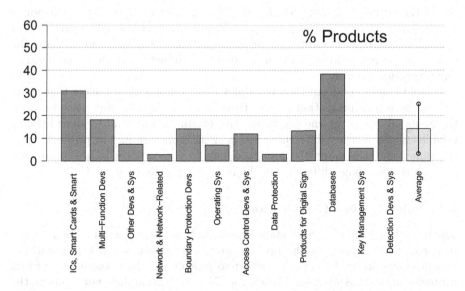

Fig. 2. Protection Profile Conformance among certified products (Right-most bar shows the average conformance to PP for our dataset, 14%, and corresponding standard deviation, 11%)Note that categories with less than 10 products are not shown

around 11 % (see Fig 2, rightmost column). This indicates that a relatively low number of certified product use CC-PPs with relevant differences among categories. Indeed, a closer inspection reveals that the products broadly related to *hardware or firmware* show higher conformance than products that fall under the software-only category. This low conformance could also be due to vendors finding it difficult to build products that conform to a particular CC-PP, while the products themselves are targeted for the general commercial market. Hence, to conform to a particular CC-PP, which is produced by specific consumer or a consumer group, does not provide any competitive advantage in the general market.

On the other hand, the low CC-PP conformance makes it difficult to compare and contrast the security requirements addressed by the certified products. In fact, the non-conformance to a CC-PP allows vendors to customize the scope of certification to features that are very different from other certified products. As an example, a product in a certain category could make claims that it addresses more SFRs related to data protection, while another certified product in the same category may have claims addressing SFRs related with access control. Furthermore, each certified product identifies different threats and makes various assumptions. Hence, comparison of certified products in such cases can become rather labour intensive and a very time consuming process.

Next, we compare products based on the number of *SFRs* that are addressed by each product in a certain category to understand the differences in certified products based on their security functionalities. Figure 3 and Figure 4 show the SFRs addressed in products for *Database* and *Operating System* categories certified at *EAL4* (and *EAL4+*) and conform to CC version *3.1*. Each shade of the bar in the figures 3 and 4 represents products that conform to a specific protection profile and the *white bars* represent products that *do not* conform to any protection profiles.

It can be observed from Figure 3 and 4 that even among products that claim conformance to a protection profile, there is a considerable difference between the SFRs addressed by the products. And products that tend to show little or no difference are either different versions of the same product or products from the same vendor. Among the products that do not conform to any protection profile there is a huge difference in the number of SFRs addressed.

5.2   Point in Time Certification

The CC scheme certifies products at a point in time, that is, certification applies to a particular version of the product and in a certain set of configurations. But products do need to evolve - either to provide new functionalities or to fix problems or both. And in such cases, the CC certification does not apply to the new version and the whole product has to undergo the certification all over again which is once again a very time consuming and expensive process, especially when the changes made to the product are very minor. In order to avoid such situations, the CC scheme allows products to be under the CC Maintenance Agreement (CCMA) where only the changes made to the product are evaluated

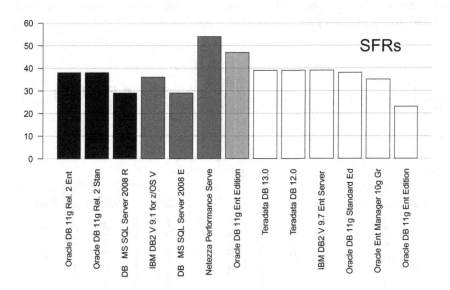

Fig. 3. SFR variation in Database Category for EAL4+ (Each shade of the bar represents products that claim conformance to a particular CC-PP, white bar implies non conformance to any CC-PP)

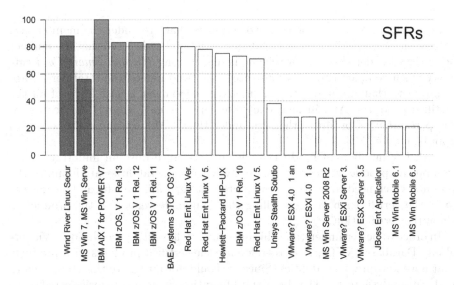

Fig. 4. SFR variation in OS category for EAL4+ (Each shade of the bar represents products that claim conformance to a particular CC-PP, white bar implies non conformance to any CC-PP)

and certified. This aspect of the CC scheme would allow the products to be certified over a *period of time* instead of a *point in time*.

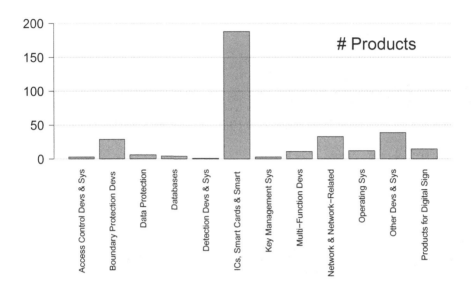

Fig. 5. Products under CCMA

From Figure 5, we see the certified products that are under the maintenance agreement across various product categories. It can be observed that the number of products under the CCMA scheme is high among *ICs and Smart Card* category when compared to the other categories. And indeed the total percentage of products that are under the maintenance agreement is just 22 % of all the certified products. And in fact, excluding the *ICs and Smart Cards* category, the percentage of products that are under the CCMA scheme comes down to approximately 15 %.

Such low numbers of products under maintenance raise an important question on the product's lifecycle, especially when vulnerabilities are found in the product which need to be fixed - can a product vendor issue a fix and technically *loose* the certification or keep selling the vulnerable version of the product to claim the certification?

In order to better understand this question, we have used the National Vulnerability Database (NVD), to cross-reference the certified products with products that have known vulnerabilities. Since we could not automate this step, we limited our analysis to the Database and Operating System categories certified at assurance level EAL4+. In the Operating System category, we found 22 % of the products under the maintenance agreement have disclosed vulnerabilities. And in the database category we found only 25 % products under the maintenance agreements are shown to have a known vulnerability. To contrast this, we cross reference products (in the database category at EAL4+) that are not under the maintenance agreement and 85 % of the products have shown to have a known vulnerability.

Though we do not claim that the vulnerability is in the certified "golden" configuration, these figures show that in practical usage of the products the issue of addressing new vulnerabilities must be discussed. And clearly, a point in time certification does not cope well with the dynamic landscape of a product's lifecycle.

6   Discussion and Conclusions

6.1   Findings about the CC Certification Practice

Comparability of Certificates. Our results illustrate some reasons behind the lack of comparability of certificates. In particular, the SFRs in the certificates with the same class of products often exhibit large differences. When products conform to a CC-PP, the variation between SFRs addressed by the products is rather low. However, many products do not conform to a CC-PP, particularly in software products. We believe that mandatory conformance to a *Standard Protection Profiles* in each product class could ease the comparison.

On a more fundamental level, we found out that without tool support it is not a trivial task to perform comparison between products based on their SFRs. In this regard, the CC-STs should be represented in a machine processable manner that facilitates automated reasoning to be performed on them.

One point in Time Certification. The low numbers of products under maintenance raise an important question on the product's lifecycle, especially when vulnerabilities are found in the product which need to be fixed - can a product vendor issue a fix and technically *loose* the certification or keep selling the vulnerable version of the product to claim the certification? It is rather obvious, that the product vendor will choose to fix issues and risk losing the certification.

Our results show that, despite the finding of new vulnerabilities, which are sometimes unknown at the time of initial certification, and the provisions made by the Common Criteria scheme to support incremental certification (CCMA), the certified products are overwhelmingly certified once and for all. While this is perfectly valid in itself, it shows that two certificates should be compared with respect to their time of issuance but also with the information from publicly available vulnerability databases (such as *NVD*).

6.2   Outlook

Contributions have been proposed in order to ease the comparability of the certificates produced by the Common Criteria evaluation process. Those approaches rely either on an extension of the CC certification scheme, or on tools to support a more homogeneous generation of certificates.

Common Criteria Framework Extensions. Countries that are members of the Common Criteria Recognition Agreement (CCRA) have recently agreed to develop internationally accepted Protection Profiles (known as Collaborative Protection Profiles - CPPs) for each class of products. Each product has to conform to the CPP that is applicable in its class, thus facilitating an easier comparison among certified products.

Computer Aided Certification. These approaches most notably aim at providing some guidance for evaluators in the production of certificates, and in making sure that their description is consistent. These approaches might be extended in order to provide the necessary support to implement the recommendations we suggest above, in particular that of rendering certificates machine readable, to comparable SFRs and TOEs.

Certification Toolboxes, such as the *CC Design Toolbox* created by Tore Nygaard [13], aim at supporting the production of CC certificates. They aim at supporting the uniform definition of protection profiles, and at certifying those profiles themselves. Other proposals have extended this approach with the use of security ontologies. Ekelhart et al. [8] and Chang et al. [4] proposed to use an ontology as the core tool to manipulate Common Criteria certificates. The main improvement of this approach over plain toolboxes is that the definition of an ontology makes the relationships between the different concepts apparent. However, the resulting security targets from these toolboxes, though structured, are still represented in a human readable form (such as PDF files).

Machine Processable Security Certificates. We believe that though a uniform production of security targets is necessary, automation support in the consumption of the certificates would improve the usefulness of the CC scheme as a whole. In [11], the authors propose a language that provides detailed, extensible and machine processable representation of the security certificates. In [12], the authors present a machine processable language to represent CC-PPs and a tool that automatically verifies the conformance of a certificate with its profile.

6.3   Conclusions

We have presented the results from a thorough analysis of the certificates of CC certified products to concretely understand the drawbacks of the CC practice. We presented evidences that highlight the variation of SFRs in products and prove that the EAL of the product should not be considered as the only metric to measure its security assurance. The limited number of certified products that conform to CC-PP makes the comparison even more harder. We believe that the conformance to a standard (or basic) CC-PP for each product category could help in allowing easier comparison between products. In addition, we also discovered that very few products are under the maintenance agreement which limits the usefulness of the CC certification, as new security patches (to counter any discovered vulnerabilities) and new versions of the product are released. Our results prove that machine processable CC-ST and CC-PP could provide significant advantages to perform a more thorough and accurate comparison of different certified products.

Acknowledgment. This work was partly supported by the EU-funded project ASSERT4SOA (grant no. 257361) and OPTET (grant no. 317631).

References

1. NIST National Vulnerability Database. National vulnerability database (2012)
2. T. C. C. R. Agreement. Common criteria for information technology security evaluation part 1: Introduction and general model revision 3 final foreword. NIST 49, 93 (2009)
3. Beckert, B., Bruns, D., Grebing, S.: Mind the gap: Formal verification and the common criteria (discussion paper)
4. Chang, S.-C., Fan, C.-F.: Construction of an ontology-based common criteria review tool. In: 2010 International Computer Symposium (ICS), pp. 907–912 (2010)
5. Cisco and Intel. Common criteria embrace, reform, extend. discussion draft 1.0. (2011)
6. Common Criteria. Common criteria portal (2012)
7. Damiani, E., Ardagna, C.A., Ioini, N.E.: Open Source Systems Security Certification, 1st edn. Springer (2008)
8. Ekelhart, A., Fenz, S., Goluch, G., Weippl, E.R.: Ontological mapping of common criteria's security assurance requirements. In: Venter, H., Eloff, M., Labuschagne, L., Eloff, J., von Solms, R. (eds.) New Approaches for Security, Privacy and Trust in Complex Environments. IFIP AICT, pp. 85–95. Springer, Heidelberg (2007)
9. Herrmann, D.S.: Using the Common Criteria for It Security Evaluation. CRC Press, Inc., Boca Raton (2002)
10. Kallberg, J.: Common criteria meets realpolitik - trust, alliances, and potential betrayal. IEEE Security Privacy PP(99), 1 (2012)
11. Kaluvuri, S.P., Koshutanski, H., Di Cerbo, F., Mana, A.: Security assurance of services through digital security certificates. In: 2013 IEEE 20th International Conference on Web Services (ICWS). IEEE (2013)
12. Kaluvuri, S.P., Koshutanski, H., Di Cerbo, F., Menicocci, R., Maña, A.: A digital security certificate framework for services. International Journal of Services Computing, p. 25
13. Nygaard, T.B.: Common criteria design toolbox. Master's thesis, Informatics and Mathematical Modelling, Technical University of Denmark, DTU, Richard Petersens Plads, Building 321, DK-2800 Kgs. Lyngby, Supervised by Professor Robin Sharp and Assoc. Professor Michael R. Hansen, IMM, DTU (2007)
14. U. S. G. A. Office. Information assurance: National partnership offers benefits, but faces considerable challenges. Technical Report GAO 06-392, Report (March 2006)
15. Shapiro, J.: Understanding the windows eal4 evaluation. Computer 36(2), 103–105 (2003)
16. Smith, R.E.: Trends in security product evaluations. Inf. Sys. Sec. 16(4), 203–216 (2007)
17. Yajima, H., Murata, M., Kai, N., Yamasato, T.: Consideration of present status and approach for the widespread of cc certification to a private field cases in japan
18. Zhou, C., Ramacciotti, S.: Common criteria: Its limitations and advice on improvement. Information Systems Security Association ISSA Journal, 24–28 (2011)

A Normal-Distribution Based Reputation Model

Ahmad Abdel-Hafez[1], Yue Xu[1], and Audun Jøsang[2]

[1] Queensland University of Technology, Brisbane, Australia
{a.abdelhafez,yue.xu}@qut.edu.au
[2] University of Oslo, Oslo, Norway
josang@mn.uio.no

Abstract. Rating systems are used by many websites, which allow customers to rate available items according to their own experience. Subsequently, reputation models are used to aggregate available ratings in order to generate reputation scores for items. A problem with current reputation models is that they provide solutions to enhance accuracy of sparse datasets not thinking of their models performance over dense datasets. In this paper, we propose a novel reputation model to generate more accurate reputation scores for items using any dataset; whether it is dense or sparse. Our proposed model is described as a weighted average method, where the weights are generated using the normal distribution. Experiments show promising results for the proposed model over state-of-the-art ones on sparse and dense datasets.

Keywords: Reputation Model, Ratings Aggregation, Uncertainty.

1 Introduction

People are increasingly dependent on information online in order to decide whether to trust a specific object or not. Therefore, reputation systems are an essential part of any e-commerce or product reviews websites, where they provide methods for collecting and aggregating users' ratings in order to calculate the overall reputation scores for products, users, or services [1]. The existence of reputation scores in these websites helps people in making decisions about whether to buy a product, or to use a service, etc. Reputation systems play a significant role in users' decision making process.

Many of the existing reputation models did not mention how good they are with different sparsity datasets, Lauw et.al [2] mentioned that the simple average method would be adequate with dense dataset supported by the law of large numbers [3]. Other models focused on robustness of the reputation score, i.e., the value is not easy to be affected by malicious reviews [4]. In general, the majority of the recently proposed reputation systems involved other factors, besides the ratings, such as the time when the rating was given or the reputation of the user who gave that rating. Usually, this data is incorporated with ratings as weights during the aggregation process, performing the weighted average method. These factors can be easily combined into our proposed methods.

C. Eckert et al. (Eds.): TrustBus 2014, LNCS 8647, pp. 144–155, 2014.
© Springer International Publishing Switzerland 2014

One of the challenges that face any reputation model is its ability to work with different datasets, sparse or dense ones. Within any dataset some items may have rich rating data, while others, especially new ones, have low number of ratings. Sparse datasets are the ones that contain higher percentage of items which do not have many ratings or users who didn't rate many items. However, with the increased popularity of rating systems on the web particularly, sparse datasets become denser by time as ratings build up on the dataset. Most of the current reputation models did not mentioned if they work well with dense or sparse datasets or both, others focused on sparse dataset only assuming they are the ones require attention only [2].

On the other hand, most of the existing reputation models don't consider the distribution of ratings for an item, which should influence its reputation. In this paper, we propose to consider the frequency of ratings in the rating aggregation process in order to generate reputation scores. The purpose is to enhance accuracy of reputation scores using any dataset no matter whether it is dense or sparse. The proposed methods are weighted average methods, where the weights are assumed to reflect the distribution of ratings in the overall score. An important contribution of this paper is a method to generate the weights based on the normal distribution of the ratings. We evaluate the accuracy of our results using ratings prediction system, and we compare with state-of-the-art methods. Our methods show promising results dealing with any dataset no matter whether it is dense or sparse.

In the rest of this paper, we will first introduce existing product reputation models briefly in Section 2, and then we will explain the proposed methods in Sections 3. We will also provide detailed experiments and results evaluation in Section 4 in order to prove the significance of our proposed method. Finally in Section 5 we conclude the paper.

2   Related Works

Reputation systems are used with many objects, such as webpages, products, services, users, and also in peer-to-peer networks, where they reflect what is generally said or believed about the target object [5]. Item's reputation is calculated based on ratings given by many users using a specific aggregation method. Many methods used weighted average as an aggregator for the ratings, where the weight can represent user's reputation, time when the rating was given, or the distance between the current reputation score and the received rating. Shapiro [6] proved that time is important in calculating reputation scores; hence, the time decay factor has been widely used in reputation systems [6,7,8,9]. For example, Leberknight et al. [9] discussed the volatility of online ratings, where the authors aimed to reflect the current trend of users' ratings. They used weighted average where old ratings have less weight than current ones. On the other hand, Riggs and Wilensky [10] performed collaborative quality filtering, based on the principle of finding the most reliable users. One of the baseline methods we use in this paper is proposed by Lauw et al., which is called the Leniency-Aware

Quality (LQ) Model [2]. This model is a weighted average model that uses users' ratings tendency as weights. The authors classified users into lenient or strict users based on the leniency value which is used as a weight for the user's ratings.

Another baseline model that we use was introduced by Jøsang and Haller, which is a multinomial Bayesian probability distribution reputation system based on Dirichlet probability distribution [8]. This model is probably the most relevant method to our proposed method because this method also takes into consideration the count of ratings. The model introduced in [8] is a generalization to their previously introduced binomial Beta reputation system [11]. The authors indicated that Bayesian reputation systems provide a statistically sound basis for computing reputation scores. This model provides more accurate reputation values when the number of ratings per item is small because the uncertainty in these cases is high. Using fuzzy models are also popular in calculating reputation scores because fuzzy logic provides rules for reasoning with fuzzy measures, such as trustworthy, which are usually used to describe reputation. Sabater & Sierra proposed REGRET reputation system [12] , which defines a reputation measure that takes into account the individual dimension, the social dimension and the ontological dimension. Bharadwaj and Al-Shamri [13] proposed a fuzzy computational model for trust and reputation. According to them, the reputation of a user is defined as the accuracy of his prediction to other user's ratings towards different items. Authors also introduced reliability metric, which represent how reliable is the computed score.

In general, some of the proposed reputation systems compute reputation scores based on the reputation of the user or reviewer, or they normalize the ratings by the behavior of the reviewer. Other works suggested adding volatility features to ratings. According to our knowledge, most of the currently used aggregating methods in the reputation systems do not reflect the distribution of ratings towards an object. Besides, there are no general methods that are robust with any dataset and always generate accurate results no matter whether the dataset is dense or sparse, for example, LQ model [2] is good with sparse datasets only and Jøsang and Haller model [8] generates more accurate reputation scores for items with low frequent ratings.

3   Normal Distribution Based Reputation Model (NDR)

In this section we will introduce a new aggregation method to generate product reputation scores. Before we start explaining the method in details, we want to present some definitions. First of all, in this paper we use arithmetic mean method as the Naïve method. Secondly, the term "rating levels" is used to represent the number of possible rating values that can be assigned to a specific item by a user. For example, considering the well-known five stars rating system with possible rating values of $\{1, 2, 3, 4, 5\}$, we say that we have five rating levels; one for each possible rating value.

As mentioned previously, the weighted average is the most currently used method for ratings aggregation, while the weights usually represent the time when the rating was given, or the reviewer reputation. In the simplest case, where we don't consider other factors such as time and user credibility, the weight for each rating is $\frac{1}{n}$, if there are n ratings to an item. No matter for the simplest average method or the weighted average methods that take time or other user related factors into consideration, the frequency of each rating level is not explicitly considered. For example, assume that an item receives a set of ratings $< 2, 2, 2, 2, 3, 5, 5 >$, for the simplest average method, the weight for each of the ratings is $\frac{1}{7}$ even the rating level 2 has higher frequency than the other two rating levels. For other weighted average methods, the weights are only related to time or some user related factors but not rating frequency.

In the following discussion, we will use the Naïve method as an example to explain the strength of our proposed method since the other factors can be easily combined into our methods to make the weights related to other factors such as time or user credibility.

Our initial intuition is that rating weights should relate to the frequency of rating levels, because the frequency represents the popularity of users' opinions towards an item. Another important fact that we would like to take into consideration in deriving the rating weights is the distribution of ratings. Not losing generality, like many "natural" phenomena, we can assume that the ratings fall in normal distribution. Usually the middle rating levels such as 3 in a rating scale $[1 - 5]$ system is the most frequent rating level (we call these rating levels "Popular Rating Levels") and 1 and 5 are the least frequent levels (we call these levels "Rare Rating Levels"). By taking both the rating frequency and the normal distribution into consideration, we propose to 'award' higher frequent rating levels, especially popular rating levels, and 'punish' lower frequent rating levels, especially rare rating levels.

Table 1. Comparing weights of each rating level between Naïve and NDR methods

Ratings	Rating Weight		Rating Weight	
	Naïve	NDR	Naïve	NDR
2	0.1429	0.0765		
2	0.1429	0.1334	0.5714	0.604
2	0.1429	0.1861		
2	0.1429	0.208		
3	0.1429	0.1861	0.1429	0.1861
5	0.1429	0.1334	0.2857	0.2099
5	0.1429	0.0765		

Table 1 shows the difference between the Naïve method and the proposed Normal Distribution based Reputation Model (NDR) which will be discussed in Section 3.1. From the second column in Table 1 (i.e., Weight per rating), we can notice that using the Naïve method the weight for each rating is fixed which is $\frac{1}{7} = 0.1429$. Different from the Naïve method, the NDR method generates different weights for different ratings, especially, the weights from rare ratings such as 2 and 5 to popular ratings such as 3 are increase and the increment is non-linear. This non-linear increase in weights for repeated ratings of the same level will result in a higher aggregated weight for that rating level. For example, rating level 2 is the most frequent level, in comparison, the aggregated weight generated by the Naïve method for rating level 2 is 0.5714, where the NDR model generates a higher value 0.604 which reflects the contribution from the frequency of rating level 2. On the other hand, rating level 3 gets a higher weight 0.186 in the NDR method than the Naïve method which generates a weight value 0.1429, however, this is not because level 3 is more frequent, but because it is a popular rating level. In contrast, rating Level 5 gets a lower weight in the NDR method because it is a rare rating level and not very frequent in this example.

3.1   Weighting Based on a Normal Distribution

Our method can be described as weighted average where the weights are generated based on both rating distribution and rating frequency. As mentioned above, we use a normal distribution because it represents many "natural" phenomena. In our case, it will provide different weights for ratings, where the more frequent the rating level is, the higher the weight the level will get. In other words, using this weighting method we can assign higher weights to the highly repeated ratings, which we believe will reflect more accurate reputation tendency.

Suppose that we have n ratings for a specific product P, represented as a vector $R_P = \{r_0, r_1, r_2, \ldots, r_{n-1}\}$ where r_0 is the smallest rating and r_{n-1} is the largest rating, i.e., $r_0 \leq r_1 \leq r_2 \leq \ldots \leq r_{n-1}$. In order to aggregate the ratings, we need to compute the associated weights with each rating, which is also represented as a vector $W_P = \{w_0, w_1, w_2, \ldots, w_{n-1}\}$. As we discussed previously, the weights to the ratings will be calculated using the normal distribution density function given in Equation 1, where a_i is the weight for the rating at index $i, i = 0, \ldots, n - 1$, μ is the mean, σ is the standard deviation, and x_i is supposed to be the value at index i; the basic idea is to evenly deploy the values between 1 and k for the rating scale $[1, k]$ over the indexes from 0 to $n - 1$. k is the number of levels in the rating system, in this paper we use the popular 5-star system, then $k = 5$.

$$a_i = \frac{1}{\sigma \sqrt{2\pi}} e^{-\frac{(x_i - \mu)^2}{2\sigma^2}} \tag{1}$$

$$x_i = \frac{(k - 1) \times i}{n - 1} + 1 \tag{2}$$

Equation 2 is used to evenly deploy the values of x_i between 1 and k, where $x_0 = 1$ and $x_{n-1} = k$. In Equation 1, the value of the mean is fixed, i.e., $\mu = \frac{(k+1)}{2}$. However, the value of σ is the actual standard deviation value extracted from the ratings to this item; hence, each item in the dataset will have different flatness for its normal distribution curve.

The purpose of using such these values for x, μ and σ is to produce normally distributed weights associated with the k-levels rating system. The generated weights in Equation 1 is then normalized so the summation of all weights is equal to 1, hence, we create the normalized weights vector $W_P = \{w_0, w_1, w_2, \ldots, w_{n-1}\}$ using Equation 3.

$$w_i = \frac{a_i}{\sum_{j=0}^{n-1} a_j}, \text{ where } \sum_{i=0}^{n-1} w_i = 1 \tag{3}$$

In order to calculate the final reputation score, which is affected by the ratings and the weights, we need to sum the weights of each level separately. To this end, we partition all ratings into groups based on levels, $R^l = \{r_0^l, r_1^l, r_2^l, \ldots, r_{|R^l|-1}^l\}$, $l = 1, 2, \ldots, k$, for each rating $r \in R^l$, $r = l$. The set of all ratings to item p is $R_P = \bigcup_{l=1}^{k} R^l$. The corresponding weights for the ratings in R^l are represented as $W^l = \{w_0^l, w_1^l, w_2^l, \ldots, w_{|R^l|-1}^l\}$

The final reputation score is calculated as weighted average for each rating level using Equation 4, where LW^l is called level weight which is calculated in Equation 5

$$NDR_p = \sum_{l=1}^{k} \left(l \times LW^l \right) \tag{4}$$

$$LW^l = \sum_{j=0}^{|R^l|-1} w_j^l \tag{5}$$

Equation 5 calculates level weights LW^l as a summation of the weights of every rating belonging to that level.

Fig. 1 shows the weights generated for the above example by the Naïve method and the proposed NDR method, where left-most region represents the overall weight for rating level 2, and the middle region and the right-most region are for rating levels 3 and 5. We can see that, the weights for all ratings are the same in Fig. 1a, which uses the Naïve method, while using the NDR method in Fig. 1b, the ratings with index near to the middle will be given higher weights.

3.2   Enhanced NDR Model by Adding Uncertainty (NDRU)

In this section we will do a modification to our proposed NDR method by combining uncertainty principle, introduced by Jøsang and Haller Dirichlet method [8]. This enhancement is important to deal with sparse dataset, because when the number of ratings is small, the uncertainty is high. The enhanced method is expected to pick up the advantages of both reputation models, i.e., the NDR method and the Dirichlet method. Inspired by the Dirichlet method in [8], the NDRU reputation score is calculated using Equation 6 which takes uncertainty into consideration:

$$NDRU_{p1} = \sum_{l=1}^{k} \left(l \times \left(\frac{n \times LW^l + C \times b}{C + n} \right) \right) \tag{6}$$

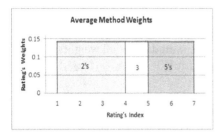

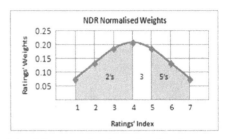

(a) Average method weights for the 7 ratings example.

(b) NDR normalised weights for the 7 ratings example.

Fig. 1. Weights generated using Naïve and NDR methods

C is a priori constant which is set to 2 in our experiments, and $b = \frac{1}{k}$ is a base rate for any of the k rating values.

The NDRU method will reduce the effect of praising popular rating levels and depreciating rare rating levels process done by the NDR model. We can say that in all cases if the NDR method provides higher reputation scores than the Naïve method, then the NDRU method will also provide higher reputation scores but marginally less than the NDR ones and vice versa. However, as we have mentioned before, in the case of having a small number of ratings per item, the uncertainty will be higher because the base rate b is divided by the number of ratings plus a priori constant $n + C$ in Equation 6. In this case, the difference between the final reputation scores of the NDR and NDRU methods is noticeable. This advantage of the Dirichlet method to deal with sparse data is adopted by the NDRU method. Yet, when we use dense dataset, the difference between the final reputation scores of the NDR and NDRU methods will be very small, which allow the NDRU to behave similarly to the NDR method.

4   Experiment

In the beginning we want to say that there are no globally acknowledged evaluation methods that appraise the accuracy of reputation models. However, we choose to assess the proposed model in regards to the accuracy of the generated reputation scores, and how the items are ranked. Hence, we conducted two experiments in this research. The first experiment is to predict an item rating using the item reputation score generated by reputation models. The hypothesis is that the more accurate the reputation model the closer the scores it generates to actual users' ratings. For one item, we will use the same reputation score to predict the item's rating for different users. The second experiment is to prove that the proposed method produces different results than the Naïve method in terms of the final ranked list of items based on the item reputations. If the order of the items in the two ranked lists generated by the Naïve and NDR methods is not the same, we say that our method is significant.

4.1   Datasets

The dataset used in this experiment is the MovieLens dataset obtained from www.grouplens.org, which is publicly available and widely used in the area of recommender systems. The dataset contains about one million anonymous ratings of approximately 3,706 movies. In this dataset each user has evaluated at least 20 movies, and each movie is evaluated by at least 1 user. In our experiment we split the dataset into training and testing datasets with 80% of the users used to build the training dataset and the rest are used for testing.

Three new datasets were extracted from the original dataset in order to test the different reputation models for different levels of sparsity. The sparsest dataset created has only 4 ratings per movie randomly selected from users' ratings to this movie. For the second and the third datasets, each movie has 6 and 8 randomly selected ratings, respectively. Table 2 summarize the statistics of the used datasets.

Table 2. Used datasets statistics

Dataset	Users	Ratings
Only 4 ratings per movie (**4RPM**)	1361	14261
Only 6 ratings per movie (**6RPM**)	1760	21054
Only 8 ratings per movie (**8RPM**)	2098	27723
Complete Data Set All ratings (**ARPM**)	6040	999868

4.2   Evaluation Metrics

In the experiments conducted in this research, we select two well-known metrics to evaluate the proposed methods.

Mean Absolute Error (MAE). The mean absolute error (MAE) is a statistical accuracy metric used to measure the accuracy of rating prediction. This metric measures the accuracy by comparing the reputation scores with the actual movie ratings. Equation 7 shows how to calculate the MAE.

$$MAE = \frac{\sum_{i=1}^{n} |p_i - r_i|}{n} \tag{7}$$

p_i is the predicted value (i.e., a reputation score) for a movie i, r_i is the actual rating given by a user for the movie i, and n is the number of ratings in the testing dataset. The lower the MAE, the more accurately the reputation model generates scores.

Kendall Tau Coefficient. Kendall tau coefficient is a statistic used to measure the association between two ranked lists. In other words, it evaluates the similarity of the orderings of the two lists. Equation 8 shows how to calculate Kendall Tau coefficient, where it divides the difference between concordant and discordant pairs in the two lists by the total number of pairs $\frac{n(n-1)}{2}$. The coefficient must be in the range of $-1 \leq \tau \leq 1$, where the value of $\tau = -1$ indicates complete disagreement between two lists, and the value of $\tau = 1$ indicates complete agreement. In addition, the value of $\tau = 0$ identify that the two lists are independent.

$$\tau = \frac{n_c - n_d}{\frac{1}{2}n(n-1)} \tag{8}$$

$$n_d = |\{(i,j)|A(i) < A(j), NDR(i) > NDR(j)\}|$$
$$n_c = |\{(i,j)|A(i) < A(j), NDR(i) < NDR(j)\}|$$

n_d is the number of discordant pairs between the two lists, while n_c is the number of concordant ones, $NDR(i)$ is the reputation score for the movie i generated using the NDR method, while $A(i)$ is the reputation score generated using the Naïve method, n is the number of items and i and j are items. The aim of using the Kendall tau coefficient method is to compute the ordering difference between the two ranked item lists generated based on the reputations computed using two different reputation models. The higher the value of τ, the more similar the two ranked lists.

4.3   Ratings Prediction

In this experiment we use the training dataset to calculate a reputation score for every movie. Secondly we will use these reputation scores as rating prediction values for all the movies in the testing dataset and will compare these reputation values with users' actual ratings in the testing dataset. The theory is that a reputation value to an item that is closer to the users' actual ratings to the item is considered more accurate. The Baseline methods we will compare with include the Naïve method, Dirichlet reputation system proposed by Jøsang and Haller [8], and the Leniency-aware Quality (LQ) model proposed by Lauw et al. [2].

The experiment is done as a five-fold cross validation, where every time a different 20% of the dataset is used for testing. This method ensures that each user's data has been used five times; four times in training and one time in testing. We record the MAE in each round for all the implemented methods, and at the end we calculate the average of the five MAE values recorded for each reputation model. We have tested the ratings prediction accuracy using the four previously described datasets and the results are shown in Table 3. The four datasets we use include three sparse datasets (i.e., 4RPM, 6RPM, and 8RPM) and one dense dataset (i.e., ARPM). The three sparse datasets reflect different levels of sparsity. In Table 3, the MAE results using the sparsest dataset 4RPM shows that the best prediction accuracy was produced by the Dirichlet method. The reason is because the Dirichlet method is the best method among

Table 3. MAE results for the 5 fold rating prediction experiment

Dataset	Naïve	LQ	Dirichlet	NDR	NDRU
4RPM	0.5560	0.5576	**0.5286**	0.5614	0.5326
6RPM	0.5610	0.5628	0.5514	0.5608	**0.5498**
8RPM	0.5726	0.5736	0.5705	0.5693	**0.5676**
ARPM	0.7924	0.7928	0.7928	**0.7851**	0.7853

the tested 5 methods to deal with the uncertainty problem which is especially severe for sparse datasets. The proposed enhanced method NDRU achieved the second best result which is close enough to the Dirichlet method result with a small difference, indicating that NDRU is also good at dealing with uncertainty. However, when we use less sparse datasets 6RPM and 8RPM, the proposed NDRU method achieved the best results.

The last row in Table 3 shows the results of ratings prediction accuracy using the whole MovieLens dataset (ARPM) which is considered a dense dataset. We can see that the proposed method NDR has the best accuracy. Moreover, our enhanced method NDRU achieved the second best result with an extremely small difference of 0.0002. In contrast, the other baseline methods do not provide any enhancement in accuracy over the Naïve method on the dense dataset.

From the results above, we can see that the NDR method produces the best results when we use it with dense datasets, and that the Dirichlet method is the best with sparse datasets. Most importantly, the NDRU method, provides good results in any case, and can be used as a general reputation model regardless of the sparsity in datasets.

4.4   Comparisons of Item's Ranking

In this experiment, we will compare two lists of items ranked based on their reputation scores generated using the NDR method and the Naïve method. The purpose of this comparison is to show that our method provides relatively different ranking for items from the Naïve method.

The experiment is conducted in 20 rounds, with different percentage of data used every time. In the first round we used a sub-list with only the top 1% of the ranked items in one list to compare with the 1% items in the other list. The number of comparisons is equal to $\frac{n(n-1)}{2}$, n is the number of items in the top 1% of each list. For The other 19 rounds we used the top $5\%, 10\%, 15\%, \ldots, 100\%$, respectively. The reason for choosing different percentages of top items is to see the difference between different percentages of top items. Usually the top items are more influential or crucial to users.

From Fig. 2 we can find that, for all datasets, the more the items taken from the lists, the more similar the order of the items in the lists generated by the two methods. However, usually users are more interested in the top items. Therefore, the order of the top items in the lists is more crucial. If we only look at the top 20% items, we can find that the behaviour of using the whole dataset ARPM (which is much denser than the other three datasets) is different from using other three sparse datasets. For the dense dataset, the similarity reaches its minimal when we only compare the top 1% items and the similarity increases when we compare larger portions of the dataset. This result indicates that for the dense dataset, the proposed method NDR ranks the top items in the item list differently from the item list generated by the Naïve method. On the other

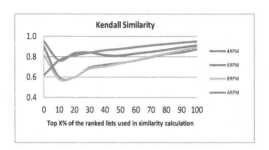

Fig. 2. Kendall similarities between (NDR) method and Naïve method using four different datasets

hand, with the sparse datasets, the ranking on the top 1% of the items shows high similarity between the two lists, which indicates that the top 1

5   Conclusions and Future Work

In this work we have proposed a new aggregation method for generating reputation scores for items or products based on customers' ratings, where the weights are generated using a normal distribution. The method is also enhanced with adding uncertainty part by adopting the idea of the work proposed by Jøsang and Haller [8]. The results of our experiments show that our proposed method outperforms the state-of-the-art methods in ratings prediction over a well-known dataset. Besides, it provides relatively different ranking for items in the ranked list based on the reputation scores. Moreover, our enhanced method proved to generate accurate results with sparse and dense datasets. In future, we plan to use this method in different applications such as recommender systems. Besides, this method can be combined with other weighted average reputation models that use time or user reputation in order to improve the accuracy of their results.

References

1. Resnick, P., Kuwabara, K., Zeckhauser, R., Friedman, E.: Reputation Systems. Communications of the ACM 43(12), 45–48 (2000)
2. Lauw, H.W., Lim, E.P., Wang, K.: Quality and Leniency in Online Collaborative Rating Systems. ACM Transactions on the Web (TWEB) 6(1), 4 (2012)

3. Grimmett, G., Stirzaker, D.: Probability and random processes. Oxford University Press (2001)
4. Garcin, F., Faltings, B., Jurca, R.: Aggregating Reputation Feedback. In: Proceedings of the First International Conference on Reputation: Theory and Technology, pp. 62–74 (2009)
5. Jøsang, A., Ismail, R., Boyd, C.: A Survey of Trust and Reputation Systems for Online Service Provision. Decision Support Systems 43(2), 618–644 (2007)
6. Shapiro, C.: Consumer Information, Product Quality, and Seller Reputation. The Bell Journal of Economics 13(1), 20–35 (1982)
7. Ayday, E., Lee, H., Fekri, F.: An Iterative Algorithm For Trust and Reputation Management. In: Proceedings of the International Symposium on Information Theory, pp. 2051–2055. IEEE (2009)
8. Jøsang, A., Haller, J.: Dirichlet Reputation Systems. In: Proceedings of the Second International Conference on Availability, Reliability and Security, pp. 112–119. IEEE (2007)
9. Leberknight, C.S., Sen, S., Chiang, M.: On the Volatility of Online Ratings: An Empirical Study. In: Shaw, M.J., Zhang, D., Yue, W.T. (eds.) WEB 2011. LNBIP, vol. 108, pp. 77–86. Springer, Heidelberg (2012)
10. Riggs, T., Wilensky, R.: An Algorithm for Automated Rating of Reviewers. In: Proceedings of the First ACM/IEEE-CS Joint Conference on Digital Libraries, pp. 381–387. ACM (2001)
11. Jøsang, A., Ismail, R.: The Beta Reputation System. In: Proceedings of the 15th Bled Electronic Commerce Conference, pp. 41–55 (2002)
12. Sabater, J., Sierra, C.: Reputation and Social Network Analysis in Multi-Agent Systems. In: Proceedings of the First International Joint Conference on Autonomous Agents and Multiagent Systems, pp. 475–482 (2002)
13. Bharadwaj, K.K., Al-Shamri, M.Y.H.: Fuzzy Computational Models for Trust And Reputation Systems. Electronic Commerce Research and Applications 8(1), 37–47 (2009)

Differences between Android and iPhone Users in Their Security and Privacy Awareness

Lena Reinfelder[1], Zinaida Benenson[1], and Freya Gassmann[2]

[1] University of Erlangen-Nuremberg
Martensstr. 3, 91058 Erlangen, Germany
[2] Saarland University
Saarbruecken, Germany

Abstract. This work compares Android and iPhone users according to their security and privacy awareness when handling apps. Based on an online survey conducted with over 700 German respondents (mostly university students) we found out that Android users seem to be more aware of the risks associated with the app usage than iPhone users. For example, iPhone users almost never consider the possibility of apps sending premium-rate SMS or causing other hidden costs. Furthermore, Android users more often mention security, trust and privacy issues as important factors when they decide to use a new app. We hypothesize that the cause of these differences they are likely to arise through differences in app market policies, in app review processes and in presentation of data usage by the apps.

Keywords: Smartphone, iOS, Android, security awareness, privacy awareness.

1 Introduction

Android and iOS are the world's most popular smartphone operating systems [17], whereas their underlying system architectures and business models differ considerably [1,4,28] (see Section 2 for more details).

It is widely believed that the corresponding user communities differ from each other. We could compile a list of differences from personal communication and different press sources [6,1]. A typical Android user is assumed to be male and technically savvy, while having an iPhone is more often attributed to women[1]. Moreover, iPhone users are said to be very loyal to Apple, they buy more apps and are more actively engaged with their devices than Android users.

In this work we assume that the differences of iOS and Android system architecture and apps handling are connected to the differences in perception and behavior of the users with respect to security and privacy. Thus, our main research question is formulated as follows:

---

[1] For example, according to a 2010 AdMob survey 73 % of Android users versus 57 % of iPhone users were male [6].

C. Eckert et al. (Eds.): TrustBus 2014, LNCS 8647, pp. 156–167, 2014.
© Springer International Publishing Switzerland 2014

Are there differences in attitudes and behavior between Android and iOS users concerning security and privacy when using apps?

Contribution. In this paper we compare Android and iOS users according to their security and privacy awareness, discuss our findings and give directions for future research. To our knowledge, this is the first direct comparison of this kind. We think that the knowledge about these differences can help in design of future security- and privacy-related features of smartphones and of app stores.

Roadmap. The paper is organized as follows: Section 2 provides background information on the differences between iOS and Android. In Section 3, we present related work on security and privacy awareness of Android and iOS users. Section 4 introduces our research methodology and Section 5 presents the results. We discuss limitations of this work in Section 6. Finally, we conclude with a discussion of ongoing and future work in Section 7.

2 Background: Android versus iOS

We focus on differences between Android and iOS that are visible to general public and non-expert users, and we do not discuss technical details of both operating systems here, as the latter are less important for our research question.

2.1 Platforms and App Markets

Apple's iOS (software) is tightly integrated with the iPhone (hardware). Moreover, Apple maintains strict control over app development and distribution. iOS apps can only be developed by subscribers to the iOS Developer Program, and can only be distributed through the official App Store.[2]

Google's Android runs on different hardware platforms. Anyone can develop and distribute Android apps, and although there is the official Google Play store, the apps can also be distributed from any other place.

App developers for either platform can earn money by integrating advertisement networks into their apps [15].

2.2 App Security

Android malware is quite numerous, as anyone can develop and distribute Android apps [26][27]. Although scanning the apps from Google Play for malicious functionality started in 2012, this was found to be not quite effectual [22]. Furthermore, Google introduced the security setting "Verify Apps" to the Google Play Store, which monitors apps at the installation process for malware [9]. This setting is going to be extended to monitor also apps during run time and to check apps that are downloaded from third-party app stores [24]. Still, this security setting can be turned off by the user. Moreover, for the usage of the functionality "Verify Apps" one has to agree to give Google a lot of information, such as

---

[2] As an exception, organizations that participate in the *iOS Developer Enterprise Program* can develop and distribute in-house apps solely to their employees.

log files, URLs related to the app and also information about one's smartphone (device ID, version of the operating system, IP address) [9].

In contrast, iOS malware is rare [7], because all apps in the App Store undergo a review process in order to ensure that the apps work according to their description. This also means that the apps should not have malicious functionality. However, Wand et al. could present a method how to get malicious apps into Apple's App store [29].

2.3   Handling of Personal Data by the Apps

Android permissions are passive warnings that are automatically generated, if the app accesses or manipulates certain data, such as contacts, messages and system settings. The warnings are presented to the users during the installation process, and they have to agree with all permission requests in order to install the app. Thus, the users only have the "all-or-nothing" choice.

iOS prior to iOS 6 required runtime consent from the users if an app wanted to use location data for the first time. Many other types of user data could be read and manipulated without user's explicit consent [25,5]. iOS 6 (released in September 2012) radically changed the handling of personal data. Now users have to give runtime consent for many more data types, such as contacts, calendar, photos, Twitter or Facebook accounts. Users can also customize their data disclosure policies.

There is evidence that the potential visibility of Android permissions may lead to a more restrictive use of personal data by the app developers [10]. Apps that are available for both Android and iOS, seem to access more sensitive information when programmed for iOS.

3   Related Work

We are only aware of two studies that explicitly mention the differences between Android and iOS users with respect to security and privacy.

In order to analyze privacy concerns and expectations of smartphone users, King [13] conducted interviews with 13 Android and 11 iOS users. The research investigates two dimensions: participants' concerns with other people accessing the personal data stored on smartphones as well as with applications accessing personal data. Almost all participants reported such concerns. King hypothesized that the Apple review process causes iOS users to exhibit more trust into the apps. However, she found out that also Android users thought that Google reviews apps before they are put into the Google Play store (this fact is also confirmed by Kelley et al. [11]), and so no difference between platforms could be observed. Users that believed (falsely or not) that the apps are reviewed felt safer when using apps. iOS users were mostly unaware of data usage by the apps (iOS 6 was not released at that time). In contrast, Android users were aware of the permission screen that is shown during the installation, although the majority of them felt that they do not quite understand what the permissions mean.

Chin et al. [3] examined differences of smartphone users' perceptions and behavior when using laptops versus smartphones. The authors conducted a survey with 30 iOS as well as with 30 Android users. They noticed that Android users had more free apps than iOS users. Furthermore, around 20 % of Android users stated that they always consider permissions when installing apps and additional 40 % stated that they sometimes considered permissions. This is an interesting contrast to the results by Felt et al. [8] that only 17 % of Android users pay attention to the permissions during the installation process.

Independently and concurrently to our work, Mylonas et al. [21] conducted a survey with 458 smartphone users in order to gain insights into their security awareness. The authors found out that most smartphone users do not feel being at risk when downloading apps from official application stores, and that this effect is independent of the smartphone's operating system. Smartphone users also do not pay attention to security messages which are shown by the devices. Further, they could only find a slight correlation between the participants' security background and their awareness of security when using smartphones [20]. In addition to the findings of Mylonas et al., we examine also privacy awareness of smartphone users and compare Android and iOS users in detail.

Android users received the most attention to date in connection with the Android permissions [8,16,2,11]. Although different research strategies and different user pools were considered, the researchers uniformly found that most users pay only limited attention to the permissions and have a poor understanding of their meaning. We are not aware of any studies that specifically concentrated on security- or privacy-related human factors for iOS users.

4   Research Methodology

We conducted a survey with 506 Android and 215 iOS users in order to analyze security and privacy behavior and attitude. We therefore designed an online survey using the LimeSurvey software[3]. The survey consisted of 21 questions including 17 quantitative and 4 qualitative (open-ended) questions and was available online from September 11th to October 4th 2012. In order to avoid priming, we called the survey "How well do you know your smartphone?". The questionnaire is available from the authors.

Participants were recruited via email from the economics department and from the technical department of the University of Erlangen-Nuremberg. Additionally, 250 flyers were distributed in the city of Erlangen in order to increase the amount of non-student participants.

4.1   Hypotheses and Survey Design

According to our research question presented in Section 1, we developed two hypotheses:

---

[3] http://www.limesurvey.org

H1: Android phone users are more security aware than iOS users.
H2: Android phone users are more privacy aware than iOS users.

The hypotheses are based on the assumption that Google's open app market makes Android users more conscious of possible malware infections and that the explicitly presented app permissions draw user attention to the possibilities of data misuse. It is also possible that security and privacy aware users choose Android because it is open source and because they can see in the permissions which data is accessed and manipulated by the apps.

We note that, on the other hand, due to the app vetting process of Apple it might be possible that security and privacy aware people choose iOS. In our ongoing work that is based on the survey presented here we are investigating whether security and privacy awareness is decisive for the choice of smartphone and its operating system, and also whether the choice of smartphone influences security and privacy awareness (see Section 7 for an initial overview).

4.2   Measuring Security and Privacy Awareness

In order to measure security and privacy awareness, we first asked the participants an open-ended question about what is important to them when choosing a new app. This question was asked before mentioning any security or privacy issues in the survey in order not to prime the participants. Users that mentioned security or privacy issues in their answers were classified as security respectively privacy aware.

Later in the survey, we asked the participants whether they have some security software installed on their smartphones, and we also explicitly asked the participants about their knowledge and concerns about the handling of personal data by the apps.

4.3   Participants

We received 917 responses to the survey. After sorting out incomplete questionnaires as well as users that had other kinds of operating systems than iOS or Android, the answers of 721 participants (258 female and 463 male) were left for further analysis.

We received answers from 506 Android and 215 iOS users. More than 80 % of the participants were between 18 and 25 years old and 14 % were between 26 and 30 years old. 93 % (674) of the participants were students, 5 % (37) were employed and 2 % (10) were neither students nor employed.

5   Analysis of the Results

We conducted quantitative as well as qualitative analysis of the answers. For the open-ended questions we used the software for qualitative analysis called

MAXQDA[4] in order to categorize the answers. For quantitative analysis we used SPSS[5].

5.1   Hypothesis 1: Security Awareness

To test hypothesis H1 (Android phone users are more security aware than iOS users), we asked the participants if they have security software such as virus scanner installed on their device. 6 % of iOS users said to have such software installed, while 38 % of Android users stated the same, see Fig. 1(a). The difference is highly significant and there is a medium correlation between the operating system of the smartphone and having security software installed (Cramer's V = .327, p ≤.001). This confirms H1.

Mylonas et al. [21] provide similar findings referring to the differences between Android and iOS users. Their survey results show that 33 % of Android users but only 14.7 % of iOS users have security software, especially virus scanners, installed on their smartphones.

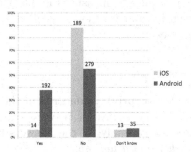
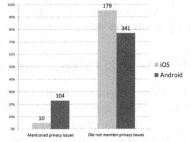

(a) Answers to the question *Do you have some security software installed on your smartphone?*

(b) Users that mentioned privacy issues as an important factor when choosing a new app

Fig. 1. Security software question (a); users that mentioned privacy issues (b)

We note, however, that it is not clear whether having a virus scanner can be considered as an independent variable, because there are many virus scanners for Android and virtually no virus scanners for iOS. One may also argue that more security aware people would probably choose iOS because of the Apple review process, and would feel that they do not need any security software in this case.

We further qualitatively analyzed responses to the question: *What is important to you when choosing a new app?* This open-ended question was asked before security or privacy had been mentioned in the questionnaire to avoid priming.

---

[4] http://www.maxqda.de/

[5] http://www.ibm.com/software/de/analytics/spss

We categorized users as being security aware if they mentioned anything connected to "security", "trust" or "permissions" in their answers (see Table 1). In total, 634 users answered this question. 9 iOS and 96 Android users were categorized as security aware (some participants mentioned more than one security-related issue). We conclude that there is a weak correlation between the operating system and the "security" category that is highly significant (Cramer's V = .206, p ≤.000).

Further categories that were derived from the answers to this question can also be found in Table 1. We divided the results into security- and privacy-related categories as well as into those that are not security and privacy relevant.

The above results confirm hypothesis H1: Android users are more security aware, if we consider having security software or mentioning of permissions as indicators of security awareness.

In their survey, Mylonas et al. [21] also asked participants about their application selection criteria, resulting in 8 categories "usefulness", "usability", "efficiency", "cost", "reviews", "reputation", "developer" and "security/privacy". Their most often mentioned category was "usefulness" with 58.8 % and the least mentioned category, "security/privacy", could only be measured in 3.5 % of the answers. In their context, the category security and privacy was e.g. related to not installing an app due to permission requests.

5.2   Hypothesis 2: Privacy Awareness

Although there are some measurement scales for privacy concerns in the literature [18,14], there are not many definitions and scales for privacy awareness [23]. As a first indicator of privacy awareness we analyzed the answers to the question: *What is important to you when choosing a new app?*

We consider users to be privacy aware if they mention anything connected to privacy or personal data, e.g. "privacy", "permissions" or "trustworthy usage of personal data". Although we previously we used the category "permissions" to analyze security awareness of smartphone users, we also use this category for analysis of privacy awareness, as permissions actually refer to both, security-critical actions and personal data access. 10 iOS users and 104 Android users were categorized as privacy aware, see Table 1 and Fig. 1(b). There is a weak correlation between the operating system of smartphones and the categories mentioned above. This correlation is highly significant (Cramer's V = .200, p ≤.000).

Here, one may be tempted to argue, similarly to H1, that more privacy aware users might choose iOS because they trust that privacy invasive apps will not pass Apple's review process. However, Apple's review criteria are kept secret and iOS apps are known to be quite privacy invasive from the literature [5,25,10].

Table 1. Most frequent categories for the answer to the question "What is important for you when you choose a new app?"

Security- and privacy-relevant	Description	Examples	iOS	Android
Security	The term "security" was mentioned	"Data security"	6(3 %)	16(3 %)
Data privacy	"Data privacy" was mentioned or handling of private data	"Protection of private data", "App should not collect or circulate personal data"	6(3 %)	33(7 %)
Permissions	Required permissions of an app; if permissions were mentioned	"Kind of permissions of an app", "If permissions are relevant for the app to function"	3(1 %)	80(16 %)
Not security and privacy relevant	**Description**	**Examples**	**iOS**	**Android**
Usefulness	Useful in daily life, functional volume	"Additionally benefit through app", "Useful benefit"	142(66 %)	318(63 %)
Costs	Costs of an app	"App should be free, because I don't have a credit card", "Free of cost"	90(42%)	205(41%)
Usability	Usability of an app	"App should be user-friendly", "Easy usage"	37(17 %)	72(14 %)
Rating	Recommendations of other users, reviews in app markets	"Experience of other users", "Apps should have good ratings in the store"	26(12 %)	67(13 %)
Entertainment	Entertaining functions such as games	"App should be fun", "Fun factor"	21(10 %)	43(8 %)
Resource usage	Storage space, battery consumption	"App should have a low battery consumption", "App should not waste storage space"	6(3 %)	47(9 %)
Absence of advertisement	No or little advertising being part of an app	"No intrusive advertisement", "No annoying advertisement"	6(3 %)	27(5 %)
N.A.			27(13 %)	61(12 %)

We also asked the participants explicitly about their awareness of data access by the apps. We found no differences between iOS and Android users here, with more than 90 % of the users stating to be aware of the fact. We note, however, one one cannot fully rely on the self-reporting by the users, as this question is suggestive.

In addition, participants were asked whether they pay attention to app accessing personal data. This question was answered by 213 iOS and 492 Android users. If one regards the answers "yes" and "sometimes" together (see Fig. 2(a)), Android and iPhone users both gain about 90 %.

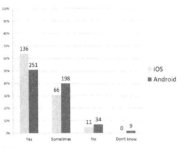
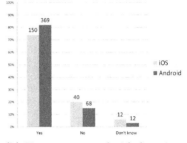

(a) Do you pay attention to whether an app accesses personal data?

(b) Have you ever decided against the usage of an app because the app wanted access to your personal data?

Fig. 2. Questions about privacy awareness

This is interesting if one considers that until iOS 6 emerged, iPhone users were only asked whether they grant the app access to the current location. For all other accesses, users were not directly asked. It remains unclear how iPhone users were able to pay attention to whether an app accesses private data or not. As iOS 6 was actually released exactly in the middle of our survey on September 19th, 2012, we could compare the answers of iOS users that were given before and after the release date. We found no difference in the answers.

Furthermore we found out that 74 % of the iPhone users as well as 82 % of the Android users state to have decided against the usage of an app because the app wanted access to their personal data (see Fig. 2(b)). This question was answered by 202 iOS and 449 Android users. 20 % of iPhone users and 15 % of Android users never decided against the usage of such apps (Cramer's $V = .103$, $p \leq .10$). These differences are not significant.

Finally, we asked the participants an open-ended question about which kind of data access would cause them to abstain from using an application. Here, some differences between iOS and Android users could be identified. "Reading SMS/MMS" is important for 1 % iOS and 12 % Android users. This reflects the corresponding Android permission.

An interesting category is "Apps causing hidden costs" (0 % iOS users and 7 % Android users) that reflects the text of the corresponding Android permission.

It seems that the Android users that pay attention to permissions are the only ones that realize the dangers of malicious apps sending, for example, premium-rate SMS.

The most often mentioned category is "Location" (named by 29 % of iOS and by 20 % of Android users), followed by "Contact data" (20 % of iOS users and 15 % of Android users), with no significant differences between the smartphone types. Moreover, around 10% of users on both platforms gave answers such as "it depends on app's functionality" or "if the data are not related to the core function of the app", indicating that these users make privacy-related trade-offs when deciding to use an app.

The results of this analysis are not straightforward. Are the Android users more privacy aware because they mention one more data type (SMS/MMS) than iOS users? Are the Android users more security aware because a small percentage of them thinks about hidden costs that an app may cause?

On the other hand, significantly more Android users stated in an open-ended question that privacy issues and permissions are important for them when deciding to install a new app (see Fig. 1(b)). They did so before any privacy-related questions were asked. So we make a tentative conclusion that Android users seem to be more privacy-aware than iOS users, confirming hypothesis H2. We note, however, that this issue needs further investigation.

6 Limitations

Our study run form September 11th to October 4th 2012, and iOS 6 was released on September 19th. Thus, the data of iOS users provided after September 19th may be biased because some of them already updated to iOS 6 which requires runtime consent for more data types than location. However, as we noticed no significant differences in the two data sets (data before the introduction of iOS 6 and afterwards), we used all data for our analysis.

Our participants sample was biased towards well-educated young people, as most of them were students, so the generalization of the results cannot be guaranteed. We are investigating other population of participants in our ongoing work.

7 Conclusion and Ongoing Work

The conducted study gave some insights into the interplay between security and privacy awareness and the smartphone choice. Android users seem to be more security and privacy aware, mostly because they notice Android permissions. This may indicate that users need to be presented with a clear overview of the data access by the apps, and that this overview may indeed improve their awareness.

To verify this assumption, and in order to further investigate the relationship between the smartphone type and the users' security and privacy awareness, we conducted in-depth interviews with 10 Android and 8 iPhone users with various demographic backgrounds and are now analyzing the transcribed interviews using structuring content analysis by Mayring [19].

Furthermore, we are going to develop a model for the interaction between the smartphone type and the security and privacy awareness and to test this model by statistical means, using, for example, structural equation modeling techniques such as LISREL [12].

Acknowledgment. This research was supported by the Bavarian State Ministry of Education, Science and the Arts as part of the FORSEC research association.

References

1. Arthur, C., Dredge, S.: iOS v Android: Why Schmidt was wrong and developers still start on Apple (June 10, 2012), www.guardian.co.uk
2. Chia, P.H., Yamamoto, Y., Asokan, N.: Is this app safe?: A large scale study on application permissions and risk signals. In: Proceedings of the 21st International Conference on World Wide Web, WWW 2012 (2012)
3. Chin, E., Felt, A.P., Sekar, V., Wagner, D.: Measuring user confidence in smartphone security and privacy. In: SOUPS (2012)
4. Dediu, H.: Android economics: An introduction (April 2, 2012), www.asymco.com
5. Egele, M., Kruegel, C., Kirda, E., Vigna, G.: PiOS: Detecting Privacy Leaks in iOS Apllications. In: NDSS (2011)
6. Elmer-DeWitt, P.: 6 ways iPhone and Android users differ (February 25, 2010), tech.fortune.cnn.com
7. Felt, A.P., Finifter, M., Chin, E., Hanna, S., Wagner, D.: A survey of mobile malware in the wild. In: SPSM (2011)
8. Felt, A.P., Ha, E., Egelman, S., Haney, A., Chin, E., Wagner, D.: Android permissions: User attention, comprehension, and behavior. In: SOUPS (2012)
9. Google: Protect against harmful apps (February 28, 2014), https://support.google.com/accounts/answer/2812853?hl=en
10. Han, J., Yan, Q., Gao, D., Zhou, J., Deng, R.H.: Comparing Mobile Privacy Protection through Cross-Platform Applications. In: Proceedings of the Network and Distributed System Security Symposium (NDSS), San Diego, CA (February 2013)
11. Kelley, P.G., Sadeh, L.F.C.N.: Privacy as part of the app decision-making process. In: ACM (2013)
12. Kelloway, E.K.: Using LISREL for Structural Equation Modeling. Sage, Thousand Oaks (1998)
13. King, J.: How Come I'm Allowing Strangers to Go Through My Phone?: Smart Phones and Privacy Expectations, under review (2012)
14. Kumaraguru, P., Cranor, L.F.: Privacy indexes: A survey of Westin's studies. Tech. Rep. Paper 856, Carnegie Mellon University, Institute for Software Research (January 2005)
15. Leontiadis, I., Efstratiou, C., Picone, M., Mascolo, C.: Don't kill my ads!: Balancing privacy in an ad-supported mobile application market. In: HotMobile (2012)

16. Lin, J., Sadeh, N., Amini, S., Lindqvist, J., Hong, J.I., Zhang, J.: Expectation and purpose: Understanding users' mental models of mobile app privacy through crowdsourcing. In: ACM UbiComp (2012), http://doi.acm.org/10.1145/2370216.2370290

17. Lipsman, A., Aquino, C.: 2013 Mobile Future in Focus (February 22, 2013), http://www.comscore.com

18. Malhotra, N.K., Kim, S.S., Agarwal, J.: Internet Users' Information Privacy Concerns (IUIPC): The Construct, the Scale, and a Causal Model. Information Systems Research 15(4), 336–355 (2004)

19. Mayring, P.: Qualitative Inhaltsanalyse, 11th edn. Beltz Verlag (2010)

20. Mylonas, A., Gritzalis, D., Tsoumas, B., Apostolopoulos, T.: A qualitative metrics vector for the awareness of smartphone security users. In: Furnell, S., Lambrinoudakis, C., Lopez, J. (eds.) TrustBus 2013. LNCS, vol. 8058, pp. 173–184. Springer, Heidelberg (2013)

21. Mylonas, A., Kastania, A., Gritzalis, D.: Delegate the smartphone user? Security Awareness in Smartphone Platforms 34, 47–66 (2013)

22. Percoco, N.J., Schulte, S.: Adventures in bouncerland. In: Black Hat USA (2012)

23. Pötzsch, S.: Privacy awareness: A means to solve the privacy paradox? In: Matyáš, V., Fischer-Hübner, S., Cvrček, D., Švenda, P. (eds.) The Future of Identity. IFIP AICT, vol. 298, pp. 226–236. Springer, Heidelberg (2009)

24. Raphael, J.: How Google's Android security is about to get even smarter (February 27, 2014), http://blogs.computerworld.com/android/23590/google-android-security

25. Seriot, N.: iPhone Privacy. In: Black Hat USA (2010)

26. Sofos: Security threat report (2013), http://www.sophos.com/en-us/security-news-trends/reports/security-threat-report

27. Spreitzenbarth, M., Freiling, F.: Android malware on the rise. Tech. Rep. CS-2012-04, University of Erlangen (April 2012)

28. Travlos, D.: Five Reasons Why Google Android versus Apple iOS Market Share Numbers Don't Matter (August 22, 2012), http://www.forbes.com

29. Wang, T., Lu, K., Lu, L., Chung, S., Lee, W.: Jekyll on iOS: when benign apps become evil. Presented as Part of the 22nd USENIX Security Symposium, Washington D.C, USA (August 2013)

User Acceptance of Footfall Analytics
with Aggregated and Anonymized Mobile Phone Data

Alfred Kobsa

Donald Bren School of Information and Computer Sciences, University of California
Irvine, CA 92617-4055, U.S.A.
kobsa@uci.edu

Abstract. Monitoring and analyzing pedestrian traffic in and around retail stores
has become an important tool for discovering underutilized operational and
marketing opportunities of retail localities. Since a large proportion of pedestrians
nowadays carry mobile phones, visual observation methods of the past could give
way to cell-tower and WiFi based capture of passers-by, optionally augmented by
aggregated or anonymized demographic data about them coming from their
service providers. A major mobile phone operator recently announced the introduction of such a service in Germany, the U.K. and Brazil, but had to cancel its
plans for Germany since the revelation caused nationwide privacy uproar.

We conducted an exploratory interview study to gauge whether and under
what conditions German consumers would accept if their mobile phone providers disclosed their personal data to retail stores they walk by, in aggregated and
anonymized individual form. Virtually all respondents wanted their data to
remain private at an extent that goes considerably beyond the protections
afforded by current privacy laws. Nearly everyone however also indicated an
interest in financial incentives in return for their consent to the transfer of their
data, and many of them at seemingly very reasonable terms.

Keywords: Footfall analytics, privacy, mobile phones, personal data transfer,
data aggregation, data anonymization, privacy laws, compensation.

1   Introduction

Monitoring and analyzing pedestrian traffic inside and outside of retail stores has
become an important means for understanding and improving customer catchment,
marketing effectiveness, sales staff allocation, and the influence of external factors
such as weather, time and nearby events. Tracking pedestrians' movements can also
help town planners, event organizers and emergency services to analyze the behavior
of crowds on different days of the week and at different times or occasions, and to
validate the effectiveness of urban developments.

Traditionally, footfall analytics has relied on visual observations by humans, either
directly or indirectly through video [1], or people-counting cameras and sensors based
on various technologies [2]. The fact that a large majority of people nowadays carry
mobile phones when they leave their homes enables new and more powerful technical

C. Eckert et al. (Eds.): TrustBus 2014, LNCS 8647, pp. 168–179, 2014.
© Springer International Publishing Switzerland 2014

solutions for foot traffic monitoring: cell-tower based positioning [e.g., 3] which is currently coarser-grained but available outdoors, and WiFi-based positioning [e.g., 4–6] which is currently finer-grained and mostly available indoors. Both technologies can deliver value beyond people counts and location information if positioning is carried out by, or in cooperation with, pedestrians' mobile network operators or WiFi access point operators. Those providers typically possess personal data about their customers, which they can convey to interested recipients together with location and time stamps, individually per pedestrian or in aggregated statistical form.

These new wireless-based technologies for footfall analytics, and specifically their potential for personal data transfer, seem however problematic from a privacy point of view. In the fall of 2012, a subsidiary of Telefónica announced its plans to introduce a "Smart Steps" footfall analytics service in Germany, the United Kingdom and Brazil, based on the location and demographical data of its mobile phone customers. The service would allow subscribers to find out, e.g., "how many customers visit an area by time, gender, and age" and to determine "the movement of crowds at any given place by hour, day, week or month" [3]. The announcement lead to a public privacy outcry in Germany [7, 8]. Telefónica thereupon pulled its plans for Germany, but introduced this service later that year in the U.K.

The applicability of data protection laws to such business models is limited, since "personal information" that is protected by these laws is narrowly defined: it denotes "any information relating to an identified or identifiable natural person" [9] or "refers to any data, including aggregations of data, which is linkable to a specific individual" [10]. Processing of data about an individual is not regulated any longer when this data is "de-identified", i.e., anonymized, pseudonymized, or compiled into statistics in such a way that it cannot be related to an individual with reasonable efforts [11–13]. Also the proposed new European General Data Protection Regulation [14] continues to maintain that "the principles of data protection should not apply to data rendered anonymous in such a way that the data subject is no longer identifiable".

It is possible to anonymize both individuals' location data from cell phone towers and personal data from customer files in such a way that both can still be merged in this anonymized form [15, 16]. Individuals' consent to the disclosure of such merged anonymized data to third parties is then no longer required. In the UK, Telefónica does not even seem to allow its customers to opt out of the Smart Steps service [17]. The situation is somewhat different in Germany where the protection of location information in telecommunications networks and services is regulated both by the Federal Data Protection Act [18] and also by the German Telecommunications Act [19]. The latter mandates a separate written (i.e., non-electronic) agreement if location data are used for value added services to third parties [20], even if the data is anonymized.[1] Users also must be alerted each time when this happens.

Against this background, we conducted an exploratory interview study among mobile phone users in Germany, to gauge to what extent they would accept if their providers disclosed their customer data to retail stores they pass by, in aggregated or in individualized but anonymized form. To the best of our knowledge, this is the first such empirical study on this topic. We aimed at answering the following questions:

---

[1] The German Telecommunications Act is stricter in this regard than the EU Directive 2002/58/EC that it implements.

RQ1. Do mobile phone users agree with the disclosure of *aggregated* demographic data to retailers they pass by, and are there differences between individuals?

RQ2. Do mobile phone users agree with the disclosure of *anonymized* demographic data to retailers they pass by, and are there differences between individuals?

RQ3. Are there differences between types of personal information in the levels of agreement with disclosure?

RQ4. What is the relationship between users' levels of agreement with data disclosure in the case of aggregated and anonymized individual data?

RQ5. Will mobile phone users agree to the disclosure of personal data to retailers they pass by if they receive compensation from their mobile phone providers?

RQ6. If so, what discount is expected for their permission to the disclosure of personal data to retailers?

RQ7. What is the relationship between consumers' expected discount and their agreement with personal data disclosure?

RQ8. Finally, we also aimed to collect participants' rationales, and their general view on footfall analytics and personal data transfer by their mobile phone providers.

2   Study Procedures

In spring 2013, announcements of a phone study on "Customer Information Through Mobile Phones" were posted on several German classifieds websites and Internet forums, and in a print weekly listing magazine. Readers could dial a German phone number, with a callback option. A €15 Amazon gift card was offered as a reward.

20 people participated in the study (13 male, 7 female), with a wide range of professional backgrounds. Their ages ranged from 20 to 60 years, with a median of 20-30 years. Their mobile phone providers spanned nearly the full breadth of pertinent German companies. 25% used resellers (virtual mobile network operators) and prepaid plans. Reported monthly mobile phone expenses ranged from €10 to €60, with €20-€30 as the median (prepaid subscribers estimated their monthly expense).

The interviews lasted between 20 and 30 minutes and were semi-structured: they contained the fixed set of questions discussed below, and participants were also encouraged to explicate and elaborate their answers. We first explained business rationales that could prompt retail stores to desire not only a numeric count of passers-by but also some of their demographic characteristics. We pointed to targeting product offerings and advertisements to the demographics of the people who tend to pass by a certain store. The remainder of the interview was then contextualized to each interviewee's personal situation [21]: the respondent's mobile phone provider and a well-known retail store in the respondent's city (typically a Karstadt or Kaufhof department store) were used as examples.

Study participants were then asked whether they would accept if their mobile phone provider disclosed eight pieces of personal data to the retail store whenever they passed by. Those pieces of personal data were chosen based on the independent opinion of two domain experts about the maximum set of personal data available to German mobile phone providers that could be currently used for data-enriched footfall analytics. We asked about the disclosure of the following pieces of data:

1. Age group (namely "below 20", "20-30", "30-40", etc.)
2. City of residence
3. Monthly mobile phone expense ("less than €20", "€20-€30", "€30-€40", etc.)
4. Payment history ("whether or not you paid your mobile phone bills on time")
5. Gender
6. Whether or not the interviewee holds a university diploma
7. Number of children[2]
8. Private or business use of the phone (based on the customer's phone plan)

We posed these questions in two rounds. First, we asked interviewees to assume that the retailer would be informed every hour about the data of all passers-by "including yourself", but only in *aggregated statistical* form ("e.g., in the past hour, 50 passers-by were less than 20 years old, 70 between 20 and 30, etc."). In the second round, we asked participants to assume that the data of every passer-by of the past hour would be disclosed individually, but in *anonymized* form ("i.e., no name, no address, no phone number")[3]. In the third part of the interview, we asked participants to indicate what discount on their monthly phone bill they expected in return for their agreement that all their data could be given to any retailer they walk by, in anonymized and in aggregated form. Finally, we encouraged participants to tell us any other comments or suggestions that came to their minds. Throughout the interviews, we used open coding, purposeful sampling, and constant comparison to generate grounded theory [22].

3   Results

3.1   Willingness to Agree with Data Transfer to Retailer (RQ1 - RQ4)

As far as the aggregated transfer of data to retailers is concerned (RQ1), 30% felt that this is o.k. for all of the polled types of personal information, while the majority (55%) gave different responses depending on the data type. 15% of participants wanted to disclose a single piece of information only (namely age group or gender), or none at all. Participants in latter group found footfall analytics "frightening", felt "like they are being followed", and deemed this data transfer "dreadful". On average, participants were willing to disclose 5.55 of the 8 polled pieces of personal data (σ = 2.53). Females agreed less than males to the disclosure of their data (4.29 versus 6.23 of 8 polled items), but the difference is not statistically significant.

As far as the individual but anonymized transfer of data to retailers is concerned (RQ2), 10% felt that this is o.k. for all polled data (all those respondents also agreed with aggregated transfer), but 30% of the interviewees felt that this was not appropriate for any of their personal data. The rest gave different responses depending on the data type. On average, participants were willing to disclose 4.08 of the 8 polled items (σ = 3.14). Female participants' agreement with disclosure was lower than that

---

[2] Information about a diploma and about children may be available to mobile phone providers if the customer has or had a student discount rate or a family/children's plan, respectively.

[3] We did not also ask subjects about the transfer of pseudonymous data (that could be linked over time) since we felt we could not easily explain its difference to anonymous data.

of males (2.14 versus 5.11 out of 8 items polled). An Independent-Samples Kruskal-Wallis test confirmed that this difference is statistically significant (p=0.048). City of residence and payment history were the two pieces of information for which female and male willingness to disclose differed the most.

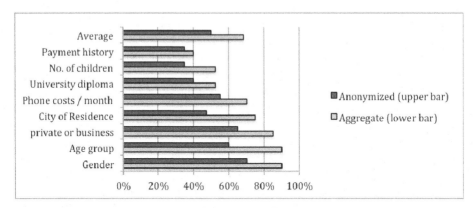

Fig. 1. Rate of consent that personal data may be disclosed to retailers passed by, by type of data and form of de-identification

Fig. 1 shows participants' average agreement rates per type of personal information requested, ordered roughly by increasing agreement (the order in which questions were posed can be gathered in Section 2). The upper bars (red) indicate the average agreement with disclosure for anonymized transfer, and the lower bars (blue) the agreement for aggregated transfer. The average agreement with disclosure clearly differs per type of personal information, in both conditions (RQ3). Agreement with disclosure is generally higher in the aggregated condition than in the anonymized individual condition (RQ4). A Generalized Estimated Equations model with data type and the form of anonymization as within-subjects factors and agreement with disclosure as binary dependent variable confirms overall statistically significant effects both for data type (Wald Chi-Square = 6.68, p=0.01) and for anonymization form (Wald Chi-Square =29.83, p<0.001). Further on RQ4, Kendall's tau shows a moderate correlation of agreement with disclosure in the two different conditions (τ=0.47, p<0.01).

3.2   Willingness to Accept Compensation for Personal Data (RQ5 - RQ7)

85% of respondents would accept a discount on their monthly phone bills in return for their agreement that the 8 items of personal data that we polled may be transferred to retailers they pass by, in aggregated or anonymized individual form (RQ5).

Fig. 2 plots the compensation requested by those 17 participants, ordered by the amount expressed as a percentage of their monthly phone bill (RQ6). Averages were chosen when participants quoted a value range, and occasionally quoted Euro amounts were put in proportion to participants' monthly phone expenses.

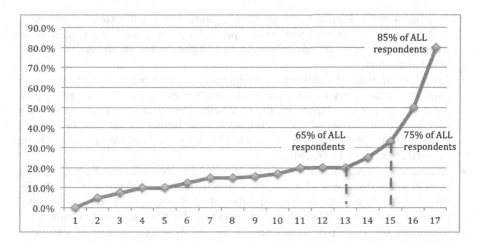

Fig. 2. Expected monthly discount for agreeing to data transfer, ordered by amount (3 respondents refused a discount)

The average requested discount is 20.9%, and the median 15.6%. As can be seen in Fig. 2, a discount of 20% would make 65% of all study participants agree to the disclosure of their data, while a discount of 33% would sway 75% of participants. With regard to RQ7, Kendall's tau shows a medium to weak negative correlation (τ=-0.35, p=0.067) between respondents' expected discount and their willingness to disclose personal data in aggregated form. The correlation between expected discount and agreement with disclosure in anonymized individual form is even weaker and not statistically significant (τ=-0.28, p=0.141).

30% of respondents indicated that they would not accept the disclosure of any of their polled data in anonymized form (see Section 3.1), and one of them not even in aggregated form. This equals roughly the proportion of "privacy fundamentalists" in Alan Westin's surveys [23]. Of those 30%, half stated that a discount on their mobile phone bill would not sway them to agree to the transfer of their personal data. The others expected discounts of 7.5%, 10% and 80%, respectively. At the opposite end, 10% of respondents had indicated that they would be o.k. with the disclosure of all of the polled data in anonymized or aggregated individual form. When asked later about a discount in compensation for their willingness, one of them did not expect any discount while the other chose 17% (pointing out this corresponds to German VAT).

3.3 Themes from Grounded Theory Analysis (RQ8)

We performed a grounded-theory analysis of the free-form part of the interviews, to collect themes relating to participants' decisions on whether or not to agree to data disclosure to retailers they pass by. We used open coding, purposeful sampling, and constant comparison [22]. While we aimed to focus on footfall analytics, i.e. the topic of this study, participants often offered their opinions on disclosing their personal data to businesses in general. The following themes emerged:

- *Personal benefits:* Participants wanted to see some benefits in return for their data: "it depends on the benefit – where is my profit?" Personalization was mentioned as one such benefit (e.g., for advertisements or tailored offers), and financial compensation as another.
- *Fair share in profit:* A subtheme of the aforesaid was the notion of participation in profits that a company makes from selling one's personal data. As one participant put it, "if my phone company profits from selling my data, then I also want to get some part of it". None of the interviewees went further though and brought up notions like property rights in one's data [24–26] or selling/renting one's data on personal data markets [27, 28].
- *"A la carte" offers*: A few participants not only wanted a financial offer for their consent to the disclosure of *all* their data discussed in the interview (i.e., a disclosure "flat rate", as one interviewee called it), but additionally also "a la carte" offers for each individual piece of data, and even offers per third-party recipient.
- *Anonymity set:* Three participants brought up that their agreement to the disclosure of their city of residence would depend on the city size. Their motivation was to hide in a sufficiently large anonymity set. City size is unimportant when walking in one's own city since the anonymity set during an hour of observation (as we had indicated) is far smaller than the population of even the smallest city. It might make sense though when walking in a different city far away from home.
- *Perceived relevance of data for recipient:* A few participants found it "daft" that a mobile phone provider would convey to retailers whether or not a passer-by holds a university diploma, as well as the number of their children ("who would need that?"). This doubt in the relevancy of these two data types for retailers aligns well with participants' low willingness to agree to its disclosure (see Fig. 1).

4   Discussion

4.1   Expected Protection of Anonymized and Aggregated Data

Footfall analytics via smartphones augmented by customer data would provide a valuable resource to retailers that can help them in their marketing and catchment efforts with regard to passers-by. The transfer of demographic data from mobile phone providers to retailers falls largely outside the scope of existing data protection laws if the data remain anonymized or aggregated (an exception is Germany since location data is involved, see Section 1). Footfall analytics may therefore be performed without notifying the data subjects or asking for their prior consent.

Our study shows however that a substantial majority of our respondents would ordinarily disagree with the disclosure of *all* their data to retailers (namely 70% of participants if it is done in aggregated form and 90% if it is done in anonymized individual form). On average, people were only willing to give out 69% of the polled data in aggregated and 50% in anonymized form. People's disclosure proclivity also varied considerably by data type, with a low of 35% disclosure for university diploma, number of children and payment history. If data protection laws are meant to reflect people's subjective desires for the protection of their personal data, then it would be worthwhile to consider widening the scope of protected data in future privacy legislation [e.g., in 10, 14], beyond the realm of identifiability. Unfettered protection of aggregated and anonymized individual data is probably out of discussion since this would have too many negative repercussions for innovations that are based on the analysis of anonymized data, ranging from value-added services to scientific research. It might be worthwhile though to give data subjects more protection in cases where data collectors reap financial gains when selling aggregated or anonymized individual data to third parties. As detailed in Section 3.3, several participants objected to such data usage unless there was some profit-sharing in place. The protections of privacy laws could be extended in such a way that data collectors would have to ask data subjects for permission before they could resell aggregated or anonymized individual data to third parties. Alternatively, mobile phone providers could voluntarily decide to ask customers for their permission that their demographic data may be used for footfall analytics. In the next section, we will discuss the implications of our study results on such a scenario.

4.2   Willingness to Accept Compensation in Return for Consent to Data Transfer

Asking mobile phone customers for permission to use their personal data for footfall analytics is likely to lead to a low rate of consent: in our study, only 30% / 10% felt that this is o.k. for all the polled types of data when done in aggregate or anonymized individual form, respectively. Our study shows that quite a few people could be swayed to agree to give out all their data if they were offered monetary compensation. The "capture rate" obviously depends on the offered amount. In our case, a 20% discount on their monthly phone bill would have swayed 65% of participants, and a 33.3% discount 75% of participants. The average requested discount was 20.9%, the median 15.6%, and the maximum 80%. Given that the median monthly phone expense was €20-€30, this roughly corresponds to average/median amounts in the 3-6 Euro range per month.

Prior studies aimed at determining the compensation people would demand for their willingness to disclose their data[4] encountered considerably higher requests:

- [33] let British university students bid on their expected compensation for their permission that precise information about their location may be collected over one month. Participants requested £32.8 on average, with a maximum bid of £300.
- [34] and [35] let European students bid on compensation for three types of location data usage: one-month academic usage, one-month commercial usage, and one-year commercial usage. The average bids were in the range of €30, €60 and €200, respectively (with a maximum bid of about €900 in the third scenario).
- [36] presented to Singaporean students websites that had different privacy characteristics, were visited in different frequencies, and offered different levels of compensation for personal data. The authors calculated that disallowing secondary use (like footfall analytics) represents a value of SGD 39.83-49.78 for subjects (equivalent to €24.65-€30.81 in April 2002).
- [37] let U.S. participants submit bids for disclosing personal data to all other auction participants. The average bid was US$ 57.56 for age and $74.06 for weight.
- [38] asked German participants what compensation they expected to "allow other companies to use data anonymized". Bids averaged €20 a month per data type.

---

[4] A very different question is how much people would be *willing to pay* for increased privacy. The results from behavioral experiments investigating this issue lie between 3% and 10% [29] or up to 17% [30] of the purchase price, or nothing at all [31, 32].

A direct comparison between those results and ours are obviously difficult, due to differences in the types of disclosed data, the number of recipients (from one to an unspecified number), and frequency of payment. Overall though, our study participants made comparatively modest requests. We attribute the sizeable difference of our responses to those in earlier studies to three factors:

- We emphasized that data would be given to the retailer in aggregated or anonymized individual form. All earlier studies except [38] assumed identified transfer.
- We introduced a point of reference or anchor [39], namely the monthly phone expense. None of the previous studies seemed to have offered a calibration point (even though in some studies the maximum possible bid was capped).
- Finally, the number of possible data recipients was geographically circumscribed, namely as businesses the participants walk by. In many prior studies, the number of possible recipients was unlimited.

Overall, these results hold promise for *consensual* footfall analytics: while a large proportion of our study participants was opposed to the transfer of all their customer data by their mobile phone providers to retail stores they walk by (even in aggregated or anonymized form), 85% of them were willing to agree to such a transfer if they received a discount on their monthly phone bill. For most of those who were open to such a deal, the expected discount seems modest (resulting in low single-digit Euro amounts per month). Even when prevailing privacy legislation would allow non-consensual footfall analytics with aggregated or anonymized data, providers who want to enter this line of business might prefer using a compensation scheme to avoid a repeat of the privacy uproars from the recent past [7, 8].

4.3   Limitations of This Study

The number of participants in our exploratory interview study was relatively small. While this is quite common in this type of research, caution must be exercised in drawing overly broad conclusions from the findings. Moreover, since our study was conducted in Germany, its results cannot be immediately applied to other countries. In a Eurobarometer survey [40], 30% of German respondents agreed with the statement "disclosing personal information is not a big issue", while the agreement in the other EU member states ranged from 23% to 51%. For the statement "you don't mind disclosing personal information in return for free services online", Germans ranked median with a 26% agreement rate in a 15%-56% pan-European range. It seems prudent to take the relative differences in those agreement rates into account when generalizing the results to other European countries.

Our study also asked participants about footfall analytics through their mobile phone provider only (who would use cell-tower based and thus relatively coarse positioning), and not about finer-grained WiFi-based footfall analytics or combinations of both technologies. None of our participants addressed the precision of locational positioning though, and hence it may not make a big difference to them. This precision also has no implications on what data get communicated to a business, but only on the amount of false negatives and positives when determining whether a passer-by is within the required range to a retail store.

Moreover, our study only asked participants about the disclosure of demographic data legitimately held by their mobile phone providers in the regular course of business. At least one U.S. wireless carrier meanwhile also links location data of customers with third-party data obtained, e.g., from credit reporting agency Experian [41]. This carrier also sells aggregates of subscribers' movement patterns and not only of their locations [42]. It is unclear whether the linkage of such data can still be performed anonymously, to avoid the purview of European data protection regulation.

As [43] points out, "estimations of the monetary value of personal data are highly context dependent", and the above comparisons with bids from study participants in prior studies should therefore be looked at with caution, even when they are about the same types of personal data. Likewise, if the purpose of the personal data transfer to retailers gets changed or widened (e.g., to displaying ads in shop windows that are highly tailored to the transmitted personal data of each passer-by), then a new study should be conducted to gauge consumers' attitudes within this new or wider context.

Finally, our study polled participants' stated willingness to agree with data disclosure, and not their actual behavior. [44] and others found that participants' actual amount of personal data disclosure significantly exceeded what they had intended to disclose when they were surveyed on the same items several weeks earlier. Those and similar findings are however also disputed, and dismissed as an experimental artifact [45]. The methodological solution for the time being is to poll both stated privacy-related attitudes and intentions, as well as actual behavior [46].

5   Conclusion

We conducted the first study of mobile phone users' attitudes towards footfall analytics that involves the transfer of personal data from their mobile phone providers to retail stores that users walk by. This is likely also to be the first privacy study that compared user attitudes towards two different methods of de-identification for shared personal data: aggregation and anonymization. We found that only very few users were willing to give out all their data in anonymized individual form, and only a minority in aggregated form. The difference in respondents' average agreement with disclosure between the two forms of de-identification was statistically significant. Agreement with disclosure also varied strongly by type of personal data.

We also found however that a large majority of users would consent to footfall analytics with data transfer by the mobile phone provider (in aggregated or anonymized individual form), provided that they receive a financial compensation. The amounts requested correlated somewhat with their levels of agreement to data disclosure in aggregate form. The expected compensation is noticeably lower than the amounts that have been reported in prior research. This may be due to the de-identified data transfer in our study, the use of an anchor point when requesting bids (namely a percentage of participants' monthly phone bill), and the narrow geographical circumscription of the set of recipients ("retail stores you walk by").

The results of our study have policy and business implications. With rare exceptions, current privacy laws do not regulate the transfer of personal data to third parties when it is carried out in aggregate or anonymized individual form. The only reason for businesses to refrain from it would be damages to their reputation, as has happened in the past. Giving data subjects their "fair share in profits", as some of our study participants put it, might be a viable way to reconcile consumer demands for wider privacy protections and business interests in leveraging and monetizing valuable but privacy-invasive technical innovations.

Acknowledgments. This study has been carried out while the author was a visiting researcher at Telekom Innovation Laboratories, Ben-Gurion University, Israel.

References

1. Nandakumar, R., Rallapalli, S., Chintalapudi, K., Padmanabhan, V.N., Qiu, L., Ganesan, A., Guha, S., Aggarwal, D., Goenka, A.: Physical Analytics: A New Frontier for (Indoor) Location Research. MSR-TR-2013-107, Microsoft Research, Banglore, India (2013)
2. Experian: People Counting Cameras (2014),
   `http://www.footfall.com/people-counting`
3. Telefonica: Smart Steps (2013),
   `http://dynamicinsights.telefonica.com/smart-steps`
4. Euclid: Euclid Analytics (2014), `http://euclidanalytics.com/`
5. Ruckus: Location Services (2014),
   `http://www.ruckussecurity.com/Location-Services.asp`
6. Little, J., O'Brien, B.: A Technical Review of Cisco's Wi-Fi-Based Location Analytics (2013),
   `http://www.cisco.com/c/en/us/products/collateral/wireless/`
   `mobility-services-engine/white_paper_c11-728970.pdf`
7. Biermann, K.: Überwachung: Telefonica will Handy-Bewegungsdaten an Werber verkaufen (2012), `http://www.zeit.de/digital/datenschutz/2012-10/`
   `telefonica-smart-steps-vorratsdaten`
8. Roman, D.: Telefónica Goes a Little Bit "Big Brother" (2012),
   `http://on.wsj.com/WJh6jb`
9. EU: Directive 95/46/EC of the European Parliament and of the Council of 24 October 1995 on the Protection of Individuals with Regard to the Processing of Personal Data etc. (1995)
10. White House: Consumer Data Privacy in a Networked World: A Framework for Protecting Privacy and Promoting Innovation in the Global Economy. Washington, D.C. (2012)
11. BDSB: German Federal Commissioner for Data Protection and Freedom of Information - Wiki, `http://www.bfdi.bund.de/bfdi_wiki/`
12. Mascetti, S., Monreale, A., Ricci, A., Gerino, A.: Anonymity: A Comparison Between the Legal and Computer Science Perspectives. In: Gutwirth, S., Leenes, R., de Hert, P., Poullet, Y. (eds.) European Data Protection: Coming of Age, pp. 85–115. Springer (2013)
13. ICO: Anonymisation: managing data protection risk code of practice. Information Commissioner's Office, Wilmslow, Cheshire, U.K. (2012)
14. EU: Proposal for a directive of the European Parliament and of the Council on the protection of individuals with regard to the processing of personal data etc. (2012)
15. Hall, R., Fienberg, S.E.: Privacy-Preserving Record Linkage. In: Domingo-Ferrer, J., Magkos, E. (eds.) PSD 2010. LNCS, vol. 6344, pp. 269–283. Springer, Heidelberg (2010)
16. Verykios, V.S., Christen, P.: Privacy-preserving record linkage. Wiley Interdisciplinary Reviews: Data Mining and Knowledge Discovery 3, 321–332 (2013)
17. BBC: Telefonica hopes "big data" arm will revive fortunes,
    `http://www.bbc.co.uk/news/technology-19882647`
18. DE-FDPA: German Federal Data Protection Act, as of 1 September 2009 (1990)
19. DE-TCA: German Telecommunications Act, as of 7 August 2013 (2004)
20. Mantz, R.: Verwertung von Standortdaten und Bewegungsprofilen durch Telekommunikationsdiensteanbieter: Der Fall Telefónica/O2. Kommunikation und Recht. 7, 7–11 (2013)

21. Stage, C.W., Mattson, M.: Ethnographic interviewing as contextualized conversation. In: Clair, R.P. (ed.) Expressions of Ethnography, pp. 97–105. SUNY Press, Albany (2003)
22. Glaser, B.G.: Doing grounded theory: issues and discussions. Sociology Press (1998)
23. Kumaraguru, P., Cranor, L.F.: Privacy Indexes: A Survey of Westin's Studies. Institute for Software Res. Intern'l, School of Comp. Sci. Carnegie Mellon Univ., Pittsburgh (2005)
24. Westin, A.F.: Privacy and Freedom. Atheneum, New York (1967)
25. Posner, R.A.: The Right of Privacy. Georgia Law Review 12, 393–422 (1977)
26. Rule, J., Hunter, L.: Towards Property Rights in Personal Data. In: Grant, R.A., Bennett, C.J. (eds.) Visions of Privacy: Policy Choices for the Digital Age. Univ. Toronto Pr. (1999)
27. Laudon, K.C.: Markets and privacy. Communications of the ACM 39, 92–104 (1996)
28. Schwartz, P.M.: Property, Privacy, and Personal Data. Harv. L. Rev. 117, 2056 (2003)
29. Tsai, J.Y., Egelman, S., Cranor, L., Acquisti, A.: The Effect of Online Privacy Information on Purchasing Behavior: An Experimental Study. Info. Sys. Research. 22, 254–268 (2011)
30. Jentzsch, N., Preibusch, S., Harasser, A.: Study on monetising privacy. An economic model for pricing personal information. Deliverable February 27, 2012, ENISA (2012)
31. Preibusch, S., Kübler, D., Beresford, A.R.: Price versus privacy: An experiment into the competitive advantage of collecting less personal information. Electron Com. Res. 13, 423–455 (2013)
32. Beresford, A.R., Kübler, D., Preibusch, S.: Unwillingness to pay for privacy: A field experiment. Economics Letters 117, 25–27 (2012)
33. Danezis, G., Lewis, S., Anderson, R.: How Much is Location Privacy Worth? In: Fourth Workshop on the Economics of Information Security, Cambridge, MA (2005)
34. Cvrcek, D., Kumpost, M., Matyas, V., Danezis, G.: A study on the value of location privacy. In: Proc. ACM WPES, pp. 109–118. ACM, Alexandria (2006)
35. Matyas, V., Kumpost, M.: Location Privacy Pricing and Motivation. In: 2007 International Conference on Mobile Data Management, pp. 263–267. Mannheim, Germany (2007)
36. Hann, I.-H., Hui, K.-L., Lee, T.S., Png, I.P.L.: Online Information Privacy: Measuring the Cost-Benefit Tradeoff. In: Proc. ICIS, Barcelona, Spain, pp. 1–10 (2002)
37. Huberman, B.A., Adar, E., Fine, L.A.: Valuating privacy. IEEE Sec. & Priv. 3, 22–25 (2005)
38. Rose, J., Rehse, O., Röber, B.: The Value of our Digital Identity. Boston Cons. Gr. (2012)
39. Tversky, A., Kahneman, D.: Judgment under Uncertainty: Heuristics and Biases. Science 185, 1124–1131 (1974)
40. EC: Attitudes on Data Protection and Electronic Identity in the European Union. Special Eurobarometer 359, European Commission, Brussels, Belgium (2011)
41. Pepitone, J.: What your wireless carrier knows about you - and what they're selling (2013), http://money.cnn.com/2013/12/16/technology/mobile/wireless-carrier-sell-data/
42. Troianovski, A.: Phone Firms Sell Data on Customers. WSJ. com (2013), http://online.wsj.com/news/articles/SB10001424127887323463704578497153556847658
43. OECD: Exploring the Economics of Personal Data: A Survey of Methodologies for Measuring Monetary Value. Report 220, OECD, Paris (2013)
44. Norberg, P.A., Horne, D.R., Horne, D.A.: The Privacy Paradox: Personal Information Disclosure Intentions versus Behaviors. Journal of Consumer Affairs 41, 100–126 (2007)
45. Rivenbark, D.: Experimentally Elicited Beliefs Explain Privacy Behavior. Univ. of Central Florida, Dept. Economics (2011), http://EconPapers.repec.org/RePEc:cfl:wpaper:2010-09
46. Preibusch, S.: Guide to measuring privacy concern: Review of survey and observational instruments. International Journal of Human-Computer Studies 71, 1133–1143 (2013)

A Protocol for Intrusion Detection in Location Privacy-Aware Wireless Sensor Networks

Jiří Kůr and Vashek Matyáš

Masaryk University, Brno, Czech Republic
{xkur,matyas}@fi.muni.cz

Abstract. Wireless sensor networks come with some very challenging demands for security – they often call for protection against active attackers trying to disrupt a network operation, but also against passive attackers looking for (potentially) sensitive information about the location of a certain node or about the movement of a tracked object. Selective forwarding is a basic yet powerful active attack. It can be detected using several existing techniques if enough information is available to an intrusion detection system. Yet when the system lacks the information due to a location privacy measure, selective forwarding detection becomes complicated. In this paper, we propose a method for detecting selective forwarding attacks and packet modification attacks concurrently with supporting location privacy. The resulting system counters a global eavesdropper capable of some active actions, such as dropping and modification of packets. We also evaluate detection accuracy of the proposed method on a small scale real-world sensor network.

1 Introduction

A wireless sensor network (WSN) is a network of tiny and resource constrained devices called sensor nodes. WSNs are considered for and deployed in various scenarios such as emergency response or critical infrastructure protection, medical, wildlife or battlefield monitoring. Some of these scenarios include tracking of monitored subjects, and this brings up not only security issues but also location privacy concerns. Research in both the security and the location privacy in WSNs has drawn a lot of attention in recent years. Yet, they have rarely been investigated together. Location privacy measures usually assume only a passive attacker that is quietly monitoring network traffic. On the contrary, security mechanisms often target also an active attacker who tries to disturb network operation. This attacker model distinction was examined by Kůr et al. in [7]. They show that location privacy protections targeting a passive attacker and intrusion detection systems (IDSs) aiming at an active one may suffer from several problems when employed together. An IDS is often rendered ineffective due to some synthetic obscurity imposed by location privacy protection. Despite the problems, it is desirable to employ both these techniques at the same time when securing a WSN.

C. Eckert et al. (Eds.): TrustBus 2014, LNCS 8647, pp. 180–190, 2014.

In this paper, we propose a modification to the link layer security scheme SNEP [9]. This modification enables one to detect selective forwarding attacks and packet modification attacks in a network where source location privacy is protected. Particularly, we consider a network that employs an existing source location privacy protection – the Periodic Collection [8]. This protection targets a global eavesdropper. Such setting was chosen since it represents, due to the strongest eavesdropper/protection, the most challenging environment for intrusion detection. Our modification equips the network with an ability to detect certain malicious actions, namely selective forwarding/dropping and packet modification, performed by a potential active attacker that captured a limited number of nodes. Though we present our modification in the context of Periodic Collection, our approach can also be used in combination with other location privacy mechanisms.

The roadmap of this paper is as follows: We summarize related work in Section 2. We describe the assumed attacker in Section 3. Then we describe Periodic Collection and analyze its potential interaction with intrusion detection systems in Section 4. The proposed modification is presented in Section 5. It is then analyzed and evaluated in Section 6. We conclude the paper in Section 7.

2   Related Work

Roman et al. [11] were among the first to consider an IDS for wireless sensor networks. They showed why IDSs designed for ad hoc wireless networks cannot be used in the domain of WSNs. They also presented a general IDS architecture for WSNs that relies on *local* and *global* IDS agents. Another seminal approach to intrusion detection for WSN was proposed by da Silva et al. [1]. They presented a decentralized IDS with several general rules that can be applied to detect a malicious behavior. Our detection technique to some extent respects both the above proposals. We employ *local* agents and apply selected rules from da Silva's work. However, both these proposals are very generic. In our work, we present a particular instance of the architecture and specific rules that enable one to detect selective forwarding and packet modification in presence of location privacy protection. We further combine our technique with an existing link layer security scheme and a location privacy technique to bring a complete security and privacy solution.

Several different principles were proposed for detecting a selective forwarding attack. Yu and Xiao [14] proposed a detection technique based on multi-hop acknowledgements. In this technique, a missing acknowledgement triggers an alarm message that flows towards both a source node and a base station. These parties then evaluate a potential intrusion. Besides relatively high communication overhead caused by the acknowledgements, this technique cannot be used in a network with location privacy protected. An attacker could easily track acknowledgements and alarm messages back to the source node or the base station.

A popular method for selective forwarding detection is the *watchdog* approach [3,6,11,12]. In this approach, selected nodes monitor the traffic in their neighborhood and analyze whether their neighboring nodes properly forward the incoming packets. However, this effort requires the monitoring nodes to be able to match the incoming and outgoing packets. This requirement cannot be usually fulfilled in the presence of location privacy mechanism due to hop-by-hop encryption which renders the watchdog approach unsuitable for our scenario.

Kaplantzis et al. [4] proposed a centralized approach. Their proposal is built on support vector machines, a class of machine learning algorithms, that are trained on an attack free traffic and then run on a base station. An advantage of this approach is that it puts no burden on sensor nodes. Furthermore, this method could be in principle combined with some of the location privacy mechanisms. However, it only detects the existence of an attack and does not identify the malicious nodes. The detection accuracy is also relatively low.

While writing up this paper, we discovered a rare example of a scheme that could, in our opinion, be easily modified to work with certain location privacy mechanisms and that is able to identify malicious nodes that drop or modify packets. This centralized IDS was proposed by Wang et al. [13]. It uses layered encryption and extra bits that are inserted to a forwarded packet by every node. These bits, together with the encryption, help a base station to reconstruct and verify the routing path. This routing information is then combined with a periodic change of routing topology to enable the base station to identify misbehaving nodes. In this approach, the detection is done in a centralized manner at the base station that must somehow notify the honest nodes in response. On the contrary, our technique adopts a highly distributed approach in which a malicious node is detected by its child or parent node.

For more selective forwarding detection techniques see Khan's study [5].

Kůr et al. showed [7] that IDSs and privacy mechanisms are likely to be in conflict when employed together in a WSN. They supported their view with several examples of problems that emerges between typical IDSs and privacy mechanisms. This suggests that most of the existing detection proposals can not be directly applied in a network with location privacy protection enabled. This fact was part of our motivation for this work.

3   Attacker Model

We model the attacker as a global eavesdropper that may have compromised and be in control of a limited number of sensor nodes. The global eavesdropper was introduced by Mehta et al. [8]. She is able to overhear all node-to-node and node-to-base station communication simultaneously for all the time. She is also able to locate the source of the transmission with a reasonable precision. We further strengthen the attacker with a possibility to capture up to 10% of sensor nodes in the network. She is able to control the nodes and use them for active attacks such as selective forwarding/dropping of packets and/or modification of forwarded packets.

The objective of the attacker is to locate sources of events monitored by the network and/or to prevent the base station from learning information about the events, i.e., to perform a denial of service attack.

4   Location Privacy Protection

In this section we describe the grounding source location privacy protection technique – Periodic Collection [8]. It was chosen as a representative technique that targets the global eavesdropper. We demonstrate both negative and positive impacts of the technique on a potential intrusion detection system. We also sketch approaches that could lead to a successful coexistence of the Periodic Collection and an IDS.

4.1   Periodic Collection

Periodic Collection provides source location privacy against a *global eavesdropper* who is able to constantly monitor all the traffic in the entire network. The main idea behind Periodic Collection is that it makes the network traffic completely independent of the events detected. Nodes employ the FIFO queue to buffer incoming real packets. Every node sends packets from the queue at a constant rate one packet at a predefined time interval. If a node has no packet to send, it creates a dummy one and sends it instead. All packets in the network are protected with pairwise keys. Thus their appearance changes hop by hop and looks random to an attacker that is not able to distinguish real packets from dummy ones. The identity of a receiving node is also protected and only the sender identity is sent in plaintext. The mechanism is almost independent of a routing technique. For demonstration purposes we assume that the topology is a tree rooted at a base station. This can be achieved, e.g., by the INSENS routing technique [2].

4.2   Problems

Periodic Collection aims at a passive attacker, leaving the IDS responsible for active attacks. Thus the IDS should detect, e.g., selective forwarding attacks where some of the packets are dropped by an attacker or an unauthorized packet modification. Although the IDS node is a legitimate member of the network, it is in a similar position to the attacker. Since pairwise keys are used to protect the packets, the IDS that is not an intended receiver of the packet can understand only an unencrypted sender identity. The rest of the packet is randomly looking. So undetectable attack vectors appear: A malicious node can simply replace a real packet with a dummy one and thus effectively drop the packet. It can also modify a packet or even inject a new packet and the IDS has no means to detect such behavior.

4.3   Intrusion Detection Support

Besides the above mentioned problems, Periodic Collection brings also some benefits for the IDSs. Since nodes are required to transmit at pre-defined time slots, the IDS can easily detect dead or malfunctioning nodes that do not fulfill this condition. If a node is silent, it may indicate a node failure or a node compromise. If a node is transmitting in other than a pre-allocated time slot, it may be recognized as a jammer. It is necessary to note that these benefits would be normally traded for energy and latency costs caused by Periodic Collection. However, once these costs are traded for location privacy, the benefits become an added value.

4.4   Towards Better Detection

The troubles of the IDS may be reduced by a modification of Periodic Collection. There are two straightforward ways to increase the ability of the IDS to detect selective forwarding and packet modification. First, packets may be protected by cluster keys instead of pairwise keys. Second, communicating nodes may share their pairwise key also with the IDS. In the first case, all nodes in the cluster, usually a one-hop neighborhood, are able to monitor and analyze the traffic. However, an attacker that controls a single node from the cluster is also able to do so. The second solution is a bit better from this point of view. In order to understand the traffic, an attacker has to identify and compromise a node running the IDS.

The common problem of such simplistic solutions is that an attack on a single node affects a group of nodes. This limitation stems from the fact that the IDS accumulates sensitive information and becomes a single point of failure. In the ideal case, only a single node should be affected by such attack, i.e., only information on packets that are forwarded directly by the node should be available to an attacker. This observation leads us to the following idea. No additional key sharing is performed and every node pays attention only to those packets that flow directly through itself and to which it has got access. Thus a simple IDS (agent) runs on every node in the network and every node becomes a watchdog for its child and parent nodes that are given by the underlying routing algorithm.

5   Proposed Detection Technique

We construct our detection technique using building blocks from a well established link layer security scheme SNEP [9]. This scheme provides node-to-node data confidentiality, data authentication, replay protection and weak data freshness. Furthermore, it provides a mechanism to derive various types of keys (e.g., encryption key, authentication key) from a given master key. The structure of the packet sent from the node X to the node Y according to SNEP is: $E_{K_{XY},C_{XY}}(M)||MAC_{K'_{XY}}(C_{XY}||E_{K_{XY},C_{XY}}(M))$, where $E_{K_{XY},C_{XY}}$ denotes encryption in a counter mode with a pairwise encryption key K_{XY} and a counter C_{XY}, both shared between the nodes X and Y. $MAC_{K'_{XY}}$ denotes a computation of a message authentication code (MAC) with an authentication key K'_{XY}, M is a data message to be transmitted and $||$ denotes concatenation. The use of the counter mode for message encryption ensures *semantic security*, i.e., that similar messages are encrypted differently each time. This is an important property for the location privacy protection. Consider the following attack scenario where semantic security is not ensured. An attacker captures a node and repeatedly sends a message M to a base station. Then she can track the message to the base station by searching for spots where multiple similar messages are transmitted. The drawback of the counter mode is that both communicating sides need to keep the counter synchronized. However, SNEP actually offers also a simple protocol for counter resynchronization.

The proposed solution employs cryptographic primitives for encryption, MAC computation, key derivation and the protocol for counter resynchronization used in SNEP. It also leverages the broadcast nature of the wireless medium and the fact that a packet can be overheard by previous and next hop nodes simultaneously. Let us demonstrate the solution by an example – a data message M is sent by a node X, then should be forwarded by a node Y and subsequently received by a node Z. The node Y can be cooperatively watched for modification/drop of this message by nodes X and Z. This watch is enabled due to a packet format that contains per-hop changing MAC verifiable by both the nodes. Furthermore, no key needs to be shared between these nodes. The format of a packet (instance sent from the node Y to the node Z) is as follows: $P_{YZ} = E_{K_{YZ}, C_{YZ}}(N_Y \| M) \| MAC_{N_Y}(M)$, similar notation as above is used and $MAC_{N_Y}(M)$ represents a message authentication code of the data message M protected with a pseudorandom nonce N_Y in place of the authentication key. The nonce is computed by the node Y as $N_Y = MAC_{K'_{XY}}(C_{XY} \| N_X)$, where N_X is a pseudorandom nonce computed by the node X and extracted from the packet P_{XY}, and K'_{XY} is a pairwise key shared between the nodes X and Y.

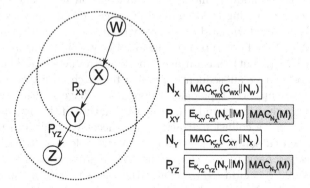

Fig. 1. The nodes W and Y watch the node X, while nodes X and Z are responsible for watching the node Y

6   Analysis of the Solution

We analyze security properties of the detection technique and evaluate its communication overhead and detection accuracy.

6.1 Security Properties

Consider the situation sketched in Figure 1. When the node Y sends the packet P_{YZ}, both nodes X and Z receive the packet and verify whether the MAC value corresponds to the nonce N_Y and the message M. Note that the message M was first sent from the node X to the node Y and thus the node X can compute the nonce N_Y and the MAC in advance. On the contrary, the node Z is not able to compute the MAC until it receives and decrypts the packet P_{YZ}. That is why the nodes X and Z have a slightly different role in the watch.

The node X watches for a message drop. It sends the message M to the node Y and expects this node to send a packet with an expected MAC in the near future. Note that the node Y needs not to forward the message immediately since it may have other legitimate messages in a buffer. Therefore the node X has to tolerate some reasonable delay until it may conclude that the message was dropped. The node X cannot detect a message modification as it has no access to the encrypted content of the packet P_{YZ}.

The message modification can be detected by the node Z. It first decrypts the packet and then checks whether the message M and the nonce N_Y correspond to the appended MAC. If not, the message is considered modified. In our experimental implementation on TelosB nodes, a 16-bit CRC code is appended by a radio to every packet. Thus if the CRC check succeeds and MAC verification fails, the chance that the message modification was inadvertent is close to $\frac{1}{2^{16}}$. Therefore, in such a situation, the packet sender is marked as malicious. If the MAC verification succeeds, the message may still be modified. It is because the potentially malicious node Y has all the information necessary to compute a correct MAC corresponding to a modified message. Yet in this case the message modification is detected with a short delay by the node X as a message drop since the expected MAC shall not appear in the air. The watching mechanism assumes that a simple IDS (agent) runs on every node in the network. The mechanism is transitive and can be subsequently applied to watch all forwarding nodes on the path. It also supports topologies where nodes have multiple child and/or parent nodes. On the other hand, the transitive nature of this mechanism makes it vulnerable against a collusion attack of two successive malicious nodes on the path. The presented solution assumes that every node has at least one parent node that receives packets and checks the message integrity. This requirement has to be ensured by additional means either as a part of a topology setting process, e.g., by the INSENS scheme [2], or by a precursory handshake.

Besides message modification/drop detection, the solution provides, similarly to the SNEP, semantic security, data authentication, replay protection and weak data freshness.

6.2 Communication Overhead

We compute the communication overhead per packet and compare it with the SNEP technique. To ensure the security properties, we set the length of both the MAC and the nonce to 8 bytes. Thus the overhead when compared to the SNEP is only 8 bytes per packet for including the nonce. Assuming a standard SNEP packet is 36 bytes long, adding the nonce results into a communication overhead of 22%. The computation overhead is negligible – a longer encryption is traded for a shorter computation of MAC, thus the only computation overhead with respect to SNEP relates to the nonce creation.

6.3   Accuracy Evaluation

We evaluated the detection accuracy on a real sensor network deployed in our laboratory. Our network consists of 29 TelosB nodes attached to ceiling in our office environment with several rooms and corridors. The average distance between communicating nodes is approximately 5 meters. The experiment setting is as follows: the communication topology is a tree routed at the base station and remains static during the evaluation. Each node sends a packet, either real or dummy, every 500 ms. There is a single source node that generates 100 real events at a constant rate one event per 2 seconds and reports them to the base station. There is a malicious node on the path to base station that performs the selective forwarding attack. This node has two ways of dropping packets. It may modify a message M and use the original message MAC. The resulting packet then misleads a node that is watching for message drop. However, the discrepancy is detected by a packet receiver. In our implementation with an additional CRC code, such discrepancy immediately puts blame on the packet sender. Therefore, in our experiments, the malicious node is only using the second mean of packet dropping. It does not forward the incoming packets (with a certain probability). We use four settings of the malicious node. In the first setting, the node behaves correctly; in three other settings the node drops incoming real packets with probability 0.03, 0.05 and 0.2, respectively. We ran the experiment 100 times for each setting.

With such experimental (and namely malicious node) settings, we evaluate accuracy with respect to the following metrics – *detection rate* and *false alarm rate*. Detection rate is defined as a number of experiment runs in which malicious activity was successfully detected divided by the total number of runs. False alarm rate is calculated only for a setting with a correct node behavior and is defined as a number of experiment runs in which a correctly behaving node was falsely detected as malicious, i.e., number of false positives, divided by the total number of runs.

The resulting accuracy is mainly dependent on two factors, on a link quality between the monitoring node X and the monitored node Y and on the IDS detection threshold. The link quality can be expressed by probability $Prob_{link} = Prob_{XY} * Prob_{YX}$, where $Prob_{XY}$ is probability of successful packet delivery from X to Y. The IDS detection threshold is an IDS parameter that is used to decide whether a monitored node is malicious or not. This threshold is compared with an IDS observation – a number of packets forwarded by the monitored node divided by a number of packets sent to that node. If the observation is below the IDS threshold, the monitored node is marked as malicious.

Consider an example, $Prob_{link} = 0.95$ and the IDS detection threshold of 0.95. The monitoring node X sends 100 packets and the monitored node Y behaves correctly. Then the expected observation of the node X is that Y forwarded 95 packets out of 100. However, due to the variance of the observation it may sometimes fall to 94 packets. Such observation is below the threshold and produces a false positive. To prevent such situations, let us lower the detection threshold to 0.9. Assume that Y is malicious and drops packets with probability of 0.05. Then the expected observation of X is that Y forwarded 90 packets. This does not fall below the new IDS threshold and produces a false negative as the malicious node remains undetected. Yet it may sometimes still lead to a successful detection depending on the variance of the number of dropped packets and the link quality. To balance the number of false positives and false negatives, the detection threshold would be around 0.925.

In our experiments, $Prob_{link}$ was measured by counting overheard dummy packets, it never fell below 0.98 and the average value was 0.993. The IDS detection threshold was then set to 0.95. For the probabilities of malicious packet drop 0.03, 0.05 and 0.2, respectively, we obtained detection rates of 12%, 40% and 100%, respectively. The corresponding false alarm rate that is independent of the drop rates was 0% as the IDS detection threshold was considerably below $Prob_{link}$. For the IDS detection threshold of 0.97, the detection rates would be 51%, 78% and 100%, respectively, with false alarm rate of 1%. The results are summarized in Table 1. Note that the most accurate IDS would have an adaptive IDS threshold based on the actual link quality. The link quality could be estimated based on the LQI (link quality indicator) value provided by the radio chip as the LQI and the packet drop rate are correlated on Telos nodes [10]. We leave experiments with an adaptive IDS detection threshold for future work.

Table 1. The average $Prob_{link} = 0.99$, IDS detection threshold is a) 0.95 and b) 0.97, respectively. False alarm rate was calculated for setting where probability of malicious drop was 0.

	Probability of malicious drop	0.03	0.05	0.20
a)	Detection rate	0.12	0.40	1
	False alarm rate	0	0	0
b)	Detection rate	0.51	0.78	1
	False alarm rate	0.01	0.01	0.01

Another factor with some impact on detection accuracy is the probability that a packet received by a node is dropped due to full internal buffers. This probability is dependent on the network traffic load. In a network with a low traffic load the probability would be negligible, therefore we omit this factor in our experiments and leave examination of this factor for future work.

7 Conclusions

Both active and passive attackers pose a real threat for wireless sensor networks. Thus intrusion detection systems and location privacy measures need to be deployed, most often at the same time. Yet this coexistence may result in a malfunction or an inefficiency of one of these components. We proposed a modification to the link layer protection SNEP that enables one to detect active attacks – selective forwarding and packet modification – in a WSN where location privacy is protected. The resulting technique provides, beside detection functionality, also usual link layer security services. We have implemented the technique in combination with the Periodic Collection measure that targets a global eavesdropper. However, it can also be used in combination with other location privacy measures. We have evaluated the proposed technique in our (real-world) sensor network, obtaining a very high detection accuracy. If the attacker drops 20% of the traffic, the resulting detection accuracy reaches 100%, with the false alarm rate at 1%. For a 5% attacker drop rate, the detection accuracy gets to 78% and the false alarm rate remains at 1%.

Acknowledgements. We are grateful to the anonymous reviewers for their suggestions that improved the paper. This work was supported by the project GAP202/11/0422 of the Czech Science Foundation.

References

1. da Silva, A.P.R., Martins, M.H.T., Rocha, B.P.S., Loureiro, A.A.F., Ruiz, L.B., Wong, H.C.: Decentralized intrusion detection in wireless sensor networks. In: Proceedings of the 1st ACM International Workshop on Quality of Service & Security in Wireless and Mobile Networks, Q2SWinet 2005, pp. 16–23. ACM, New York (2005)
2. Deng, J., Han, R., Mishra, S.: INSENS: Intrusion-tolerant routing for wireless sensor networks. Computer Communications 29(2), 216–230 (2006)
3. Hai, T.H., Huh, E.-N.: Detecting selective forwarding attacks in wireless sensor networks using two-hops neighbor knowledge. In: Proceedings of the Seventh IEEE International Symposium on Network Computing and Applications, NCA 2008, pp. 325–331 (2008)
4. Kaplantzis, S., Shilton, A., Mani, N., Sekercioglu, Y.A.: Detecting selective forwarding attacks in wireless sensor networks using support vector machines. In: Proceedings of the 3rd International Conference on Intelligent Sensors, Sensor Networks and Information, ISSNIP 2007, pp. 335–340 (2007)
5. Khan, W.Z., Xiang, Y., Aalsalem, M.Y., Arshad, Q.: Comprehensive study of selective forwarding attack in wireless sensor networks. IJCNIS 3(1), 1–10 (2011)
6. Krontiris, I., Dimitriou, T., Freiling, F.C.: Towards intrusion detection in wireless sensor networks. In: Proceedings of the 13th European Wireless Conference (2007)
7. Kůr, J., Matyáš, V., Stetsko, A., Švenda, P.: Attack detection vs. privacy – how to find the link or how to hide it? In: Christianson, B., Crispo, B., Malcolm, J., Stajano, F. (eds.) Security Protocols 2011. LNCS, vol. 7114, pp. 189–199. Springer, Heidelberg (2011)

8. Mehta, K., Liu, D., Wright, M.: Location privacy in sensor networks against a global eavesdropper. In: IEEE International Conference on Network Protocols, ICNP 2007, pp. 314–323 (October 2007)

9. Perrig, A., Szewczyk, R., Tygar, J.D., Wen, V., Culler, D.E.: SPINS: Security protocols for sensor networks. Wireless networks 8(5), 521–534 (2002)

10. Polastre, J., Szewczyk, R., Culler, D.: Telos: Enabling ultra-low power wireless research. In: Fourth International Symposium on Information Processing in Sensor Networks, IPSN 2005, pp. 364–369 (2005)

11. Roman, R., Zhou, J., Lopez, J.: Applying intrusion detection systems to wireless sensor networks. In: Proceedings of the 3rd IEEE Consumer Communications and Networking Conference, CCNC 2006, vol. 1, pp. 640–644 (2006)

12. Stetsko, A., Folkman, L., Matyáš, V.: Neighbor-based intrusion detection for wireless sensor networks. In: Proceedings of the 6th International Conference on Wireless and Mobile Communications, ICWMC 2010, pp. 420–425 (2010)

13. Wang, G., Zhang, W., Kim, J., Feng, T., Wang, C.: Catching packet droppers and modifiers in wireless sensor networks. IEEE Transactions on Parallel and Distributed Systems 23(5), 835–843 (2012)

14. Yu, B., Xiao, B.: Detecting selective forwarding attacks in wireless sensor networks. In: Proceedings of the 20th International Parallel and Distributed Processing Symposium, IPDPS 2006, pp. 1–8 (2006)

Author Index